Women and Economics

*For Shyamala
In sisterhood
& shared struggles

Prue Hyman*

Women
and
Economics

A New Zealand Feminist Perspective

Prue Hyman

First published in New Zealand in 1994 by
Bridget Williams Books Ltd, PO Box 11-294, Wellington

© Prue Hyman, 1994

This book is copyright under the Berne Convention. All rights reserved.
No reproduction without permission.
Inquiries should be made to the publishers.

ISBN 0 908912 61 7

Cover design by Mission Hall Design Group, Wellington
Internal design by Afineline, Wellington
Typeset by Archetype, Wellington
Printed by GP Print, Wellington

Contents

Preface — vii

Introduction — 1

Part I: *How Feminist Analysis Could and Should Change Economics*

1. Feminist Critiques of Orthodox Economics and Why They Are Neglected — 13
2. 'Mitigating Misery': the Co-option and Twisting of Feminist Arguments — 61

Part II: *Equal Pay and Pay Equity Struggles*

3. The History and Concepts of Equal Pay and Pay Equity in New Zealand — 79
4. Job Evaluation and Levels of Industrial Bargaining — 101
5. International Comparisons: the Earnings Gap and Pay Equity — 124
6. Equal Pay for Women After the Employment Contracts Act — 136

Part III: *A Modest Safety Net? Women, the State and Social Policy*

7. The State, Income Maintenance and Economic Independence for Women — 157
8. Income Adequacy for Older Women — 189
9. Women and Housing Policy — 206

Part IV: *The Future*

10. The Last 100 Years and Prospects for Positive Change — 219

References — 231

Index — 249

Preface

Many thanks to all my friends in the New Zealand feminist and lesbian communities whose existence has helped sustain me through the years of fun and struggle and the writing of the articles which came together in this book. Women's Studies at Victoria University and the Women's Studies Association have been stimulating and warm places to exchange ideas. Thanks also to my colleagues in the Economics Department, many of whom I like or respect, even though it is not the easiest place in which to be a feminist economist. The department and the university, notwithstanding my criticisms of the discipline and of powerful institutions, have allowed me the physical and mental space, a salary and (just!) the time to write this book, and I am grateful. A special thanks to my students who, over the last four years, have participated in the course which covers the topics in this book: they have brought varied experience and much enthusiasm to discussing the issues, challenged me frequently, and undertaken excellent and interesting project work. I want particularly to mention Nan McDonald: her many stimulating class contributions included reminding me of the Sarah Hoagland passage quoted in Chapter 1 and pointing out the *Hecate* article quoted in the Introduction. Many thanks also to my publisher, Bridget Williams, and her editor, Jane Parkin.

Among my friends, four women and a dog have to be singled out for special mention. First my mother, Greta Hyman, who has struggled bravely and well to understand her daughter through all the changes. Friends, especially those whose mothers find it harder to accept and understand their lesbian daughters' choices, tell me how lucky I am to have her as a mother. They are right, but we've also both worked hard to get our relationship to that stage! At age 80, she even helped me in the production of this book, checking typing, grammar, references and its ability to be understood. This, and all she has done over the years, is much appreciated.

Second, my dear friend Ann, without whom I might have taken much longer to find myself, I might not have ended up in New Zealand, and I almost certainly would not have bought my house at beautiful Paekakariki, which has been a haven for over 20 years. Third, my good friend Sue, who kept me young, made me laugh, shared some transitions, persuaded me I should activate my desire to buy a dog and, having agreed to access rather than custody, has always been happy to look after J while I am overseas. Fourth, my dog J, in the past swimmer, ball and stick chaser *extraordinaire*, as greedy as ever, and loving and loved companion for 16 years: still with me, as I write this, for a little longer.

Fifth and last, my best friend and partner Bronwen Dean, with whom I've shared the joys and sorrows of the last eight years and who has endured fairly patiently the writing of the papers that grew into this book.

Prue Hyman

Introduction

The two major themes of this book can be simply outlined. The first is the contention that feminist analysis has made depressingly little impact on economic theory or on economic and social systems and policies in Aotearoa/New Zealand. While most economic analysis and the resulting policies may appear to treat men and women equally (and thus appear gender-neutral), they do not adequately allow for differences between women's and men's lives and perspectives.

The second theme concerns the economic and social outcomes which result from the lack of impact of feminist critiques. Maori and people with disabilities, as well as women, do less well than white, middle-class, middle-aged men on a range of economic and social indicators of well-being.

In this introduction, I place the book in context, outlining my own background and why I find it important to mention it. This raises issues within feminism over identity politics, commonalities and difference, and coalition-building. Then I move to my participation in the public arena, and reflect on working inside and outside government, in pressure groups and on advisory bodies. Finally, I explain how the book arose and refer to articles on which it is based.

I write as a white, middle-class, Jewish, lesbian feminist trained in economics. The personal and political influences, events and changes in my life and thinking are relevant, because we are all shaped by our upbringing, personal circumstances and choices/constraints. For me, at least, there are chicken-and-egg issues in this, with personal and political changes interlinked.

My upbringing in London was privileged and largely happy, despite the early death of my father. Awareness of the oppression of the Jewish people was of course an early reality, but was hardly ever a personal experience, as we mixed in a largely Jewish (and some non-Jewish) liberal, middle-class London; my school was at least 10 per cent Jewish. The full extent of the Holocaust was revealed when I was too young to understand, but it was part of the awareness that grew among family, community and religious (weekend) schooling. I was five when the need for a Jewish homeland in Israel was recognised.

Paradoxically, it was in New Zealand, when I had moved away from adherence to Judaism as a religion but was feeling a revival of cultural and historical pride, and identification in my Jewishness, that I became more aware of anti-semitism. Overt discrimination has not been totally absent in New Zealand, with some incidents reported in the media and a background of immigration discrimination (Beaglehole, 1988). However, I was more affected by a lack of Jewish milieu and a sense of invisibility which paralleled my invisibility as a lesbian than by an overt anti-semitism. The world tends to assume universality of the dominant non-Jewish and non-lesbian culture, unless one throws one's identity in its face. This, as a lesbian, I often do, as a political decision, not because I could not 'pass' as straight – an option which was not always available to lesbians of different eras or cultures.

Increasing identification as lesbian and Jewish inevitably led to my growing realisation of the extent of discrimination against many groups seen as different or as minorities. Earlier I was sheltered by my middle-class background, tertiary education and a type of paid work which minimised the personal experience of bigotry, except at some political demonstrations. Hence I came, perhaps rather late, to understand analyses of structural power. This involved seeing the need both for justice for all groups suffering discrimination and for the reduction of inequalities in opportunities and outcomes – which I argue in Part IV requires radical changes to society. It also involved my belief that groups are as important as or more important than individuals. This leads to interdependence and co-operation as a major element of human motivation and the mainspring of society, with the individualistic, competitive, selfish model of economic orthodoxy relegated to a secondary level. Both have their place for women and men, but the first should not be thought of as the province of a female-dominated private world and the second of a male-dominated public world. This issue is discussed further in Part I.

An 'out' lesbian academic is subject to far less direct discrimination than many in less privileged occupations, but visibility is still an issue, and prejudice by no means absent. Further, the more political noise one makes in an institution (and I probably have not made enough), the more discrimination will appear. Lesbian identity is for me and many others a political issue, not simply a personal choice. Thus visibility is essential not only to personal comfort, but also to show younger staff and students that we are around, and to enable us to form groups to act as a political force. Lesbian feminist theory and politics is crucial to feminist theory; for example, in its analysis of how heterosexism has constrained both straight women and lesbians. Sadly, it is hard to be totally free of internalised homophobia, and from constraints on what can be accomplished while working in an institutional setting.

Hence in this book and elsewhere my writing has been almost entirely 'general' (there is no such thing!) feminist economics. It is only very recently that I have have started to explore the specific contribution that a lesbian feminist economics might make, and to point out the heterosexist assumptions of much previous work. For example, the importance of economic independence rather than total dependence on a spouse is rightly emphasised by feminist economic writing. However, this often assumes that all women are married for part of their lives, and ignores the experience of many lesbians.

Identifying as a white, middle-class, Jewish, lesbian feminist trained in economics is itself controversial. The meaning (if any) of such categories is questioned by post-modern thought. However, considering such aspects of oneself to be important does not necessarily contradict the realisation that identities are 'provisional and relative: historically, culturally, politically constructed' (Guy *et al*, 1990: 13). Specifying my background in this way is a reaction to false depictions of universal sisterhood which ignores differences between women. This is now recognised by almost all feminists as having been a mistake. 'Feminist discourses, while claiming truths for and about "women", have in fact represented the universalised perspectives of the white, Western and middle class' (Jones, 1993: 23).

A growing awareness of the multi-faceted nature of power and structural difference has greatly improved feminist theory. It has led to the recognition of important insights in each of radical, lesbian, socialist, post-structural and Maori feminist thought, as well as the writing of other women of colour. It did, however, have one unfortunate by-product. This was the construction of a hierarchy of oppressions which could be silencing and paralysing rather than constructive. Recognising the importance of different facets of identity does not, however, necessarily involve a hierarchy of oppressions or identity politics. The former has helped in the production and appreciation of writing which recognises the simultaneous importance of sameness and difference. Visions of a democratic, socialist-feminist future address all the structural inequalities, including gender, race, class and sexuality, and draw on the separate strands (Ferguson, 1991).

In my view it remains useful to organise partly within tight groups, using separatist space to organise politically and to share common understandings. Both lesbian space, for political and social purposes, and woman-only space have been important to me personally and to New Zealand theory and politics. Certainly issues of inclusion/exclusion, representativeness, multi-faceted identity and the ability to work on the struggles of others cannot be avoided. 'It is necessary for those in relatively powerful or privileged positions to analyse their own speaking positions, and to resist appropriating other people's struggles. But using identity politics or category politics to exclude or fragment can paralyse politics in a process of exclusive insiderism' (Meekosha and Pettman, 1991: 78). However, if these problems are recognised, they should not prevent coalition politics or the attempt to understand and recognise difference. 'If we are to move beyond identity politics and a hierarchy of oppressions, we need first to know how to celebrate each other's differences. The most detrimental pressure ... is the pressure to "pass" ... Once our differences are acknowledged and affirmed we can begin to look for common ground and negotiate our needs' (Cockburn, 1991: 238-9).

Turning to my working life, my English university degree was in mathematics, economics, philosophy and politics, and I spent a few years in research and industry before coming to New Zealand. I was recruited to the Economics Department at Victoria University during a period of expansion. It was also a time of emphasis on modelling and the use of mathematics and statistics in economics. The expansion phase and my reasonable mathematics background by the standards of that time (1969) compensated for the lack of a doctorate. Staff mentoring or advice was then undeveloped, and I was unsure what I wanted to do beyond teaching. Faintly left-wing politics was not strongly motivating until the arrival of the second wave of feminism. With the advent of women's studies and a somewhat late emergence as a feminist, my research and community involvements began to come together. I was lucky enough to have tenure at the university before this; many academics with strong feminist beliefs and research programmes have had difficulties in New Zealand universities and overseas. Even with tenure, concentrating on feminist critiques of economics has consequences: my writing is often discounted as not really economics.

For nearly 20 years I have been involved in the development of women's studies teaching at Victoria, and in research on women's participation in the labour force, equal pay issues and other related areas. There are few academics for whom this is a major area, in economics or elsewhere. Inevitably and with enthusiasm I became involved in policy debates, and gradually spent increasing amounts of time on advisory bodies to government, in giving advice to organisations with some feminist agendas, and in public speaking. I have always avoided party politics, preferring pressure group involvement.

Soon after the Ministry of Women's Affairs was established by the incoming Labour Government of 1984, I became a part-time consultant on a range of economic issues and projects, and worked for the ministry on secondment during 1989 and 1990. Prior to that I served on a number of government advisory bodies (quangos), with five years on the National Housing Commission (NHC). A six-year term on the National Advisory Council on the Employment of Women ended in 1993. I have also been a member of the Social Science Research Fund Committee and its successor, the Social Science Committee of the Foundation for Research, Science and Technology, assessing research proposals.

I have some ambivalence about these experiences. Governments basically want advice within very narrow parameters, based on their philosophy and current wisdoms. Alternative views are not sought, and research which may give them support often fails to find funding. The Ministry of Women's Affairs attempts to give advice on differential gender impacts over a wide range of policy areas. However, its resources are few and its position can easily be marginalised. During Labour's period of office (1984–90) there was a somewhat greater formal commitment to policies to improve the position of women, and in particular Maori women, than there is now or was prior to 1984. This involved the use of at least limited interventionist policies, which are much less favoured by subsequent National Governments. Nevertheless, even these interventionist policies were often contradictory to, and overwhelmed by, the general trend to deregulation and emphasis on the market.

These contradictions account for the delays and major fights which occurred between departments and ministers before the Employment Equity Act 1990 was passed. Inevitable compromises were involved (see Part II). Further, the Ministry of Women's Affairs, as a policy department only, cannot itself sponsor or administer legislation. Thus it was constantly in the position of responding to Department of Labour and minister's office drafts, rather than taking the initiative.

Feminists are bound to have mixed feelings about what can be achieved by working within the bureaucracy. 'Femocracy', a term for such feminist participation, has received much discussion in Australia, where it originated, and a little here (McKinlay, 1990). Even in advisory bodies, I question whether much worthwhile is accomplished, although some useful research and media attention is generated. At times advice is toned down to what might be reasonably palatable to avoid abolition. It would indeed be interesting to analyse which quangos survived the 1980s, and why. For example, the National Housing Commission and the Women's Advisory Committee on Education were abolished, while the National Advisory Committee on the Employment of Women survived. Were these and other such decisions really related to relative importance, performance and efficiency, or more a matter of how outspoken the committees were and ministerial whim? Governments also, of course, influence what advice they will get by the power of appointments to these bodies.

I have spent much energy working on a liberal feminist agenda which can at times achieve some immediate gains (though they are often far from secure), and I still argue that feminists need to be everywhere. At times, though, we feel in a token position, and are there to make the Government look as if it is listening rather than really achieving a great deal. For me, therefore, such work should not be so absorbing as to distract from the longer-term aims for more radical change.

While still retaining a minor link with the Ministry of Women's Affairs, my current preference is to advise pressure groups, including unions and women's organisations. One recent example is work on behalf of midwives. Midwives had gained parity with doctors in fees for normal birth, thanks largely to then Health Minister Helen Clark's commitment to equal pay for work of equal value. Giving evidence on behalf of midwives seeking to retain this position and advising unions on gender-neutral job evaluation are among my better memories.

Another difficulty with full-time work in the public sector is the inability to participate fully in public debates on policy issues. Prior to

1989 I had a reasonable amount of media involvement on some of the issues raised in this book, but this was lost while I was at the ministry. Most of those links have gone, and I hope that this book will help me regain them. Links between academic research and community groups are also essential for the development of real alternatives to current wisdom.

This book should be of interest to a number of audiences. There is little similar New Zealand writing over the full range of topics discussed here, and virtually none on feminist critiques of economic theory. The book should therefore be a useful resource for teachers and students in courses in economics, women's studies and other social sciences which focus on feminist analysis of economic theory and economic/social policy. It should also be read by a full range of economics students, although many of the points made later about the marginalisation of feminist critiques indicate that this may not occur. However, *Women and Economics* is not just for an academic audience. I have tried to write accessibly, and have aimed the book at any woman or man wanting to know something about feminist analysis of economic policy, even if they have no economics background whatever.

The book has taken shape from a collection of articles, many of them written in response to current concerns. When preparing them for publication and undertaking the necessary updating and elimination of overlaps, I became dissatisfied with what would result from making minimal changes. Hence there is a fair amount of new material, particularly in Chapter 1. Nevertheless, the book naturally shows its origins. I have therefore included below a list of the articles on which it is mainly based, with the chapters to which each principally contributes (given in brackets after each entry). Some of the articles are fuller than the versions included in this book, so may be worth consulting by readers with a particular interest.

This background also influences the choice of topics. *Women and Economics* is not a systematic account of New Zealand women's position in the labour force and treatment by the state, although it covers many issues in this area. However, its focus is unique in that it combines theoretical and applied economic analyses. Hence it first argues that economic theory itself embodies a systematic inability to avoid biases against the groups with less power in society. It then shows the ways in which economic systems and policies built on such theory reinforce these gender and other biases.

The book starts with a lengthy section (Part I) which discusses orthodox economic theory and explains the neglect of feminist criticism. For those less interested in theory, the labour market and social policy sections (Parts II and III) may be a better starting-point. Part II concentrates mainly on issues related to equal pay, and gives some attention to occupational segregation and the impacts of government policies and industrial relations systems. The role of the state is discussed in Part III, with superannuation and housing the main application areas. Part IV suggests positive directions for change.

Articles relevant to particular chapters

Hyman, P. (1981), 'Women and Low Pay – A Review Article', *New Zealand Journal of Industrial Relations* 6, 2, pp. 78–89. (Ch 3).
___ (1985), 'Equal Pay for Work of Equal Value – Is it a Goal Desirable, Achievable, Both or Neither?' in *Women's Studies Conference Papers, '84*, Auckland: Women's Studies Association NZ, pp. 129–46. (Ch 3).
___ (1986a), 'Perspectives on Equal Pay for Work of Equal Value' in *Proceedings of Seminar on Equal Pay for Work of Equal Value*, Wellington: Victoria University of Wellington Centre for Continuing Education, pp. 1–19. (Ch 3).
___ (1986b), 'Housing Needs, Research and Policy: What are the Priorities for Women?' in *Women's Studies Conference Papers, '84*, Auckland: Women's Studies Association NZ, pp. 44–57. (Ch 9).
___ (1987), 'The Fight for Equal Pay for Work of Equal Value (Comparable Worth) in New Zealand – Lessons from Past Campaigns in New Zealand and Elsewhere', paper delivered to Seventh Berkshire Conference on the History of Women, Wellesley, Massachusetts. (Ch 3).
___ (1988a), 'Equal Pay for Work of Equal Value – Job Evaluation Issues', *New Zealand Journal of Industrial Relations* 13, 3, pp. 237–55. (Ch 4).
___ (1988b), 'The Advantages of Intervention in Housing Markets', *Victoria Economic Commentaries* 9, pp. 35–7. (Ch 9).
___ (1989), 'The Impact of Social Policy on Women – the Royal Commission, Government Policy and Women's Lives', *Women's Studies Journal* 5, 1, pp. 37–59. (Ch 7).
___ (1990a), 'The Royal Commission on Social Policy (NZ) and the Social Security Review (Australia) – A Comparison of their Reports and Recommendations, Particularly in Terms of their Implications for Women' in *Social Policy in Australia: What Future for the Welfare State? Proceedings of the National Social Policy Conference*, Sydney: University of New South Wales 4, pp. 51–64. (Ch 7).

___ (1990b), 'Women and Superannuation Policy', *Victoria Economic Commentaries* 7, 1, pp. 50–2. (Ch 8).

___ (1991), 'Enterprise Bargaining and Pay Equity in New Zealand' in *Work, Work, Work: Women in the Nineties, Proceedings of the Fifth Annual Conference of the Women's Directorate*, Sydney: New South Wales Department of Further Education, Training and Employment, pp. 42–56. (Ch 4).

___ (1992a), 'The Use of Economic Orthodoxy to Justify Inequality: A Feminist Critique' in R. du Plessis *et al*, pp. 252–65. (Ch 1).

___ (1992b), 'Income Adequacy for Older Women: Why Government and Private Provision are Both Failing and Some Possible Improvements', *Women's Studies Journal* 8, 1, pp. 95–111. (Ch 8).

___ (1992c), 'The Role of Orthodox Economic Methodology in the Justification of Inequality: A Feminist Critique' in N. Armstrong, C. Briar and K. Brooking (eds) *Proceedings of August 1991 Conference on Women and Work: Directions and Strategies for the 1990s*, Palmerston North: Massey University, pp. 132–51. (Ch 1).

___ (1993a), 'Women's Economic Position' in *Walking Backwards into the Future*, Hamilton: Women's Electoral Lobby, pp. 9–21. (Ch 10).

___ (1993b), 'Equal Pay for Women after the Employment Contracts Act: Legislation and Practice – The Emperor with No Clothes?', *New Zealand Journal of Industrial Relations* 18, 1, pp. 44-57. (Ch 6).

___ (1993c), 'Mitigating Misery – How to Co-opt and Twist Feminist Arguments', *Broadsheet* 197, pp. 26-30. (Ch 2).

___ (1993d), 'The Earnings Gap and Pay Equity: Developments in Five Countries' in P. S. Morrison (ed) *Labour Employment and Work in New Zealand – Proceedings of Fifth Conference*, Wellington: Victoria University of Wellington Geography Department, pp. 113–20. (Ch 5).

___ (1993e), 'Women in the Political Economy – Address to Women's Electoral Lobby 1992 Annual Conference', *Victoria Economic Commentaries* 10, 1, pp. 57–64. (Ch 10).

___ (1993f), 'Equal Pay for Women in New Zealand – History and Evaluation', *Victoria Economic Commentaries* 10, 1, pp. 65–8. (Ch 6).

___ (1993g), 'Paid and Unpaid Work, Independence and Interdependence – Towards Gender-Specific Analysis of Tax and Income Maintenance' in C. Scott (ed) *Women and Taxation*, Wellington: Victoria University of Wellington Institute of Policy Studies, pp. 156–71. (Chs 1 and 7).

___ (1993h), 'The Impact of Feminist Analysis on Economics: A Case Study in Exclusion and Proposals for Change', paper delivered to New Zealand Association of Economists Conference, Dunedin. (Ch 1).

—— (1993i), 'One Hundred and Fifty Years of Feminist Critiques of Orthodox Economics, in New Zealand and Overseas', paper delivered to Suffrage and Beyond Conference, Wellington. (Chs 1, 3 and 7).

Part I

How Feminist Analysis Could and Should Change Economics

1
Feminist Critiques of Orthodox Economics and Why They Are Neglected

Economic conditions, systems and policies are of critical importance to the realities of women's lives, and yet feminist theory has made fewer inroads into the discipline of economics than into most other subjects. Each wave of feminism has been aware of the need for economic and social change, but its impact on economic orthodoxy has been minimal.

Recent New Zealand feminist writing has given considerable attention to analyses of the state, of new right philosophy, and of contradictions in policy relating to paid employment of women and to the welfare state (Armstrong, 1992; Else, 1992; Du Plessis, 1992). It has also analysed the negative implications of the lack of recognition given to unpaid household, caring and voluntary work (Waring, 1988b). However, less emphasis has been placed by New Zealand feminists specifically on the problems and shortcomings of the assumptions and methods of analysis used within economics. A notable exception is the Wellington Women's Studies Association submission (1988) to the Royal Commission on Social Policy, which critiques the free market model and in particular its focus on rationality, economic incentives, competition and individualism, demonstrating its male and monocultural biases, and its costs.

My major contention is that orthodox economic analysis is more often gender blind than gender neutral. (I owe the terminology of this distinction to Sharp and Broomhill, 1988: 33. Gender is now the term used for social differences; sex is the term used for biological differences.) Gender-blind analyses, systems and policies appear to be universal, but in fact use methodologies, assumptions and practices which systematically disadvantage women. Thus, they are not gender neutral in effect.

Feminists argue that social forces and structures cause women as a class to be subordinate to men. However, the language of gender blindness or subordination and of social forces or structures can be seen as too mild. It obscures any group and individual responsibility, and the need for change. 'Women active in grass-roots feminist activities, such as Women's Aid and Rape Crisis Centres, have suggested to me that it is also a language which is too academic, too sanitised, too polite. It is time to stop talking about gender subordination and start talking about male bias' (Elson, 1991: 2). Economic theory and many policies based on it exhibit this male bias, often disguised by non-gendered language. The 'level playing field' is the current jargon for the need for competition, with no incentives or advantages accruing to any participant. There is, in my view, no level playing field in economic theory and policy between women and men.

Five sub-categories of feminist criticisms of orthodox economics can usefully be identified, although they inevitably overlap. The first is the overall framework of consumer theory, in which the economically rational agent maximises individual or household satisfaction. This ignores or inadequately analyses interdependence and conflict, and gives legitimacy to the dichotomy between the private world of households and the public world of markets.

The second issue is the methodology of orthodox analysis, which claims to be based on value-free, positive analyses and scientific status, but disguises the underlying normative structure and values involved.

A third area of criticism is the definitions of economic activity integral to orthodoxy which omit unpaid work of all types and deal inadequately with activity detrimental to the environment.

The fourth issue is the analysis of discrimination within orthodoxy which is based on circular explanations of occupational segregation and pay differences. It thus reinforces status quo distributions of paid and unpaid work and resources, and justifies inequalities based on factors such as gender, race, class and age.

Finally, orthodoxy pays insufficient attention to economic and social outcomes. Its frameworks for analysing differential gender impacts of economic systems, circumstances and policies, including the role of the state, are inadequate. As a result of this, most feminist critiques are located outside orthodoxy, within the general area of political economy, although some criticism is possible even within the orthodox tradition and using its tools. Political economy spans a variety of approaches, including institutional economics which puts considerable emphasis on the political, economic and social institutions that structure our lives and affect economic outcomes.

This chapter will concentrate on the first two and last of these five areas, with the third discussed in the next chapter and the fourth in Part II. It will be helpful first to outline the orthodox or neoclassical economic approach, making some comments on the issues of scarcity and choice, and to contrast it with the broader approaches of some political economists. The three areas of feminist criticism of orthodoxy discussed in this chapter then will be considered in detail. This is followed by a discussion of why and how orthodoxy resists feminist ideas. The chapter concludes with a section arguing that a momentum is building in feminist economic analysis which has the potential to make a substantial and positive difference.

Contrasting orthodoxy and political economy

Orthodox micro-economics taught in most elementary economics courses analyses consumer and producer behaviour on the basis of standard assumptions. Equilibrium prices are established by the forces of supply and demand in perfect competition (this assumption is then relaxed). Individual producing units maximise profit; consuming units maximise satisfaction, utility or well-being, given the constraints of prices and available incomes.

Most orthodox definitions of the scope of economics start from a concern with the allocation of scarce resources. Choices made in situations of scarcity are the key issue. In practice, orthodox economics often appears obsessed with the market at the expense of alternative exchange mechanisms, and of production and distribution. A range of problems which result from over-emphasis on choices, and from glossing over constraints, are discussed in this chapter.

First, even the basic concept of scarcity should not be taken for granted. Whether resources are scarce is a matter of time and place, as well as of their desirability. Hence the usually low price of essential water, which is scarce only in a few places such as deserts. More fundamentally, some human wants or needs, such as love, need never be in scarce supply, even if we often behave as if they are. Whether the essentials of life, and even access to standards of living beyond those, would be scarce with different economic and social systems and more equal distribution within and between countries is open to question. However, environmental considerations, the uneven distribution of resources, and the reality of political and economic life make it necessary to accept that scarcity is a genuine problem.

In conditions of scarcity, whether real or created, market price, based on supply and demand, is the standard method of valuation and, for orthodoxy, the only meaningful one. Hence the low valuation of water and the high valuation of inessential but scarce diamonds. A useful distinction that arises from this example is between exchange value and use value, with the former often inflated relative to the importance of a product to human life (Lewenhak, 1992: 15). The valuation issue is a key one. On the one hand, realism dictates that in practice nothing can be ascribed infinite value or be beyond price. Economics has to try to put a value even on human life itself, and on extra years of life, to assist sensible and consistent decisions on expenditure in areas like road improvements, traffic safety enforcement and health policies. Yet the notion that market price is the only measure of value can appear crass, offensive and contrary to human beliefs and actions. That wisdom is more precious than rubies (Proverbs 3:15) should not be meaningless even to economists. A major challenge to alternatives to orthodox economics is to find ways through these issues, so that human endeavours and attributes which are not priced in the market are valued and taken into account in policy initiatives.

Institutional economists, unlike orthodoxy, do not take market values as sacrosanct. A comparison of the analyses and solutions proposed on waste and pollution is illuminating. For orthodoxy, there can be no wastage in competitively operating markets. If someone is willing to pay, that amount is the value. Environmental problems often arise from the presence of externalities. These externalities allow a polluter, for example, to avoid incurring the cost of the activity to others, who themselves bear these costs. The preferred solution is to internalise these costs, in order to make the market work optimally. For the institutionalist, by contrast,

> The problem of waste takes on a very different look ... Further inquiry into the operational implications of the market solution is precluded by the traditional limited scope and alleged value neutrality of orthodox economics. Externality and waste are all too often attributed to physical causes alone ... This is unfortunate for it precludes analysis of social causes, most specifically the institutionalization of externality and waste through the market, the professed solution ... It will be slim comfort to our children and grandchildren to know that we fouled the world they will inherit 'optimally'. (Hickerson, 1988: 187–8)

In addition to scarcity, the concept of choice also needs careful examination. Those who have a near religious belief in the efficacy and equity of the free market assume or argue that transactors, both buyer and seller, are always better off as a result of their transaction. Otherwise they would not have taken part in it. Thus, free choice is by definition involved in market transactions. This ignores or slides over the fact that different people enter the market with very different access to resources and power, so that there are quite different ranges of options and constraints on their choice. It is therefore little or no more than a tautology to say that all transactors are made better off. 'It seems invalid to explain human behaviour in terms of free choice when we are all products of the social, political, cultural and economic order that we are born into' (White, 1983: 9).

Much greater emphasis is placed by economics on the wonders of choice than the realities of constraints. Yet at some stages of life, such as infancy, people are totally dependent and have no ability to choose. This ability is low at all life stages for those who, often through no fault of their own, are more dependent and have less market power than others. Those who see outcomes largely as the consequences of choice and individual responsibility, rather than constraints and systems, will be able to justify the resulting inequalities to themselves. But this type of thinking may prevent adequate attention being given to social problems. This has been suggested as a factor in the United States' poor record on child poverty and infant mortality (Strassmann, 1993b: 63). New Zealand, too, is slipping down the international league table on these measures, at least partly as a result of a shift away from community assumption of responsibility in these areas.

Examples of the way in which a lack of real options makes the concept of choice almost meaningless arise in the labour market. In 1991 the New Zealand Minister of Labour, Bill Birch, argued the virtues of the Employment Contracts Act 1991 partly in terms of the increased choices it gave employers and employees. The theoretical symmetry of the Act's explanatory note is appealing, but totally spurious:

> This Bill . . . (c) enables each employee to choose either – (i) to negotiate an individual employment contract with his or her employer; or (ii) to be bound by a collective employment contract to which his or her employer is a party (d) enables each employer to choose either (i) to negotiate an individual employment contract with any employee: (ii) to negotiate or elect to be bound by a collective employment contract that binds 2 or more employees.

In practice, there is an inherent power difference between employers and individual employees, with those who sell their labour (unless it is particularly scarce) in the less powerful position. A combination of co-operation and conflict is inevitable in employment relationships, but a desirable shift towards greater co-operation cannot be achieved simply by legislative fiat, particularly when there is no guaranteed sharing of any gains. Recognition of this power difference was one important factor which led to the development of trade union movements, collective bargaining and separate labour law. Current policies appear to ignore historical lessons. Power differences mean that employees may have very little or no choice over coverage by an individual or collective contract or over who should represent them under the legislation, and this shifts the balance of effective decision-making further towards employers. This applies particularly in firms, industries and occupations in which bargaining power and ability to engage in industrial action are low and employer goodwill is not guaranteed. Small workplaces and lower-paid groups are particularly vulnerable. Women and Maori are over-represented in such workplaces.

Similarly, the terms of any contract are in principle to be agreed after bargaining between the parties, who may be represented by an organisation if they wish. In practice, categories of employees with low bargaining power, including younger workers, may well have to accept any terms presented, particularly under the threat of a six-month stand down period for the unemployment benefit. Transactions and contracts can be legally set aside as unfair only in very narrow circumstances, such as extreme coercion or when particular types of misinformation are involved.

Two key claims are frequently made, explicitly or implicitly, about the virtues of the neoclassical economics approach. The first is that there are no viable alternative economic frameworks. The second is that its analysis is based on an entirely descriptive and analytical (known in the jargon as positive) method, and is thus value free, rather than prescribing what ought to be (normative). Feminist challenges to these claims receive attention later. The claims are also attacked by other perspectives within political economy, as the following extract illustrates:

> Orthodox economics typically rests upon particular axioms (e.g. utility maximization) which are fed in at the start of the analysis. Political economy, by contrast, seeks to situate economic analysis within an analysis of society and its institutional structure which is itself well developed intellectually. In this sense, political economy can claim to be less directly shaped by the influence of ideology. Of course, this is not to say that ideological elements are absent. (Stilwell, 1988: 15)

Political economy rejects orthodoxy's view of society and the associated expectations of convergence to an equilibrium. Instead it sees society as being based on 'class divisions and with tendencies towards recurrent economic crises' (*ibid.*: 15). It is more concerned with understanding how surpluses are generated, how capital accumulation occurs and how distribution is determined than with the narrow focus of orthodoxy on market exchange. 'Orthodox economics tries to show that markets allocate scarce resources according to relative efficiency; political economics tries to show that markets distribute income according to relative power' (Nell, 1972: 95). Political economy is characterised by its adherents as involving a broader scope and methodology, and a more interdisciplinary character than orthodox economics.

> If we are to understand why human beings act as they do in their economic roles in various societies, we need to learn all we can from psychology, sociology and anthropology, i.e. that people's economic roles and behaviour are culturally and socially determined, and people are not to be regarded as maximising automatons, reacting mechanistically in an institutional vacuum. (Wheelwright, 1976: 179)

These characteristics make political economy more receptive to feminist challenges than orthodoxy, with a common thread being the recognition of systematic power differences between groups. This is not to assert that feminist critiques are impossible within orthodoxy and its language, nor that all or most writers of political economy have paid adequate attention to gender issues. However, orthodox analyses of issues such as discrimination, occupational segregation and lower wages for women are conservative and limited. Discussion of similar areas using feminist perspectives and/or other political economy positions are broader and more realistic.

Critiques of orthodox economics include those which come from environmental, radical, feminist and institutional perspectives. Current orthodox policies, together with their assumptions and underlying ideology, are being questioned in New Zealand and overseas, but the influence of critics is muted and possibly even decreasing. The moves towards market economies in Eastern Europe and the imposition of approved policies in developing and developed countries all involve the ever-extending influence of orthodoxy. This is the price of loans from international institutions and adequate ratings from credit agencies. Multinational companies and agencies such as these reduce the autonomy of national governments, particularly in small and debtor countries. A focus on individualism, self-reliance and the virtues of competition is evident in many western countries, giving rise to retrenchments in the welfare state, a retreat from state-run economic activity and a totally market-oriented system. In this climate, critics of orthodoxy of any school are marginalised.

An unhealthy tendency is evident among current adherents of orthodoxy, who claim not only the high ground of correctness in theory, prescription and philosophy, but also that there are no alternatives worthy of consideration. Thus Roger Kerr, executive director of the New Zealand Business Roundtable (on an *Insight* documentary on the New Zealand Treasury in March 1991), claimed that Treasury had improved since his time there, owing to a greater congruence of opinion and higher overall standard of analysis. This simply means that alternative views have been eased out. He further asserted that Keynesianism was dead, and that anyone propounding alternative views to his own were simply ignorant, misinformed and/or not up to date. Such abusive tactics are prevalent, and the arguments based on one over-simple variant of theory. The analyses and resulting conclusions are either unencumbered by any appeal to empirical data, particularly New Zealand-based information, or refer only to selective overseas studies to support the position taken (Easton, 1988).

A full analysis of the methods and causes of the takeover of orthodoxy among influential economists in New Zealand and elsewhere is beyond this discussion. However, the influence of American orthodoxy, and particularly the Chicago school, through direct contact with New Zealand policy-making economists can be traced out (*ibid.*). This influence extends to macro-economic ideas and modern adaptations and extensions of micro-economics (Goldfinch, 1990). Such refinements are responses to the oversimplicity of models which cannot account for real-life phenomena, such as the persistence of unemployment and the behaviour of institutions. The areas include public choice theory, transaction costs and principal agent theory, and the developments attempt to incorporate realities within the basic framework of orthodoxy rather than to alter its overall approach.

In claiming the high ground of correct analysis, orthodoxy has also subtly instigated a takeover of ordinary language into a form of doublespeak. The term 'incentives' is a good example. The need for appropriate 'incentives' to influence behaviour is frequently argued by politicians. The supposed 'poverty trap' caused by an 'insufficient' gap between benefit levels and wage opportunities is said to reduce the incentive to be in paid work and to encourage welfare dependency. But this is a form of doublespeak. Incentives to be in paid work in fact become punishments for not being in paid work. Sole parents, for example, may find considerable difficulty in rejoining the paid workforce through a shortage of vacancies, a lack of suitable training, the unavailability or unaffordability of childcare and discrimination against women with dependants. They might then be justifiably cynical about the need for an incentive for them to rejoin the paid workforce in the form of a lower benefit.

Feminist critiques of orthodoxy

Turning to the specifically feminist critiques of orthodoxy, a political economist summarises the major feminist challenges posed within economics as 'the need to analyze the relationship between capitalism and patriarchy, to account for the differential position of men and women in respect of waged labour and non-waged labour, to reappraise the role of the household in the production process, and to broaden the analysis of economic activity to include the role of the household in the process of reproducing the economic and social order' (Stilwell, 1988: 20). However, even this does not go far enough. Feminist economists argue for a reappraisal of almost all the bases of economics. 'Add women and stir' is quite insufficient.

This is not to imply that there is a homogeneity of approach among those who consider themselves to be feminist economists. All see the need for changes to the discipline, and all are motivated by a concern that the quality of women's (and men's and children's) lives could be improved by better analysis, systems and policies. Most would agree that feminist economics should also pay attention to ethnic, class and other structural characteristics which orthodox economics ignores or analyses in an inadequate manner.

However, feminist economists differ among themselves, and take up liberal, Marxist, radical and other approaches linked to positions, beliefs and schools within economics and feminisms. It is beyond the scope of this chapter to discuss in detail the different analyses of those writing in these various traditions. However, some of the differences will be touched on, and will emerge also in the different visions sketched in Part IV – and it will become apparent that I am in greater sympathy with more, rather than less, radical positions. But the main focus here is on common elements within the feminist critiques of neoclassical economics, even though they differ in some respects. Feminists working mainly within a Marxist framework have shown that feminist ideas within socialist writing predated and were marginalised by Marx (Folbre, 1993b). They have also criticised some later Marxist writing for ignoring gender issues, and have attempted to remedy this (Matthaei, 1991). Similarly, institutional economics has the potential to incorporate feminist ideas, but only recently have feminist writers in this genre returned to exploring their earlier interest (Jennings, 1993). Ways of building a positive feminist economics will be considered after an examination of three of the five areas of critique outlined earlier, their longevity and their comparative neglect by orthodoxy.

Frameworks

The overall orthodox framework of economically rational man (*sic*) maximising individual (or household) satisfaction ignores or inadequately analyses the relationships between independence and interdependence/co-operation. It thus fails to deal with the problem that, at times, interdependence breaks down and conflict occurs.

The early economic models of rational decision-making based on the maximisation of utility ignore interpersonal relationships in a fundamental way. The models of behaviour stress selfishness and competition. Non-economic motivations, interdependence between individuals and concern for others are ignored. Time allocation models based on maximising satisfaction focus on the choice between leisure, valued intrinsically, and paid work, valued for the consumption purchased with the remuneration. As well as omitting other reasons for working for pay (Lane, 1991), this ignores unpaid household, caring and community work, which is neither leisure nor paid work.

Orthodox economists now apply their tools to almost all economic and social questions involving scarcity and choice, from marriage and children to crime, from time allocation to discrimination. The 'new home economics' is the term used for applications to the family, although it is no longer new, dating back to the early 1960s. For example: 'The basic underlying assumptions of the neoclassical analysis of the family are that it is a unit whose adult members make informed and rational decisions that result in maximising the utility or well-being of the family' (Blau and Ferber, 1986: 40).

More generally, as the founding father of the new home economics, Gary Becker, puts it:

> Scarcity and choice characterize all resources allocated by the political process, by the family (including decisions about a marriage mate, family size, the frequency of church attendance, and the allocation of time between sleeping and waking hours) . . . What most distinguishes economics as a discipline . . . is not its subject matter but its approach . . . which assumes maximising behavior more explicitly and extensively than other approaches do, be it the utility or wealth function of the household, firm, union, or government bureau . . . The combined assumptions of maximizing behavior, market equilibrium, and stable preferences, used relentlessly and unflinchingly, form the heart of the economic approach as I see it. (Becker, 1976: 4–6)

He even claims that: 'Economic theory may well be on its way to providing a unified framework for all behaviour involving scarce resources, non market as well as market, non monetary as well as monetary, small groups as well as competitive' (Becker, 1974: 299).

There are some worthwhile features of the attempt to extend the sphere of economics, in that it reduces somewhat its unreality and concentration on only a small subset of economic and social life. Further, some genuine insights result. For example, economic explanations of the long-term decline in fertility in western countries emphasise the increased relative price or cost of children. The decline in traditional agriculture reduced the need for children's economic contribution, while the increasing value of adult time raised the opportunity costs of childcare, with higher expenditure per child substituting for large numbers of children. These explanations complement medical and social analyses (Becker, 1985: 16).

However, such analyses are much enhanced when they are combined with a feminist perspective. A deconstruction of the work of a 'housewife', in this tradition, examines her duties, general and sexual: the physical hazards, including risks of physical abuse from the male partner, and the pay, in a non-cash form (Bergmann, 1981). Barbara Bergmann makes an arresting impression by putting into the jargon of labour economics some of the obvious disadvantages of being a full-time housewife during marriage:

> The housewife's attractiveness to her husband can be thought of as a component of the human capital needed for her job, and she may be in the position of seeing this part of her portfolio of assets wane in value either gradually or suddenly. Her husband's attractiveness to her may also suddenly

or gradually diminish, reducing the value of the intimacy fringe benefit, possibly changing it from positive to negative. These possibilities obviously make for high risk both with respect to 'working conditions' and tenure. (*ibid.*: 82)

She then goes on to ask why an occupation which has so many disadvantages is chosen by so many people, and answers her own question by saying that the alternatives facing the women who 'choose' it are worse or made to seem so. Barbara Bergmann also notes that a declining proportion of women are in fact choosing the occupation in developed countries, since few women are now full-time housewives for all their adult lives. She welcomes the demise of the occupation.

This is an example of a stimulating feminist application within a neoclassical framework. However, a number of problems are evident both in the colonising efforts of neoclassical economics and its immodesty. The difficulties with given, stable preferences, all of equal validity, are discussed later. Another of its problematic implications is that all behaviour, including the unexpected, must be rational and based on these fixed preferences. Hence unexpected behaviour must be explained by some element in the environment, such as hidden costs which account for a firm, worker or household failing to exploit an apparently profitable opportunity. This is regarded as a strength by adherents of the genre, since it avoids the need to 'take refuge in assertions about irrationality, contentment with wealth already acquired, or convenient ad hoc shifts in values (ie preferences)' (Becker, 1976: 7). However, this can easily degenerate to circular reasoning, as Becker himself recognises. He argues, nevertheless, that useful predictions have resulted.

Circular reasoning, with preferences taken as given, can, however, simply reinforce and justify the status quo – for example, in the division of labour within households. If men earn more on average than women, specialisation of roles, with men doing all or more of the market work and women more of the household and caring work, emerges appropriately from rational household decision-making. In turn, this expectation can justify less education and training for women, which will perpetuate their lower average earnings. This analysis of course deals in averages, and ignores the role of discrimination and the undervaluation of female-dominated occupations which reinforce the circular justification of the division of labour.

Thus too much is taken as given in the conventional explanations, including the existence of discrimination, the extent of the occupational segregation of men and women, and women's responsibility for child rearing (MacDonald, 1981). Weighing up the pros and cons of applying neoclassical analysis to the family, Isabel Sawhill argues that:

> To anyone who has been trained as an economist, the charms of economic analysis are almost irresistible. It is intellectually clear, challenging and rigorously deductive. In addition, the methodological sophistication of most economists, although not essential to good theory, gives them a competitive edge in empirical work. Most importantly, the economic paradigm does have a certain 'unifying power' because it is highly general – highly abstract. This power, however, has been gained at the price of obliterating most of the trees from the forest. (Sawhill, 1977: 120)

Rational decision-making is central to neoclassical analysis, but the nature of the decision-making unit is frequently glossed over. Are expenditure and consumption decisions made by the individual, the household, the family, iwi, community, or any of these? And how are they defined? In practice, some decisions are taken at each level, with variations between people and over time. Economics started to confront these questions when it turned to marriage and children. However, the first approach was simply to assume a joint household or family utility function, which allowed for co-operation or altruism but assumed away any possibility of different preferences or conflict. Such a family utility function could, of course, instead reflect dictatorship rather than co-operation, with any conflict simply hidden.

This has been rightly criticised. 'The people marching through the household of the economist are an enviable group: they are motivated by love and caring and rarely by hate or fear. Very little attention is given to the nature of conflict or to the use of power within the family. Why is it that marriage leads sometimes to positive and sometimes to negative caring among family members? The economist has no answers' (*ibid.*: 121). There are many examples of the absence of altruism and sharing under patriarchal structures in the household. Family violence is overwhelmingly perpetrated by men on women and children in western countries, while the impact of similar gender power imbalances on the distribution of resources is demonstrated by undernourishment of children, especially girls, in India and elsewhere (Sen, 1984). The greater valuation of male children even leads to selective abortion of female fetuses and infanticide of baby girls, while the practice of suttee has not completely disappeared. These and other areas of greater relative deprivation for women resulted in a decline in the male/female population ratio in India from .972 in 1901 to .935 in 1981 (Sen, 1990: 142).

All this was ignored by the earliest writing of the new home economics school. In this tradition, Becker assumed parents are altruistic toward their children, with the utility of the former dependent on that of the latter: 'The main characteristic that distinguishes family households from firms and other organisations is that allocations within families are largely determined by altruism and related obligations, whereas allocations within firms are largely determined by implicit or explicit contracts among selfish members' (Becker, 1985: 7).

More recent writing has responded to the obvious inadequacy of a single utility function by considering conflict and its consequences. Three later modifications can be distinguished, which meet some of the problems discussed above, but only imperfectly. Two of them use game theory, an approach which models decision making as a game between players who decide their strategies on the basis of possible outcomes, taking account of the likely behaviour of the other player(s). The first modification was based on bargaining models of allocation and distribution within families, treating marriage as a co-operative game. The bargaining process should resolve conflicting preferences, with the threat of the dissatisfied party leaving the marriage if no satisfactory compromise is reached. The second uses non-co-operative games, with each spouse having independent preferences while also showing some altruism towards the other (Woolley, 1988). A feminist evaluation of these two approaches to gender relations in the household concludes that non-formalised versions have some potential, but that game theory models are not likely to contribute a great deal, as they involve over-arbitrary rules and mostly yield solutions that are already well known (Seiz, 1991).

Finally, the transaction cost approach is broader, in that it can deal with change over time, and concentrate on the internal organisation and structure of the household or family. Transaction cost analysis within firms 'focuses on the role of institutions in structuring complex, long-term relationships' (Pollak, 1985: 583). In extending the approach to households, parallels between marriages and firm mergers, insurance concepts and the role of implicit or explicit contracts throw light on the advantages and disadvantages of family organisation. The greater complexity inevitably implies a structure unsuitable for rigorous statistical testing, and this was seen by Pollak as a defect. It may instead reflect the reality of a complexity unsuited to such an approach.

Noting that Becker's model of marriage is based on the metaphor of free trade between producers, and Pollak's on the merger of independent firms, Elaine McCrate (1987) proposes a third metaphor, based on the hierarchical employment relation in the Marxian theory of the firm. This brings together feminist and Marxist writing on the family, in which unequal gender power relations are critical. She points out that the merger analogy, if to a slightly lesser extent than that of trade, falls short of acknowledging the systematic bias towards men's having more power in marriage. From this power, men can extract economic benefits from the dependent group, their wives. Thus McCrate, like Bergmann who was quoted earlier, attributes high marriage rates to lack of alternatives until the capitalist expansion of labour demand provided opportunities for women's economic independence. She shows the link between an increasing measure of economic independence for women over a 30-year period and the declining proportion of women in marriages, with greater prevalence of divorce and lower marriage rates. The increasing possibility of economic independence is measured by the ratio of average income inside and outside marriage.

McCrate's analysis has more resonance for feminists than the previous models. However, even the transactions cost approach is a move towards recognising that a combination of self-interest and the interests of others prevails in the private world of the household, with a blend of individual and collective means of meeting needs. Feminist analysis argues that this is the case in both the private world and the public world of the market, and so attempts to break down the artificial separation and address its adverse consequences for many women.

This separation, with altruism assumed to be the main driving force in the female-dominated private domain and self-interest in the male-dominated public domain, has underpinned much economic writing, old and recent (Pujol, 1992). 'Feminist economic approaches, however diverse, are all suspicious of any rhetoric that describes women as less self-interested than men or automatically places gender interests on a lower level of analysis than family interest or class interest ... Much contemporary feminist research focuses on the causes and consequences of unequal power between men and women' (Folbre and Hartmann, 1988: 193). Nancy Folbre and Heidi Hartmann go on to argue that this research provides a better explanation of economic trends in households and in the labour market than simple neoclassical and Marxist perspectives. The implications of the public/private split are under scrutiny in a number of strands of thought, influenced by post-structuralist arguments that all knowledge is socially constructed and dualisms suspect. This school of thought will be discussed later.

Recognising the co-existence of independence/self-interest and interdependence/concern for the interests of others in all spheres clarifies a number of issues. Some degree of interdependence and sharing of resources within and between various levels, including nuclear and extended families, communities and the state, is inevitable and desirable. However, interdependence is more acceptable if it occurs by near consensus (the welfare state is an example) or voluntarily than if it reduces to forced dependence on a spouse or the state. Hence individual independence or separation forms the basis of interdependence or connection. A good summary of recent writing on these lines suggests that:

> Separation and connection are both integral to human identity. While, on the one hand, 'no man or woman is an island', on the other hand, no person can give up an individual identity without great cost. The separation/connection dualism as seen through the dominant world view, however, with individuality prized and attributed to men, and connection seen as requiring the dissolving of identity and linked to women and inferiority, represents a perversion of this dialectic nature. (Nelson, 1991: 13)

Instead, Nelson argues for a balance, seeing both men and women equally as 'individuals in relation'.

It has been in men's interests to see women as naturally altruistic; this then involves them in little or no sacrifice. There are also some feminist schools of thought which see women either by nature or nurture as more altruistic and bound to an ethic of caring for others than men (Gilligan, 1982). The arguments with respect to the existence or otherwise of these and/or other differences between women and men, and whether, if they exist, they arise from nature, nurture or a combination, are beyond this discussion. Certainly gender role differences exist. It is their exploitation through the public/private split, and the gender power and role differences which accompany it and disadvantage women, that are the focus here.

The whole area of selfish versus unselfish or altruistic behaviour is a complex one, with many different situations and interpretations, and no simple contrast between the two. For example, giving some time to helping a friend may not feel like a sacrifice: there may be no conflicts of interest (Hoagland, 1988: 88). In a worse situation, self-denial by a woman acting under actual or threatened dominance by a man can be simply for self-preservation. However, acting in the interests of others can be regarded as always simply self-interest, either to make oneself feel good or by definition. In this way, by tautologically making it just another neoclassical taste, economists can ignore it altogether. Economics teaches us that all choice involves sacrifice, through the opportunity cost of time and/or money involved which cannot be used elsewhere.

Sarah Hoagland suggests that instead we may see choice not as involving sacrifice but as the creation of activity and value in a particular direction:

> Understanding choice as creation, not sacrifice, helps us better understand choices we make typically considered 'altruistic'. We often are drawn to helping others. That's one reason so many are drawn to healing, to teaching, to volunteering to work at shelters, to practicing therapy, to working at community centers or in political campaigns, to going to Nicaragua – to all kinds of political work. In doing such work, we feel we are creating something, that we are participating in something; we engage and we make a difference. (*ibid.*: 93)

This may seem to contradict earlier discussion of the capitalist and patriarchal, or male structural, power. This power, together with the policies supporting it, was argued to impose constraints on the choice of less advantaged groups, including women. However, Hoagland's analysis is more concerned with positive choices made within the context of feminist and lesbian community and is thus not incompatible with concern about outside constraints on choice which do involve sacrifice.

Another important aspect of the broad application of orthodox economics relates to the possession and acquisition of adequate information. The economic approach is that investment in information can be analysed, as it is for other investments, in terms of costs and benefits. Thus, one would expect a greater investment in information to be made before taking major decisions rather than minor ones: 'the purchase of a house or entrance into marriage versus the purchase of a sofa or bread' (Becker, 1976: 7). However, in personal areas, full information may be impossible to obtain. Thus the situation is not that simple.

> In economic terms, it is generally assumed that people have sufficient information about alternatives to make reasonably intelligent choices. In some areas it is easy to obtain such information either before one acts or through experiences and mistakes are not very costly. For example, if one chooses a restaurant and it serves a poor meal, one need not go there again. On the other hand, if one

marries or has a child and the decision turns out badly, the solution is not so easily corrected. Furthermore, one's own reaction to it can have serious ramifications for others. Unfrequented restaurants will and should go out of business; unloved spouses and children are not so easily written off. (Sawhill, 1977: 122)

In principle, extending economic analyses of households could be helpful and incorporate feminist perspectives. In practice, the education, language, leanings and, in most cases, gender of the writers make this unlikely or rare. 'Each marriage can be considered a two person firm with either member the "entrepreneur" who hires the other at ... salary and receives residual "profits" ' (Becker, 1974: 302). Such a symmetrical framework fails to reflect the realities for many women. Unfortunately, this type of approach is much more common than the analyses of feminist economists.

Methodology

The claims that orthodox economics is objective and value free have been touched on earlier. For those who believe that the claim is false and the desire fruitless, economics has attempted to make itself into a pure science, at the expense of dealing with most important questions. A number of influential economists have made similar points: 'To eliminate value judgements from the subject-matter of social science is to eliminate the subject itself' (Robinson, 1971: 122)

By contrast, the orthodox view is on these lines: 'Economics, as a positive science, has no status as ethical or political prescription ... Political economy in my vocabulary is not scientific economics, a collection of value-free generalisations about the way in which economic systems work' (Robbins, 1976: 2). This view rests on the argument that theoretical economics consists wholly of descriptive statements and their logical consequences, and is therefore necessarily value free. Thus welfare economics has been obsessed with seeking an equilibrium in which no one can be made better off without making someone else worse off. In practice, almost all change makes some better off and others worse off, absolutely or at least relatively. In theory, orthodox analysis attempts to predict the distributional effects of economic or policy changes but not to evaluate distributional change, thus avoiding interpersonal comparisons.

The investment in avoiding interpersonal comparisons has several aspects. Utilities which can involve my increased satisfaction from your better position make the simple theory much more intractable. Thus, 'If you understand that I am deeply injured by your taking action X as compared to Y, you may very well refrain from taking X even though you are marginally injured by Y. And if economists are forced to take such behavior into account, then all the fine optimality theorems about competitive capitalism are lost' (Ward, 1972: 199–200).

Ward also argues that economic texts typically concentrate on trivial choices which make social factors of little importance, and that the market divides choices in such a way that few have discernible impacts on others, thus circularly reinforcing the assumption of independence. In practice, of course, policy has to make interpersonal comparisons, or at least decisions with distributional and thus interpersonal implications. Further, 'the idea that we do know something usable, something "publicly testable" about the belief-systems of other people, must seem rather banal and obvious' (*ibid.*: 204). While higher incomes are not the only, or even the most important, contributor to happiness (Lane, 1991), a positive relationship is usually found between income level and reported self-rated happiness (Scitovsky, 1986).

Orthodox economists avoid judging distributional change, but they do discuss the costs of redistribution policies. It is suggested that significant efficiency losses arise from income transfers through tax/welfare systems. Such losses come from administrative costs and behavioural changes as a result of reduced incentives to seek paid work. In advocating considerable gaps (or, in the jargon, a lowering of replacement rates) between benefit levels and wages because of the alleged labour market incentive effects, the positive and normative start to elide, and the values of such writers emerge. This is particularly so when the argument is based on thin or non-existent empirical evidence.

Contrast the tenor of the discussion repeated several times and without empirical references in *Government Management* (New Zealand Treasury, 1987) with the conclusion of a careful review of the evidence. Treasury asserts, 'The likelihood of undertaking paid employment is inevitably reduced by the offer of income support for those without paid employment' (*ibid.*: 404). By contrast, Brosnan *et al* conclude: 'we have shown that the assertion that disincentives in social security programs have substantial effects on actual labour supply appears to be an "economic myth". Accordingly, attempts to reduce unemployment or poverty by cutting benefits or limiting their duration to reduce labour supply disincentives are largely mistaken, and it is misleading to present reforms that are essentially cost cutting measures as the solution to increasing welfare dependency' (Brosnan, Wilson and Wong, 1989: 33).

Concentration only on the efficiency costs of redistribution, while avoiding the attempt to evaluate changes in distribution, is inadequate. This is accentuated if the distributional effects of a policy change are much larger than the efficiency gains, particularly if these are only speculative. Easton quotes evidence that these problems were present when the case was made for trade liberalisation and some elements of labour market liberalisation in New Zealand. He concludes: 'We are now beginning to see an insidious side to the advocation of the recent policies of liberalisation. They have been presented in terms of "value free" efficiency, and of somehow being above politics. But the reality is that they have had an extremely value laden agenda' (Easton, 1989: 188).

The supposed value-free position of economic orthodoxy has a high price, at least to non-adherents, in an additional way, in that all ends or wants must be regarded as equally valid. Economists study means, not ends. Rationality simply requires that purchases are made in accordance with relative preferences for the various ends, subject to the constraints of income and prices. The 'black box' of preferences can be investigated by other disciplines, but the economist takes them as given. Institutional theorists, critical of neoclassical economics, regard this as absurd. 'Values, or ends, are an "output" of the larger cultural milieu and they are not all equally valid or legitimate. We do, because we must, choose among wants, desires and preferences' (Hickerson, 1988: 176 and 188).

The assumptions of consumer behaviour have received considerable attention in discussions of methodology. Given that any model is an abstraction from reality, there are lively debates about whether the axioms or assumptions need to be a close approximation to reality or whether, as Milton Friedman among others argues, accurate predictions of behaviour are sufficient to validate the model or at least render it useful. (For a range of views, see Hahn and Hollis, 1979.) With many of the assumptions both contrary to reality and gender blind, and the resulting analyses and policy prescriptions far from gender neutral in effect, the Friedman view is open to strong feminist criticism.

Another useful way of examining rationality and consumer choice is by looking inside the 'black box' of preferences and using contributions from psychology and sociology to illuminate the decision process. This means, formally, that an individual's utility function should not be taken as given, or exogenous. What is valued by individuals is created by a combination of nature, nurture and the environment. To assume that this is of no importance in economics is absurd. Tastes also change in response to individual experience (England, 1993). Advertising has a large role in the creation of consumption desires; it raises prices, and is a weapon for the market system's control over individuals (Schmookler, 1993). It is highly doubtful that a socially desirable amount of advertising results.

Taking utility functions as given may also be gender biased. Social conditioning and the resulting acceptance of gender-biased values may make women accept a smaller share of access to resources than their partners. Men's very slow acceptance of a more equal sharing of household tasks, even if they have equal or more time free from paid work, is a preference which women are challenging as it constrains their labour force participation and/or gives them a double burden. Hence, 'because preferences in part determine women's economic position, understanding the forces that shape men's and women's preferences is high on the feminist economics agenda' (Woolley, 1993: 3). Further, if women's economic position is to be improved, it is important that some of these preferences can and should be changed.

It is rather new for economists actually to ask people what they value, but not for psychologists. Answers often indicate that material well-being is by no means the most important determinant of personal happiness and that most of the assumptions made about utility functions are invalid. Socio-economics is attempting to explore this further. (See Maital, 1988; Etzioni, 1988b; Scitovsky, 1976 and 1986.) The overwhelming and exaggerated importance of economic motivations and incentives is crucial to neoclassical economics. Those imbued with formal economics (too much and too little else?) may imbibe its assumptions and act on its predictions more than other people.

One example which has been investigated empirically is that of free-rider behaviour. With narrow self-interest as the main motivator, free-rider behaviour, in the form of a selfish unwillingness to pay for public goods or reveal one's true preferences for them, is predicted. These are areas such as street lighting or defence, from which no one can easily be excluded once they are provided. However, in experimental situations, free-rider behaviour has been found to be significantly more prevalent among economics graduate students than other students (Marwell and Ames, 1981). Similarly, selfish behaviour in an experimental game was more common both among economics majors than others and among men than women; in each case the other variable was held constant. This result was observed in a study of a 'prisoners' dilemma' game, the outcome of which depends on whether each of the two participants behaves co-operatively or competitively (Frank et al, 1993). Such behaviour can be self-defeating. These authors also report a tendency for economics professors to give less than others to charity. They ask whether mean people become economists or economics training makes you mean, and conclude that it is a bit of both! This is far more than just fun or a debating point: if, unlike the economists who influence policy, people generally are far less selfish and incentives-oriented than economic orthodoxy assumes and predicts, those policies are likely to be misguided.

It has been stated earlier that the set of economic analyses which I have broadly defined as political economy is more concerned than orthodoxy with questions of economic power, including differential access between sets of people to markets and resources, and the resulting distributions of wealth and income. Orthodox economics does not ignore power completely. Monopoly power has received attention in terms of the resource misallocation it may permit, and this has been extended to the bureaucracy and other areas. The focus is, however, on the distortion caused to perfect market behaviour and on ways to overcome this, rather than on the power imbalances inherent in different positions within supposedly well-operating markets.

Economists frequently talk past each other on issues related to power, because they use totally different concepts and implied definitions. For orthodoxy, power involves coercion whereas markets by definition involve free exchange. For institutionalists, by contrast, power is central and may be just as strong when it is wielded without explicit coercion. Trade unions can be seen as an attempt to introduce countervailing power, while the employment contract can be viewed as the purchase by the employer of the right to exert power or authority. In terms of 'power over', power may be defined as the ability to implement one's interests when they conflict with those of others. The possession of economic power can be defined simply in terms of resources, wealth and property rights, or in terms of the ability to exercise significant control over decision-making processes with respect to allocation of resources (Klein, 1988).

Klein argues that orthodox economics has consistently taken the prevailing power system as appropriate and institutionally sanctioned, whereas institutionalists argue that the realities of deploying economic power require the regulation, control and in some cases supplanting of private allocation mechanisms. The current state of technology and total resources would permit performance on many social indicators such as infant mortality, pollution and illiteracy to be improved with different forms of organisation and power distribution. Orthodox economics will not or cannot tackle these major questions.

Even within orthodox economics there has been a recent study which tackled power within markets as a central concept. It concluded that:

> Evolving technology increases the stock of information relevant to market exchange. When that expanding knowlege is unevenly owned and unequally interpretable, the old adage that 'knowledge is power' takes on a wholly new meaning ... Some actors in markets, if they are self-interested and rational, will be able to exploit the situation to their advantage, and perhaps to the detriment of their trading partners ... Rational maximizers, even if they enter the world with identical, immutable, and invariable preference functions, will thus find themselves in a complex system of power relationships. Markets per se are not themselves enough to prevent this. (Bartlett, 1989: 193–5)

Earlier questioning of the tendency for orthodox economics to assert that it is both value free and objective may have given the impression that these concepts are equivalent. This is not the case. Some recent writing in the feminist theory of sciences argues that value neutrality is neither possible nor desirable. However, it suggests that while objectivity is rarely seen in conventional science, it is possible and desirable to work towards a new and better version of objectivity (Harding, 1991). This necessarily brief account is based largely on Sandra Harding's discussion, but she draws on many other feminist theorists.

Orthodox economics is based on the positivist approach of the natural sciences. Feminist critiques of science see this approach as imbued with erroneous notions of value neutrality, objectivity and dualistic thinking. Dualisms such as mind/body, abstract/concrete, objective/subjective, rational/emotional and, by inference at least, male/female, with the first involving a superior level and manner of thinking, are criticised as limited, hierarchical and gender biased. The separation of knower from known, with detachment a major virtue, means that scientific measurement alone can contribute to knowledge, with no supplementation from experience or from sensual, spiritual or emotional knowledge (Bordo, 1986). Thus positivist knowledge is established largely by scientific methods of quantitative measurement. Social sciences aspire to be as close as possible to the natural sciences, to improve their position in a hierarchy based on objectivity and quantitative measurement as key virtues. Hence economics, which uses these methodologies and technologies more than, say, sociology or anthropology, emerges higher in such a hierarchy. However, Harding argues that it is possible to develop 'natural as well as social sciences that are not systematically blinded to the ways in which their descriptions and explanations of their subject matters are shaped by the origins and consequences of their research practices and by the interests, desires and values promoted by such practices' (Harding, 1991: 15).

Harding distinguishes three major feminist approaches to science – feminist empiricism, standpoint theory and post-modernism – which have attempted to start on such a reformation. Feminist empiricism involves the least radical challenge to scientific method, arguing that while much research has been sexist and androcentric, this is simply bad science, because it bases generalisations for humankind on data about white men. This violation of science's own rules of method and theory could be remedied by better research, without necessitating any change to the underlying notions of value-neutral objectivity. Harding argues that this school of thought has made positive contributions, but that in fact one cannot simply add feminist work into existing structures, since it ends up challenging the overall framework.

Feminist standpoint theory sees more basic flaws in positivism's dualisms and assumptions, which fit the experience of white men from elite classes. On parallel lines to Marxist analysis, it sees so-called scientific knowlege as socially constructed by its makers and dependent on their position. This does not reduce to total relativism, for it is argued that while there may be no universal truths for all times, some theories are nevertheless better supported by evidence than others. 'We can tell some stories about ourselves, nature, and social life which can be shown with good evidence to be far less partial and distorted – less false – than the dominant ones' (*ibid.*: 59-60). Thus research has to start from the lives of women and other previously marginalised groups to generate more inclusive theory and description. This does not mean that feminist standpoint theory rests on claims about biological difference or essentialism, but rather that women's lives are different from men's in important ways scientifically and epistemologically.

Post-modernism argues that standpoint theory is insufficiently destructive of science. A highly simplified treatment of these ideas is that in the absence of universal truths, all categories and knowledge are social constructs and relative, including gender. Hence there is no more (or less) justification in feminist arguments than there is in the claims of the dominant culture. The deconstruction of dualisms, including those of gender and race, is a key aspect of post-modern theory. Feminism, and feminist economics, has been little freer than other analyses of false universalising and of class and race bias (Williams, 1993). However, a critical problem of post-modern thought is that it can be interpreted as making no real challenge to current power structures, since no perspective can be judged as superior to any other. This is a serious issue when a great deal of scientific writing has refused, within its own paradigms at least, to consider the ethics and consequences of inhuman uses of science.

Harding sees value and limitations in all three of these feminist approaches, and attempts some synthesis through the creation of a new form of strong objectivity to replace the weak objectivity of conventional science. Attempting to separate objectivity from its 'shameful and damaging history' (Harding, 1991: 159), she argues that although research is socially situated, it can still be more objectively conducted without aiming for or claiming value neutrality. This strong objectivity aims at improved, not lessened, rational standards for choosing between theories, with inclusiveness seen as critical. The separation of the knower, researcher or subject from the known, researched or object is rejected. With women and men located in every class, race, sexuality, culture and society, feminist thought is multiple and sometimes contradictory, and must start from the lives of all women.

Economics in particular needs to be concerned with the reality of people's lives and not hide behind a false detachment. Nelson points out the narrowing over time of the American Economic Association statement of principles, with its increasing emphasis on detachment as against earlier statements about the promotion of human progress by the state and the need for study of the actual conditions of economic life by the profession (Nelson, 1993a). The Econometric Society's 1933 definition of scope is even more imbued with the notion of scientific objectivity. It includes: 'The Society shall operate as a completely disinterested, scientific organization, without political, social, financial or nationalistic bias. Its main object shall be to promote studies that aim at the unification of the theoretical-quantitative and the empirical-quantitative approach to economic problems and that are penetrated by constructive and rigorous thinking similar to that which has come to dominate in the natural sciences.' As Nelson asks, 'Are the terms "penetration" and "domination" really value-free and gender-neutral, or do they indicate something else about the mind-set of the founders of this school?' (Nelson, 1993b: 27).

Nelson is not alone in looking beneath the use of language for hidden meanings. Susan Feiner's brilliant deconstruction of possible unconscious meanings in neoclassical economists' analysis of exchange mechanisms in the market uses psychoanalytical theory, building on Susan Bordo's work (Feiner, 1993). She argues that economic theory, building its perfect market system which works best for all, plays an important role in generating unconscious notions of gender, sexuality and class, which then prevents it from recognising exploitation. Its community participates in a shared group fantasy of a fair and objective system. Feiner's symbolic deconstruction likens the market to a mother, the individual purchaser to an infant and the lack of a perfect functioning market to separation anxiety: 'The vision of the perfectly empathic mother is enthroned in neoclassical economics as the perfectly competitive market. In such markets, as with fantasy mothers, all wishes are fulfilled. Gratification is total, instant and infinitely repeating' (*ibid.*: 10).

This throws a different light on the question posed by Nancy Hartsock (1983) of why exchange, which draws on the notion of isolated individuals with some competing and some common interests, is seen as basic, when our first relation is the dependent one of mothers and infants. Feiner attributes the survival of neoclassical economics in the face of criticism from many sides to a potency derived from these unconscious symbolisms: 'It is not the capitalist market which meets needs, but it is instead the neoclassical representation of that market which meets needs' (Feiner, 1993: 17). Ways of using the ideas of feminist theory to develop a feminist economics are discussed at the end of this chapter.

Analyses of outcomes

Analysis of the impact of economic systems and policies on different groups should be an important part of economic discussion, and include the assessment of policy changes. However, the assumed universality of orthodox methodology results in analysis by gender and ethnicity being less common than analysis by factors such as income, age or household structure. Where gender is discussed, differential impacts are more likely to be seen as consequences of differences in women's behaviour than as partly a result of biases in systems or policies.

Since outcomes are heavily dependent on policies at the level of the whole economy (macro-economic policies), it is important for feminist economics to come to grips with this level of analysis. Most of the criticism of orthodox economics discussed so far has been at the micro level, which analyses the behaviour of individuals and specific markets. Feminist economic analysis has recently started to pay attention to macro-economics. General economic policies, covering macro and micro areas, and including labour, industry, government sector and international trade policies, have more impact on the economic status of women than specific policies aimed to improve that status. Thus the impact of equal opportunity policies, for example, may be significant alongside a favourable economic situation and policy climate, but can be negligible if other policies are causing job losses and reduced union and employee bargaining power.

In Australia, the Federal Government and several states prepare, in conjunction with the Budget, a supplementary Women's Budget in which government departments are required to assess the gender impacts of policies under their control. This does not, of course, yield an immediate diagnosis of, let alone cure for, any gender biases. Feminist critics of the process argue that Treasury sees growth as the automatic solution for all groups, and ignores criticisms of the coverage, omissions and distribution of measured national income (Power *et al*, 1988). Claims of gender neutrality for the tax system ignore the ways in which women's dependency is built in. Where little thought has previously been given to gender aspects of analysis and policy, departments can argue that: 'Macro-economic policies have a major impact on the living standards of all Australians through, for example, policies which determine the overall level of Government spending or the level of interest rates. It is difficult to determine a particular impact on women as there are no accurate means by which to measure the relative burdens and benefits of macro-economic decisions on the basis of gender' (Australia Department of the Prime Minister and Cabinet, Office of the Status of Women, 1987: 279). Such departments should rather be attempting to develop such an accurate means.

With the importance of macro and international policies to outcomes, a brief discussion of policy directions in New Zealand over the last ten years is a useful background to the assessment of gender impacts. During the 1980s global recession, the rise of the Asian economies, the aftermath of the oil crisis and technological change were among factors creating economic problems in a number of countries, with fiscal and overseas trade deficits common to many western economies. A common response included ideological conservatism, an attempt to balance the government budget through expenditure cuts, attempts to secure real wage cuts for low-income earners and a focus on reducing the rate of inflation. A full treatment of the New Zealand new-right swing towards less government in terms of a more-market approach incorporating deregulation, corporatisation, privatisation, lower taxation and lower public expenditure is beyond the scope of this discussion. (For more extensive criticism of these economic and social policies in the last ten years, see Kelsey, 1993; O'Brien and Wilkes, 1993; Rosenberg, 1993.)

Advocates of major change in the New Zealand economy were well placed to take over power following economic stagnation and the exchange-rate crisis which accompanied the 1984 general election. Assertions of lack of accountability and inefficiency in the public sector, of distortions and lack of neutrality caused by intervention in the private sector, of government failure matching market failure and of capture of social services by the middle class could be used to rationalise many of the changes (Bertram, 1988; Jesson, 1987).

These developments have of course been in the name of securing a leaner, meaner, more productive economy, improving international competitiveness and achieving medium-term growth. Inflation has been beaten and there is at last a resumption of growth in output, but unemployment remains very high, with extensive restructuring and redundancies costing jobs in both the private and public sector. Unemployment has replaced hidden underemployment, which saw many employees not fully utilised. Thus productivity levels were low. Restructuring has raised productivity, but cut many jobs. From 1980 to 1987, part-time jobs increased by 41.5 per cent, but full-time jobs by only 5.6 per cent. However, the new part-time, casual and temporary jobs, many of which replace full-time work, rarely have good pay, conditions or security. Women and Maori suffer disproportionately in this situation, with benefit and other government expenditure cuts reinforcing the labour market effects. The dual labour market is accentuated, with people at the top doing well, and the unemployed and low paid missing out.

There have been similar trends in Australia to those implemented in New Zealand. A feminist analysis was doubtful whether implementation of a new-right strategy in Australia would lead to the growth and improved competitiveness hoped for. It was unequivocal that 'trickle down' to those adversely affected by job loss and expenditure cuts was unlikely, and that women were particularly badly affected by the strategy (Sharp and Broomhill, 1988). Even the Australian Labor Government, which was in theory sympathetic to equality for women, implemented policies that worsened their economic position, 'particularly for young women, low and middle-income earners, and those in poverty' (*ibid.*: 94). Cuts were made to areas of importance to women, such as welfare, housing and education, while the Accord between government and the trade union movement produced very little, if any, net benefit to women in paid work. Arguing in the short term for a more interventionist macro strategy and trade and industry policy, Sharp and Broomhill considered that in the long term gender equality 'is incompatible with the unequal market and class systems that are the defining features of capitalism. Therefore, a feminist economic strategy must be integrally linked with a socialist economic strategy' (*ibid.*: 95). Socialism may currently be unfashionable, but it is argued in Part IV that some form of radical change involving more control by individuals over their lives and the systems which affect them is essential.

Another issue of concern is the reduced autonomy of governments, with small countries increasingly dependent on the international economy, multinational companies and institutions, and credit-rating agencies. This is not to oppose the idea of interdependence extending between as well as within countries, or some degree of specialisation. However, globalisation can result in negative outcomes, especially for women, and a lack of accountability. With the emergence of a global assembly line, 'Research and management are controlled by the core of developed countries while assembly line work is relegated to semiperiphery or periphery nations that occupy less privileged positions in the global economy' (Ward, 1990: 1).

This means that low-waged women in one country are effectively pitted against those in another. For example:

> In Australia a Victorian-based car parts maker recently closed shop and moved to Western Samoa to produce there and export to Australia. More than 2000 jobs were lost. In Australia the unionised workforce was paid a minimum of $8 an hour. In Western Samoa the Company was given a tax holiday, rent-free accommodation and a non-unionised workforce of village women who

had never worked in a factory before – and are now paid $A1.25 an hour. (ICFTU-APRO, 1992: 15)

The near unanimity of the enthusiastic response in New Zealand to the General Agreement on Tariffs and Trade (GATT) and the freer trade which will result ignores these issues. New Zealand is currently far more open to imports from elsewhere than many countries are to some of our key exports. Agreements which improve this situation are welcome. However, enthusiasm for reduced prices to consumers (and profits to multinationals) which may result from freer trade and use of the cheapest possible labour markets should be balanced by the tradeoffs involved. The implications for the jobs and incomes of those in the lowest-paid sectors of the labour markets of each country involved need also to be considered.

In the newly industrialised countries, labour services, especially those of women, are cheap, unionisation is at a low level, options are few, social control easy, and regulations over conditions such as health and safety limited. Further, women are praised for their ability accurately to perform repetitive tasks, but this ability is rewarded minimally. Since women's labour turnover is no problem to the firms, conditions injurious to health are common. Thus, some work is made available for women, but at a high cost and with less privileged women disadvantaged. 'Class and race mediate the processes of global restructuring as capitalists seek women of color and working-class women to meet their needs for a flexible labor supply' (Ward, 1990: 3).

Structural adjustment policies, implemented through institutions like the World Bank and the International Monetary Fund, have paid little attention to the needs of women and have been enforced as a condition of loans. Such structural adjustment involves a shift in production of goods for local consumption to those traded internationally through changes in relative prices. Although there is increasing evidence that investment directed to women may have higher rates of return, strategies to tackle gender barriers and channel resources to women are still rare (Elson, 1991). Most structural adjustment policies are imbued with male bias and result in high costs of adjustment for women. This male bias arises because 'it is assumed that human resources may be treated as if they were a non-produced factor of production, like natural resources; and as if they were costlessly transferable between different activities' (*ibid.*: 166). Thus costs of change are ignored, while it is assumed that women's capacity to undertake extra work is unlimited. This strikes a chord with similar assumptions in New Zealand, where worthwhile-sounding policies, such as the deinstitutionalisation of psychopaedic, psychiatric and other patients, in fact mean greater burdens being placed on female relatives, because insufficient primary community health resources accompany the change.

Even allowing for the limited power of government in a globalised world, the role of the state is one key element in economic and social outcomes. Many feminists would argue that it is essential for the state to have a continuing, leading role in helping all New Zealanders achieve social well-being, including a standard of living sufficient for participation and fulfilment in the community. This is discussed in more detail in Part III. Marilyn Waring points out that standard models of the state ignore sexism, racism and ageism, New Zealand conditions and power considerations:

> When Nozick argues that the only legitimate forced extraction of income from citizens through taxation is for protective purposes, he did not have in mind protection from hunger or homelessness, nor did he have in mind making sexual harassment a criminal offence or introducing compulsory self defence classes for girls throughout our secondary schools ... It is clear that this model of the state is a description of liberties available for individual men inside the patriarchal power process. (Waring, 1988a: 6–7)

Instead, Waring's conception of the state involves rights to services and 'survival rights', individual entitlements and a respect for differences: 'the role of the state is to mirror every fragment' (*ibid.*: 29). The conception involves freedom 'from and to' many things, not just freedom from interference and freedom to choose. A man's freedom from interference may mean a woman cannot walk safely in the streets.

When considering the ability for women to lead satisfying and happy lives, Waring's points are reminders that elements on the edge of economic analysis, but with clear links to it, may be as crucial as the strictly economic. The residue of the framework that women are owned by men, especially their husbands, continues to have a major influence on many women's lives. Expectations of sexual ownership, and different standards for male and female behaviour, have ongoing impacts on women, reinforced by legal interpretation. For example, rape in marriage has only recently become illegal, and alleged provocation by women of male violence is given an amazingly wide latitude by male judges as an excuse, even for murder (McDonald, 1993). Similar attitudes are often exhibited by police (Busch *et al*, 1992). Male violence, and the threat of it, exerts considerable constraints on many women's freedom. Discussion which simply labels as unfortunate the increasing rate of marriage breakdown and which advocates attempts to work at improving and continuing relationships ignores gender-specific reasons for breakdown. Increasing demands on women's refuges and the growing number of applications for non-molestation orders attest to the high incidence of violence within marriage perpetrated almost entirely by men.

Another major factor constraining many women's lives is the differential impact of the diet and beauty industries. Male-imposed ideas of what a woman should look like, supported by extensive wasteful advertising, condition many women into misery and/or time and expenditure wasted on attempting to conform. Even women largely immune to this propaganda often have to pay more than men for many goods purchased on the market – for example, haircuts, personal hygiene products and some clothing. Thus macro and micro policies, as well as social assumptions and priorities with economic impact, contribute to unequal gender outcomes which are often hidden and require feminist analysis.

Why are feminist critiques of orthodoxy neglected?

Few of the main points made in this chapter are new: most have been made by each wave of feminist writing, though in different language and largely neglected in standard histories and the teaching of economic thought. This is now being remedied by feminist scholars who are writing more inclusive history. A wonderful example is the analysis by Michelle Pujol (1992) of the equal pay debates in the nineteenth and early twentieth centuries, and the contrasting positions of feminists and orthodox male economists. Here I briefly show the continuity of the critiques and some of the factors contributing to their past and continuing neglect. Many are common across academic disciplines, but in some respects worse within economics.

We should note, 100 years from the achievement of female suffrage in New Zealand, that the linked problems of the public–private split and the undervaluation of unpaid work have long been recognised by feminists here and overseas. One practical move towards gender equality advocated last century and now is a more equal sharing of both market and household work.

Our strong conviction is that until a true and perfect equality is recognised between men and women that will apply to any and every relation in life, the highest happiness cannot exist ... But this will never be accomplished while they live such separate lives as they do so largely at present; while men are supposed to have little or nothing to do with 'home,' and women nothing at all to do outside it; while coarseness is condoned in the one sex, and helplessness encouraged in the other, and entitled 'womanliness'; and while the one sex assumes superiority and accords to the other tacitly, if not openly, inferiority. (Sheppard, 1892: 6)

In the same article, Kate Sheppard wrote strongly about the reality of household work. In discussing the statistical categorisation in 1892 of women into 'breadwinners' and 'dependents or non-breadwinners', she noted that 124,454 of the 248,364 women in the latter category were described as 'persons performing domestic duties for which remuneration is not paid'. She went on: 'As we suppose that wives are included in this latter category, we feel inclined to take exception to their being classed as "dependent", for she earns her living, in many cases far more hardly than her husband does, although he is the actual wage receiver' (*ibid.*, 1892: 6).

Past neglect of feminist critiques: a case study of Harriet Taylor and John Stuart Mill

A fascinating case study is provided by the work, life and times of Harriet Taylor and John Stuart Mill, and their appearance in the works of largely male commentators. Few graduates in social sciences or economics will not have heard of Mill and utilitarianism, and most will have studied his work and/or others' interpretation of it in some detail (though this may be too optimistic a hope for economists, since the training of many has become so narrow that it avoids underlying philosophies and the history of the discipline). Probably far fewer social science graduates, however, will have studied Harriet Taylor. (This is verified by small surveys generated when discussing their work at conferences.) Yet Taylor's independent work and her influence on Mill, both before and after their marriage, are of great importance. His acceptance of feminist ideas, albeit less radical than hers, owes a great deal to their relationship.

Harriet Taylor and John Stuart Mill met in 1830 or 1831, when both were in their early 20s. Mill was single, while Harriet had married John Taylor, eleven years her senior, at 19, and had two children (a third was born the following year). This was the start of a 28-year relationship which ended with Harriet's death in 1858, after seven years of marriage to Mill: the marriage took place two years after John Taylor's death. From soon after their meeting, their relationship 'was one of intellectual and spiritual intimacy' (Rossi, 1970: 6). The two worked together on most of the books published under Mill's name and he, unlike others, fully acknowledged her influence.

The general works published under Mill's name on which Harriet's influence was considerable include the *Principles of Political Economy* and *On Liberty*. On specifically feminist analysis, her impact on Mill is clear as early as 1831–32, when each wrote an essay for the other on women and their position in marriage. However, Mill states that his belief in gender equality in legal, political, social and domestic relations predates his relationship with Harriet, although it remained somewhat abstract until that time, and that this belief was, indeed, a major cause of her interest in him (Mill, [1873] 1924). These two essays remained unpublished until Hayek's book on their correspondence and marriage (1951). The two major published feminist works from the partnership are *The Enfranchisement of Women*, first published anonymously in the *Westminster Review* in 1851, and *The Subjection of Women*, largely written in 1861 but revised and published in Mill's name in 1869. *The Enfranchisement* is Harriet Taylor's work, although Mill doubtless had some influence, but considerably less than Harriet's on *The Subjection*.

Rossi argues that Harriet's authorship of the former is contextually clear from its greater radicalism, particularly with respect to equal opportunity in paid work for self-development and treatment as a fully contributing partner (Rossi, 1970: 41–3). *The Subjection* is based more on individual rights and a theoretical intellectual commitment to removal of all forms of sex discrimination, while still being, in partial contradiction, resistant to any change in the traditional division of labour.

Mill's own acknowledgement of Harriet's contributions and demonstration of his commitment to equality (on his understanding, at least) are unequivocal. With respect to *The Subjection* he said, 'In what was of my own composition, all that is most striking and profound belongs to my wife; coming from the fund of thought which had been made common to us both by our innumerable conversations and discussions on a topic which filled so large a place in our minds' (Mill, [1873] 1924: 173). However, her influence has been given much less weight by many later commentators, mainly male. It is ironic that the mutual respect and complementary vision which appears to have existed between Harriet and Mill has subsequently been discounted by those who have argued over their individual contribution to the published works (Soper, 1983: iii). Rossi discusses the reasons why Harriet's influence has been questioned, including nineteenth century aversion to assertive women questioning the traditional role. She shows that opinions are also correlated with the writer's own stance, with those of more radical views more likely to defend Harriet's positions and influence.

Hayek correctly asserts that after Harriet's death Mill withdrew from some of the 'more advanced' (read, feminist and socialist) positions he espoused earlier. For Harriet Taylor was well ahead of her time, and of Mill, who was nevertheless himself a radical thinker. *The Subjection* was not well received and has, not surprisingly, received far less attention and analysis than most of his other works, while *The Enfranchisement* was largely ignored. Even if today both come across as somewhat liberal documents, containing little systematic analysis of patriarchy, they are still highly impressive.

Present neglect of feminist critiques: the number and position of women economists within the profession

A critical mass of women economists may not be sufficient to guarantee that feminist critiques receive adequate development and attention, given the other constraints discussed below. However, numerical strength and representation throughout the profession is probably a necessary condition, particularly as it has been the catalyst for the explosion in feminist economic analysis published overseas in recent years. It should also be mentioned that a (small) number of men are taking seriously and adding to such critiques (for example, Sen, 1984 and 1990; Klamer, 1991; McCloskey, 1993).

While higher proportions of women in the profession do not guarantee widespread adoption of feminist perspectives, there is evidence in New Zealand (admittedly from a small sample) that women in the profession do on average think differently from men. The 184 replies from men and 33 from women to a 1990 survey of members of the New Zealand Association of Economists showed significant, and perhaps predictable, differences in positive and/or negative responses to 14 of 43 questions (for example, women had less faith in the market and were being less supportive of recent government policy). In particular, more women gave negative responses to the following questions: 'the economic power of trade unions should be significantly curtailed' (44.07 per cent male; 70.97 per cent female) and 'the educational voucher system is better than supplying education free of charge to the user' (37.08 per cent male; 70.97 per cent female). Similarly, women economists were more inclined to think that 'the free market underpays women workers', with 19.35 per cent answering negatively as against 50.28 per cent of male respondents.

The author of the survey report comments that 'the existence of very significant differences between men and women on questions which touch upon gender issues throws doubt upon the objectivity of economists. It may suggest that our theoretical positions are merely rationalisation of underlying sentiments . . . Alternatively and more optimistically, we could interpret these gender based differences as reflections of differences in what parts of the world the sexes know about' (Coleman, 1992: 55). He also asks, 'To what extent are the judgements of economists correlated with their personal circumstances and characteristics (e.g. place of employment, gender, age, branch of specialisation)? To what extent are their judgements "impersonal"?' (*ibid*.: 48). Few feminists would believe in 'impersonal' judgements.

The centre of gravity, at least, in the thinking of women economists is thus somewhat different from that of men, with the former less supportive of recent, more-market government policies. There is some evidence that gender difference is mirrored in the population as a whole. An Insight Research survey conducted for the Council of Trade Unions in 1993 found less enthusiasm for more market and other policy changes since 1984 among women than men. In particular, 72 per cent of women, as against 61 per cent of men, opposed the main changes to the education system, and 61 per cent of women, compared with 54 per cent of men, opposed the Employment Contracts Act (NZCTU Women's Conference, 1993).

Similarly, the results of a national post-1990 election survey found small but important gender gaps. 'This gap consisted essentially in women's relatively more compassionate view of the state. The evidence for this was their concern for health, welfare, education and the environment, reinforced by their slightly greater willingness to see more money spent in these areas and to countenance a more interventionist conception of government than men' (Aimer, 1993: 120). The gap widened when the sample was divided into a few coherent groups. Of the 11 per cent described as 'new left' or anti-nuclear, pro-union, Maori, women and environment, and strongly favouring redistribution of wealth and public ownership, 63 per cent were women. By contrast, of the 6 per cent described as 'new right', with reverse opinions, only 32 per cent were women. Aimer points out that it may be possible for the gender difference to be mobilised in a more crucial way under a proportional representation electoral system. In the United States, feminist pressure groups have put major effort into investigating and publicising the views of individual candidates and supporting the campaigns of those, particularly women, with views which conform with their own. These efforts have borne some fruit in recent years, with the election of more women of liberal views, for example on abortion rights, and also in broader economic and social areas, such as health policies.

In a recent symposium, three feminist economists discussed the difference it would make to economic thought and its history if practitioners took feminist theory seriously. Evaluating their contributions, Janet Seiz points out that 'all three authors see important links between the social identities of inquirers and the methods and content of their scientific work' (Seiz, 1993: 193), as would also be suggested by the argument here. However, Seiz is wary of making too sharp a contrast between men's and women's thinking, including that between male and female economists. Class, race and other aspects of identity and position cut across gender, so that there is no unitary male or female standpoint. In addition it is crucial and in the interests of positive change for feminists to believe that it is possible for individuals to transcend their personal experiences and interests. 'If such transcendence were impossible, feminists would have little hope of persuading nonfeminists of the truth of their own knowledge-claims' (*ibid.*: 197).

There is little possibility, moreover, of the differentiated thinking of women economists with feminist perspectives making a major impact in New Zealand universities unless they can influence their male colleagues. In 1992 only two out of 30 senior staff (professor/associate professor/reader) in economics departments in the seven universities were women, with 9 per cent at senior lecturer level and 25 per cent at lecturer level. How many of these would describe themselves as feminist can only be speculated.

There are factors in economics as elsewhere in academia which inhibit women's access to lecturing positions and promotion. These add to workforce-wide issues around differential time, responsibilities and expectations concerning household and caring work. Promotion issues include evidence that time spent on teaching-associated work, including assistance to students, may be a higher priority on average for women academics than it is for men. The 'publish or perish' admonition often means that research and publication are of more importance than teaching evaluations in tenure and promotion decisions. Informal departmental networks and mentoring may be more geared towards men, albeit unintentionally. The relative valuations of particular methodologies and areas of the discipline are also unlikely to favour feminist and other critiques compared with safer mainstream topics.

In New Zealand these processes have been best documented with respect to a university geography department (Johnson, 1987). This contrasts the dominant, intensely competitive group 'pervaded by a macho culture geared around physical geography, quantification, publications and the survival, not to say the speedy promotion, of those within it' (*ibid.*: 142) with the stimulating and supportive Marxist Geography Reading Group which had a more even sex ratio, but was poor in resources, time and status, and less conventionally productive or successful. Louise Johnson argues that she is describing 'some details of a systematic process, structured by institutional rules and procedures, individual assumptions and particular constellations of people and events, whereby a sexual division of labour is created and sustained in a university department'. With all except one lecturer male but five of the seven untenured tutors female, 'sexual politics were inevitably played out. And such politics are always about status and about power, with men usually holding power over women' (*ibid.*).

The construction of knowledge: gatekeeping and marginalisation

It has been argued that what counts as important and valued knowledge is socially constructed. Many feminist theorists have pointed out the mechanisms for, and results of, the exclusion of women's experience, perspectives and writing. Fewer women than men obtain positions in the top US universities. The rankings of these institutions and of individual economists on the basis of citations, associated networks of and mentoring among scholars, and number of articles, especially in top journals, are interlinked areas into which it is hard for women to obtain even a footing. The top 25 economists in a study by Medoff (quoted in Colander, 1989), judged by mean citations per year, were all men, with 24 located at only 12 universities.

The extra difficulties for female economists of being published, especially in top journals, are exacerbated if articles are in areas not seen as mainstream and/or if they use methodologies and techniques not totally based on the building and fitting of formal models. There is now a large literature within economics which discusses its own rhetoric and expresses dissatisfaction with its methodology, the nature of graduate training, the concentration on building and fitting ever narrower models, and the resulting incentives within the profession. Alternative approaches, with their own networks and journals, are growing, and may now exceed the 25 per cent of dissenters estimated to exist and disagree with the 75 per cent orthodox core (Blaug, 1988), but they are still marginalised. There is by no means perfect competition in the marketplace of ideas, with entry to the discipline and its publications filtered by the need to conform to a core conceptual structure (Strassmann, 1993a and 1993b). Further, the judges of the permitted ideas, framework and rhetoric are themselves 'not produced in a vacuum, but are chosen through a complex set of highly selective processes of intellectual and professional socialisation' (Strassmann, 1993a: 153).

Incentives, graduate training, models and mathematics

Ironically, for those ambivalent about orthodoxy, neoclassical analysis of utility maximisation within the profession is useful in questioning the importance to economists of the search for truth. It suggests that risk-averting behaviour means conforming to current practice, which is reinforced by peer review and related processes which exclude non-orthodox approaches. Techniques, rather than ideas and real economic problems, are the main focus of graduate training.

This is confirmed by US graduate students' assessment of what is important to placing them on a fast track in the academic profession. Sixty-five per cent believed ability at problem-solving and 57 per cent believed excellence in mathematics to be very important (3 per cent and 2 per cent respectively believed these to be unimportant). By contrast 3 per cent believed knowledge of the economy and 10 per cent believed knowledge of economic literature to be very important; 68 per cent and 43 per cent respectively believed these to be unimportant (Colander and Klamer,

1987: 100). According to Colander, these results show a profession which has lost its bearings and many members of it their excitement and joy at discovery. Instead it allows one-upmanship and self-interest to govern the choice of theories and models, based on how publishable they are, not how illuminating: 'One knows as little literature as possible, because to know literature will force one to attribute ideas to others' (Colander 1991: 70).

Texts and courses

Women students who, despite these issues, decide to persist with economics at undergraduate and graduate level next confront the problems of framework and methodology mentioned earlier, including female invisibility and gender bias in definitions of areas of study, curriculum and textbooks. Inevitably, most widely adopted textbooks are within the orthodox canon and pay little or no heed to feminist and other critiques. A number of reviews have appeared of both the quantity and treatment of race and gender in economics textbooks. One concludes that scant attention is paid to these issues, and identifies the 'gender and race blindness of the theory' and the resulting tendency to define the economic experiences of white men as the norm. Hence minorities and women are most frequently portrayed in stereotypes, and their experiences are treated as 'anomalous or deviant' (Feiner and Morgan, 1987: 387). Some texts, like some individuals, appear to take the view that the use of gender-neutral language is sufficient to remove biases in content and theory. Neither this nor a few gender role reversals in labour market examples deals with the major issues. The issue of basic paradigms and approaches is addressed more directly by Feiner and Roberts (1990), who argue that the biased treatment of gender and race is inevitable when neoclassical philosophical premises and equilbrium structures are assumed. Emphasis on the constrained choice model and maintenance of the positive-normative distinction discussed earlier means that 'at present, race and gender are hidden by the invisible hand' (*ibid.*: 180).

Feminist economists are now showing these biases in detail. A deconstruction of some extracts from a standard labour economics textbook designed to illustrate standard labour/leisure choices for two families provides an excellent example. Ironically labelling them the Enjoyable and Other Families, the critique draws out the implications of stated and unstated contrasts between them. Discussing the Enjoyable Family, 'the language in the text draws attention to the family's enjoyment of meals, of the children. The vacuum cleaner, the microwave, the clean home, the well brought up children, the pleasant mealtime tell us a great deal more than merely these few facts: from these facts an entire world is conjured into being . . . – of an American family, the stuff of television sitcoms and popular fiction' (Polyani and Strassmann, 1993: 10).

The Other Family has a wife with a low wage who needs to combine paid work and considerable home responsibilities, because her disabled husband is unable to be in paid work. It is therefore suggested that she will specialise in time-intensive meal preparation activities, including weeding, tilling, canning and freezing. Polyani and Strassmann suggest that such an image conjures up a shabby rural setting (where else would the weeding and tilling occur?) but that the reader sees the family as able to live a reasonably comfortable life, rather than one of desperate poverty. They may not have as much as the Enjoyable Family, but can still provide for themselves through rational choice.

Full justice cannot be done in a paragraph to the wry humour yet serious message of this critique. The authors find complacency and incoherence in the story of the Other Family. Its unremarkable nature within economics writing suggests that expected and actual readers, like the writers, experience no dissonance with the default assumptions. 'The story presents an unrealistic picture of the situation, thereby revealing itself to be written from a perspective of privilege . . . The political agenda suggests that poor people accept and work within the status quo' (*ibid.*: 12–13).

Specific courses on gender and the economy are still comparatively rare. I argue in this connection (as I do about both women's or feminist studies courses in general and equal employment opportunity organisation) that a combination of 'mainstreaming' and specific initiatives has the best chance of success. There may be difficulties in persuading students to take gender courses not seen as crucial, and it is necessary to reach all students in core courses. My own course on gender roles in the economy at Victoria University has been offered since 1990 at third year undergraduate level to both economics and women's studies students, and I give a few sessions to earlier women's studies courses and raise the issues where I can (insufficiently!) in other economics courses. The 12 such North American courses surveyed by Conrad (1992) are assessed to be first and foremost rigorous courses in economics, with typically one previous economic course required. Both from what is said and what is omitted, it appears that, perhaps in order to be regarded as sufficiently 'respectable', they insufficiently challenge orthodoxy – for example, in the 'lack of rigorous scrutiny of the economics of the family' (*ibid.*: 568).

Individual survival

The problems of survival for feminist economists in a frequently hostile world may produce a variety of reactions, including bending over backwards to appear respectable. The issues discussed above have led some women economists to conform to orthodoxy by conviction or necessity, or to compromise. Others who stick to feminist ideas and analysis have been eased out, left the profession in exasperation, moved to the periphery within it, or partially or totally withdrawn to their own resources. In the words of one presumed 'survivor', 'Feminist economists thus face a particularly difficult task, a task which is both intellectual and political, and which is fraught with the dangers of academic censorship, collegial ostracism and professional demise' (Pujol, 1992: 5).

It is argued that 'disagreements among economists are mostly fought on methodological grounds. These are fights on how to do economics; they produce most vicious insults, such as that the others do not do science, use "ad hoc" assumptions, or are ideologically biased' (Klamer, 1990: 133–4). Hence there are inevitably concerns about not being considered academic or respectable enough, especially when power imbalances are involved and tenure decisions looming. There is insufficient space for real, rather than stylised talk: for frank, friendly criticism and exchange, with minimum hurt or consequences.

It is not usual in economic writing to discuss personal survival strategies. However, feminist theory recognises personal and political links so it seems appropriate to outline my own experience. Recently I have been excited to discover international feminist economics networks, especially given the feeling of comparative isolation in New Zealand within academic economics. There are of course feminists with related interests outside economics departments, but only one or two within. My own survival has been assisted by these and other feminist theory contacts, while I mostly exchange ideas and give papers at women's studies and related forums, rather than at economics gatherings. I also find myself using a large number of direct quotes as well as references, largely as protection to show I am not the only ('wrong, value-laden') academic writing on these lines!

Towards a positive feminist economics

At this stage of its development, feminist influence on economic theory has largely been in terms of its critiques, rather than building new structures. Nevertheless, feminist actions and community initiatives, some helped by feminist economic insights, have had major positive impacts on economic outcomes for many women, as discussed in Part IV. Further, feminist economists are starting to structure positive alternatives based on a wider view of economics' scope.

A broad definition, from a male economist, is that 'economics is about the quality of human lives' (Bartlett, 1989: 3). One feminist economist's view is that economics should remain differentiated from other social sciences, perhaps implying a somewhat narrower field of study than that suggested by a literal reading of Bartlett but nevertheless with a focus on all the ways by which 'humans try to meet their needs for material goods and services' (Nelson, 1992: 119). Even this definition can be seen as a major shift of emphasis, encompassing market, household, government, mutual exchange, coercion and gift. It 'dethrones choice, scarcity and rationality as central concepts, and relegates them to the status of potentially useful tools. It brings previously taboo or fringe subjects like power and poverty into the core' (*ibid.*). This is in fact a return to earlier broader views of economics.

Notions of scientific objectivity and gender and other dualisms have been discussed earlier. Julie Nelson argues for a positive use of traditional gender dualisms in broadening the scope and methodology of economics. 'Scientific' attributes, such as logic and precision, are culturally defined as masculine. This is not to accept that in fact women are less logical, for example, than men. Myths can persist, and be fostered by social conditioning, despite a lack of theory or evidence. However, logic and precision are rightly valued in economics and elsewhere, while positive feminine-attributed characteristics are not. Hence Nelson uses masculine/feminine and positive/negative contrasts in suggesting that progress demands a blend of the positive side of the characteristics associated by such cultural attribution with each gender. For example, on the spectrum of mathematical rigour as a form of understanding, precision is pictured as positive and masculine, vagueness as negative and feminine. However, understanding requires use of language as well as mathematical rigour. On the use of language spectrum, richness is seen as a positive, feminine attribute and thinness as a negative, masculine one (Nelson, 1992). Hence, blending precision and richness would lead to better methodologies.

Whatever else is controversial, there is general agreement among feminist economists that progress requires a broadening of the main concern of orthodoxy with choice theory to encompass insights from other disciplines. This has overlaps with incorporating positive feminine attributes. 'A truly feminist economics, as opposed to economics done by feminists or economics about women, will necessarily be the result of feminist explorations in epistemology and methodology' (Waller and Jennings, 1990: 613). It involves questioning ideological concepts such as economic rationality, and basing theory 'in the material reality of women's lives' (Pujol, 1992: 203).

Such approaches fit reasonably well with other recent strands of thought outside neoclassicism, some of which build on institutional, radical and socialist analyses. Robert Lane also uses an interdisciplinary approach in suggesting that we should work on how to make the market a better agent for promoting happiness and human development. These two attributes are claimed to be the final goods for which people strive, with goods, services and income simply among the intermediate goods which may help produce them (Lane, 1991). Cognitive complexity, a sense of being in control of one's life and self-esteem are seen as the elements of human development. With satisfying paid work (and unpaid work, less emphasised by Lane) contributing to these elements, it should be valued for itself, not just for the income it produces. Lane argues that many elements of the market are antithetical to a change of focus from consumption to happiness and human development. Competition and conflict, rather than mutual gain, is often market reality; intrinsic satisfactions are not valued by market price, and outcomes rather than processes are the only focus.

Like feminist analysis, socio-economics argues that altruism and moral values cannot be reduced to tastes. It attempts to incorporate both personal and social goals into its models (Etzioni, 1988a). Humanistic economics argues that needs cannot be reduced to wants, different kinds of satisfaction are not commensurable, and it is worth examining how tastes are formed (Lutz and Lux, 1988). Altruism is not simply another neoclassical taste, but reflects a dual self not dominated solely by maximising personal satisfaction. The broader motivations allowed for in humanistic economics can encompass the free-rider results discussed earlier. So can a variety of shared ideals, socialisation, enforcement and customs and/or habits which encourage co-operation, as discussed within feminist analysis and elsewhere. 'A growing body of interdisciplinary feminist research complements the efforts many economists are making to develop a more complete theory of economic interests, one that can encompass concepts like cooperation, loyalty, and reciprocity' (Folbre and Hartmann, 1988: 197). Arguing against wage labour and in favour of worker-managed enterprise, Lutz and Lux cite the large self-managed Spanish community at Mondragon as an example of co-operative activity along the lines of the humanistic approach.

However, socio- and humanistic economics do not necessarily take sufficient account of feminist critiques of standard economic and dualistic reasoning. Economic man's replacement by an individual with a higher and lower self still involves a hierarchical dualism, with reason seen as above nature and altruism above self-interest (Nelson, 1994). Further, Lutz and Lux ignore the role of the development of higher attributes in children of parental teaching and example, usually overwhelmingly by the mother.

This analysis may be very little advance on the confining of altruism to the home front and seeing it as natural to women, discussed earlier. It is not far removed from Adam Smith's attribution of humanity to women and generosity, which unlike humanity requires self-sacrifice, to men. 'He is telling a familiar story: Women's sacrifices for husbands and children are not really virtuous because they come naturally' (Grappard, 1993: 17). Grappard also notes that Smith gives as evidence of women's lack of generosity the rarity of their making considerable donations (footnoted as *Raro mulieres donare solent*). She asks, 'Is the mere translation into Latin enough to yield an aura of truth and authority to a rather trivial observation in a world where few women have any claims to wealth?' (*ibid.*)

Lutz and Lux's advocacy of co-operative enterprise also needs to be tempered by the results of research which show that women may be disadvantaged in this setting as much as in standard companies. Mondragon demonstrates three major obstacles to gender equality despite its being 'on many counts astounding, vibrant, effective' (Hacker, 1989: 120). These are women's major responsibility, here as elsewhere, for unpaid labour in the home, the devaluation of collective social goals, and men's control over decisions about technology and management. Hacker suggests that only degendering or desegregating knowledge and skill among the young can deal with the first issue, and this must be in the context of a feminist and co-operative community overall, not confined to the workplace, if all tasks are to be shared.

The broadening of types of reasoning to include attributes culturally regarded as feminine implies the use of analogy, metaphor, experience and intuition (Nelson, 1993b). It is clear that natural sciences have themselves often made advances by such methods (Nelson, 1993a). Broader economic methodologies also require a greater variety of detailed methods of inquiry, not confined to building and fitting from secondary data ever more refined mathematical models. Deriving suitable methods from the nature of the question may mean consideration of primary data collection, ethnographic studies, questionnaires, interviews and case studies more common in other social sciences (McDonald, 1993).

The last ten years have seen a new awareness among even mainstream economists that the discipline's method of knowledge construction involves the use of its own conversational metaphors, rhetoric or stories, to convince the audience (McCloskey, 1985). McCloskey's analysis has features in common with some of the criticisms of orthodoxy made in this chapter, debunking the notion of value-free positivism. It has been suggested that it goes part-way towards a deconstructionist approach, examining the forms of the conversation, but not going as far as to suggest that truth and objectivity are unattainable and persuasion all there is. 'McCloskey leaves room for the reader to continue to believe in some form of objectivity being possible, while arguing it is not important because it is not in fact what we do . . . Objectivity is "overrated"; not non-existent or impossible' (Rosetti, 1992: 222).

The dualisms recognised by McCloskey include objective/subjective, positive/normative, precise/vague, fact/opinion and hard/soft, but not clear-headed/emotional, public/private, individual/family or dominant/subordinate (Grappard, 1993). Thus, Grappard argues, McCloskey's analysis is apolitical, ignoring power differences arising from gender, race and class. His later work, however, pays more attention to gender issues (McCloskey, 1993), and he has coined a new term, 'conjective economics', for analysis which uses the ways of knowing thought of as feminine as well as those regarded as masculine in the manner argued by Nelson. He argues that this would be 'better science, because it would be more complete and persuasive', involving 'coherence in story as much as in axioms; of relevance in Bureau of Labor Statistics questionnaires administered as much as in its regressions' (*ibid.*: 76). Discussing some examples where this would make a difference, he argues that government intervention might be less necessary in some areas.

We have seen earlier that experimental evidence indicates that free-rider and selfish behaviour is less common among women and non-economists. If feelings of solidarity for others reduce negative externalities such as rubbish dumping, even though no cost falls on the individual, there is less need for central clean-ups. By contrast, in some areas where interventions are needed, they might have to be more intensive than at present. As mentioned earlier, valuation of human life in dollar terms is needed in many policy areas despite the discomfort this may cause. The most common way of deriving such a value is through observing behaviour in areas such as purchase of insurance and wage differentials needed to attract people to risky jobs. However, this allows only for personal valuation of one's own life. If the value placed on one's life by others was added, the higher value would justify more expensive interventions to save lives (*ibid.*: 79–80).

Another emerging strand of a positive feminist economics is to see wellbeing less in terms of a neoclassical utility function and more in terms of access and capability to be and do many things, such as eat, be adequately and warmly sheltered, read, write, be free of violence and take an active role in one's community. The capabilities approach, developed by Amartya Sen (1984) and discussed by Frances Woolley (1993), relates closely to Marilyn Waring's analysis of the role of the state and its need to provide positive freedoms, discussed earlier. Using criteria such as lack of food and shelter to measure poverty is hardly new, but making a full list of capabilities the basis of economic analysis is more radical, and the implications are considerable. If some people derive satisfaction from the nourishment of their children and others only from their own nourishment, efficient resource allocation, defined as maximisation of total utility, will devote more resources to the selfish and less to the altruistic (Woolley, 1993). Hence the unequal division of resources may be seen as less of a problem within neoclassical analysis – as the outcome of rational choice – than within the capabilities approach. The latter thus provides an underpinning for studies of the distribution of food and health care within the family as well as between families.

Capabilities, as a measure of positive possibilities, and poverty, as a measure of negatives, need therefore to be assessed within households, families and other groupings, not only between them. Woolley points out that what is seen as a necessity or need is itself culturally defined. For example, broad categories like nutrition are narrowed to access to particular types of food, but not all of these may be desirable or needed for a balanced diet. In response to a British study which used as one measure access to a weekly roast joint, she comments that, 'There is room for a feminist analysis of what men and women from different socio-economic backgrounds view as necessities' (Woolley, 1993: 16).

Neoclassical economics is more comfortable with wants in utility functions and demands dependent on price than with basic needs. One can recognise that 'the line between needs and wants is not distinct, and yet one can certainly say that a Guatemalan orphan needs her daily bowl of soup more than the overfed North American needs a second piece of cake. A refusal to recognise such a distinction on the basis of its logical ambiguity leads to an abdication of human ethical responsibility' (Nelson 1993b: 33). Women need to be in a position themselves to evaluate what their real needs are, and which capabilities are important to them. This relates closely to the notion of self-reliance, community development and empowerment, developed further in Part IV.

Thus feminist science and economics must have a major concern with self-assessed quality of life for all and ways of improving it. This means that it must draw on all types of research and knowledge, and be linked to all the struggles for radical liberation and change (Harding, 1991). While there is room for feminist perspectives within all types of economics, the elimination of gender, race and class bias will require changes in both content and form. 'If economists wish not to support the dissemination of falsehoods that impede progress toward a more just world, they (like other scientists) will have to become more responsible about the stories they contribute to society's discourse on social relations' (Seiz, 1992: 301).

Finally, Julie Nelson's vision of a feminist economics which is useful in bringing about positive social change is neither of a female economics different from an unchanged male economics, nor of a feminine economics which replaces masculine-associated concepts with feminine ones. Instead her feminist economics is 'a better economics, which rejects the negative aspects and builds on the positive aspects of characteristics traditionally associated with both masculinity and femininity, and which, since it is recognized that these concepts are only metaphorically associated with actual women and men, is practiced by men and women alike' (Nelson, 1993c: 19).

2
'Mitigating Misery': The Co-option and Twisting of Feminist Arguments

This chapter starts by developing the third area of feminist criticism of orthodoxy mentioned in the previous chapter – that orthodox definitions of economic activity, which exclude all unpaid work, are gender biased. Feminists argue that household, caring and community work deserves recognition as real work, even though unpaid. Earlier, I have argued that feminist critiques of orthodox economics have had a limited, but slowly increasing, influence on economic debate and policy. While I very much welcome the influence of feminist thought on orthodoxy, there are also some dangers. This discussion goes on to demonstrate the inappropriate co-option of feminist arguments around unpaid work by an influential advocate of current micro-economic orthodoxy (more market, deregulation, less government). Acceptance of his ideas would exacerbate inequalities, to the detriment of women and other lower-income groups. This type of twisting is one of the reasons why some feminists have doubts about including unpaid work in national income statistics, even though vehemently agreeing that it is real work.

The paper discussed is entitled 'Mitigating Misery – A Preliminary Assessment of New Zealanders' Capacity to Absorb Cuts in Real Income', issued by Infometrics Business Services Ltd, April 1991. The primary author, Gareth Morgan, is seen often in the New Zealand media and has some influence in economic policy-making circles; paying attention to his arguments is well justified.

Unpaid work and measures of economic activity

In recent years there has been an increased or revived awareness, by most women at least, that unpaid work in the home and community is real work, even if much of it is seen as obligation and/or pleasurable. For the lucky, the latter applies as well to paid work. Feminist analysis of the dependence of the market economy on women's productive and reproductive work has made some impact. However, all standard measures of national income, such as Gross Domestic Product (GDP), continue to exclude these 'goods', while including 'bads' such as pollution and defence industries (Waring, 1988b). New Zealand's statistical accounting system, like most, is based on the United Nations System of National Accounts (UNSNA), and our quoted annual growth rates in GDP are calculated from the increase (or decrease) in monetary transactions recorded and measured. Hence it matters a great deal what is included and excluded. While GDP is not directly a measure of welfare, it is frequently used as such. The fact that it excludes much economically productive work and includes environmentally damaging activity means that policy measures based on increasing its growth rate may be misguided.

While such standard measures are in theory based on market activity only, in practice some estimates are included of activity where no money changes hands, such as the rental value of owner-occupied housing. In addition, a number of transactions hidden from official statistics, such as barter, undeclared and/or illegal activities, are estimated in some countries, as well as some subsistence agriculture. Thus the arguments against inclusion of unpaid work based on consistency or difficulty of estimation are somewhat specious.

Economists increasingly agree that the omission of unpaid work from national income statistics is problematic (Eisner, 1988; Ironmonger, 1989) although their rationale is not based on feminist principles. Orthodox economists' arguments are based more on the misleading nature of the statistics which result from current practices than on equity considerations. The counter-cyclical nature of such work means that the impact of boom and recession, in aggregate and on individual households, is overstated. All types of unpaid work, including household, barter, voluntary and under-the-counter activities, are likely to be relatively greater in periods of recession than in growth periods.

Marilyn Waring is convinced that inclusion in measures of economic activity is an important aim (Waring, 1988). She vividly documents the ways in which statistical and economic systems based on the 1953 UNSNA have deleterious effects on the way the world is described and run. Her analysis spans the 'developed' and 'third' worlds, and a continuing example concerns Tendai, a young Zimbabwean girl who works a 17-hour day fetching water and firewood, collecting and preparing the family meals, and looking after her siblings. 'Tendai is considered unproductive, unoccupied and economically inactive. According to the international economic system, Tendai does not work and is not part of the labour force' (*ibid.*: 13).

Waring reminds us that when international reports refer to women as statistically or economically invisible, and when it dawns on us that militarism and the destruction of the environment are recorded as growth, it is the UNSNA that has made it so. Similarly, when we yearn for a breath of fresh air or a glass of radioactive-free water, the UNSNA says that both are worthless. The theme of profits from death spans military expenditures amounting to almost one-third of industrial production, the Bhopal 'accident', and unsafe pharmaceuticals and pesticides foisted on third world markets. And the developed world damages itself as well as the third world: poverty is as important an element in child deaths in the developed world (compared with the better-off, 12 times as many poor children die in fires and eight times as many from disease in the United States) as in the more obviously appalling African famines.

A lesser value is placed on life and the economics of reproduction, including not only birth but also reproduction of the labour force and of social relations within the household. Waring details the religious, legal and cultural beliefs and practices that define women as the property of men. From surrogacy to abortion of female fetuses, from breastfeeding to sexual slavery, from population policy to the cost of children, she shows the generally low value put on women's lives and time, and the control of decisions by limited economic visions and male policy-makers.

There have been a number of attempts to estimate how much would be added to national income by the inclusion of unpaid work. They indicate that including unpaid work in national income would add between a quarter and slightly more than a half to measured income, depending on the method used and country/time period – the unpaid sector is certainly extremely large. Most methods are based on valuing the time and money inputs, although there have been some attempts to value the output directly (Goldschmidt-Clermont, 1972 and 1983; Australian Bureau of Statistics, 1990). Input valuation methods multiply the time involved by an estimate of the value of that time. Three such methods can be distinguished. The first, the opportunity cost method, calculates the income lost by not spending the time in the paid labour force, usually using average female incomes rather than the income of specific individuals. With the second method, the wage rate in the market for a specific role, such as childcare, is multiplied by an estimate of time spent on it. Adding over all household tasks gives a total value for the work. The third method uses the overall average wage for a housekeeper.

The question of what range of unpaid work should be included is normally resolved by the third-party criterion. If the activity could be done by a third party and paid for on the market, it should be included. Hence all childcare, housework, cooking, gardening and so on falls under this definition. International organisations and pressure groups are considering the use of amended or 'satellite accounts' to supplement the current ones and include unpaid work.

Some more radical economists who share feminists' concern about sustainability, distribution questions and the importance of unpaid work have attempted to develop more complete indicators of economic welfare than current national income statistics. One strand in this is the construction of a number of social indicators, including such measures as infant mortality, and educational and health status. These are used to assess progress over time and to make inter-country comparisons, alongside more traditional economic indicators. Another strand is the construction of a single index which is more comprehensive than Gross National Product (GNP).

For example, the Index of Sustainable Economic Welfare modifies personal consumption for distributional inequality, adds in the services of household labour, consumer durables and streets and highways, and includes public consumption expenditure on health and education (Daly and Cobb, 1989). It also subtracts costs of vehicle, water, air and noise pollution, depletion of non-renewable resources, costs of commuting and urbanisation, and expenditures on advertising. This study found that the index had risen by only 20 per cent per capita in the USA between 1951 and 1986, with no increase during the 1970s and a decline in the 1980s. Daly and Cobb suggest that appropriate policies can improve results on their measure of welfare: reduced income inequality in the 1960s, and reductions in car accidents and air pollution more recently, had resulted from deliberate policy and had improved quality of life and the index.

As economists start to consider including non-market work in GDP, some feminist analysts have begun to have doubts. There are boundary issues about what should be counted, with the third-party criterion involving practical and conceptual problems. Reproductive services are one example: sex, children, eggs, sperm and their rearing can all be bought. Should they be included in GDP? Valuation of time also raises problems, when work as a housekeeper and much other female-dominated work is undervalued. More fundamental is the argument that attempting to fit unpaid work into current definitions of economic activity, and of what is valuable, is retrogressive. It encourages both using money as the only measure for valuing activity and seeing national income levels and growth as the main measure of welfare, when they are totally inadequate for this purpose. In addition to the inclusions and omissions mentioned, the same level of national income can occur with many different distributions of that income among individuals and households. Thus a focus on aggregate levels of GNP alone ignores concern over inequalities of income.

'Mitigating Misery': assessing the net value of a second family income

The use in 'Mitigating Misery' (hereafter 'MM') of arguments about the omission of unpaid work reinforces the concern that using money to value caring and household work may be retrogressive. The paper comes to two strong conclusions. The first is that earners of lower second incomes (usually women) would be more productive at home, and it would be economically rational for them to return there. The second is that efficiency in home production should be encouraged, with time substituted for money, and moreover that such efficiency should be assumed, with some benefits able to be lowered still further.

The focus in 'MM' is on measuring the total costs of acquiring an income rather than just the value of the household work, though the latter is needed to estimate the former. Two different methods are used for estimating the costs in households with two parents and two children, one pre-school and one school-age.

The first calculates the direct costs of acquiring the second income, adding to the transport and clothing costs the entire costs of daycare for the children. To these are added an estimate of the extra costs of buying in some specific household services and/or using less labour-intensive, more expensive options − a less detailed variant of one of the methods of valuing household production in national income described above.

The second method is the more aggregated version. It adds the weekly cost of a housekeeper, assumed to cover both childcare and household services, to the direct transport/clothing costs of working. Both methods, quantified below, yield the result that if the second income earner is paid less than about the average wage of $521 per week gross (November 1990 figures) or $399 net, there is little or no net benefit to the household in money terms.

The estimates are very much back-of-envelope figuring, with some components explained more fully than others, and in practice would of course exhibit great variability between families. Transport is estimated at $32 per week – $22 to work and $10 to daycare – while clothing for work is included at $18. Daycare is given as $130 for the pre-school child, at a commercial rate of $33 per half day, plus $33 for the school-age child. This yields a weekly direct cost of $213. The cost of substituting hired help or more expensive materials for personal time is estimated at $148 per week: $35 for house cleaning (three hours per week at $10 per hour, plus $5 for more expensive materials); $35 for 'clothing maintenance' (two hours washing and ironing per week at $10 per hour, plus $15 higher clothing bills), and $78 for extra food expenditure. The extra food expenditure is calculated by assuming that women at home full time could feed a family of four for $47 per week (one of Alison Holst's lower food budgets). Those in paid work are likely to spend closer to $120 per week on food for four. (This figure is based on a typical newspaper budget.) Even the figure of $47 did not allow for further savings from preserving fruit and vegetables, so $5 extra is subtracted. This gives a total figure of $361 per week which would be spent in acquiring the second income, as against $398 received post tax by those on average earnings.

The second method simply takes $10 per hour as a housekeeper wage for 37.5 hours per week and adds clothing/transport costs, and this gives a slightly higher figure than the previous method. The case of two school-age children is also discussed. With lower childcare costs, a wage of only about $261 after tax per week is estimated as the break-even point, with earnings above this giving a net monetary benefit.

There are a number of conceptual and factual problems with these calculations and the conclusions drawn, apart from the gender bias disguised as economic rationality. Firstly, as recognised in the text but not in the calculations, most women in paid work do most of the essential home production themselves in addition to their labour force activity (with varying degrees of participation by male partners, where relevant). Only a minority of those in more highly paid work employ home assistance. Australian evidence is that women in paid work have a longer working week in total than those engaged full time in home production, although they spend less time than the latter on household work (Sonius, 1989). More recent pilot time-use data for New Zealand yields similar conclusions. While many women, especially the majority who are in paid work out of economic necessity, might prefer more leisure, they are not in a position to exercise that preference. Thus, the typical weekly salary of a housekeeper should be used as a cost of paid work only for the minority of women (mainly those with higher earnings) who use one. Certainly this salary is a justified, or even minimum, estimate of the value of home production. However, most women in paid work supply the majority of the hypothetical housekeeper's services themselves, and do two jobs: the well-known 'double burden'.

Similarly, few lower-paid women can afford even subsidised formal childcare, but must manage with extended families, hours different from those of the spouse, or informal low-price minding. Thus, for most women, both childcare costs and opportunity costs are overestimated in the first method and the housekeeper costs are overestimated in the second.

In addition, attributing the full cost of childcare to the second income earner, in accordance with economists' marginal analysis, is more than just a technical nicety. It supports the status quo position in which there is a secondary earner, normally the woman, with full responsibility for childcare, and neither the primary worker, the employer of either worker nor the community shares this responsibility.

Thus, while 'MM' is correct that lack of jobs may force some women back into home production during recession, the costs to such families are underestimated. There is also the loss of market production from women's withdrawal from paid work to be taken into account. This would increase in importance if the economy recovered to a situation nearer to full employment. Further, 'MM' neglects the negative multiplier effects on economic activity of any reduced purchases of household goods and services which occur. As more goods and services are produced and sold, and wages earned, successive rounds of spending and income result – with a corresponding negative spiral from reduced spending.

In addition, for many of those who would be affected, a job is more than only an economic necessity. Thus there may be severe psychic costs in losing it, including the loss of social contact with fellow workers and others, of stimulation and feelings of self-worth gained from paid work, and of work experience important for later employment prospects. In addition, the extra expenditure on food and other household areas, some necessities and some luxuries by those in paid work are at least in part a net addition to well-being and standards of living.

At times feminism has been accused of devaluing unpaid work and the choice of those who wish to bring up children full time, while concentrating on equality in paid work. Only seldom have feminists in fact been guilty of this. Properly valuing unpaid work is not incompatible with advocating full equality of opportunity in paid work. Many would argue that the desirable situation is one in which there is neutrality towards the options and adequate support for each, with recognition that bringing up the next generation is a shared responsibility for both parents (where possible) and the community. Arguments for encouraging women to take as short breaks as possible from paid work are discussed in Part III.

Certainly, women should not be pushed out of the labour force by overestimates of the monetary and other costs of being in paid work, nor by underestimates of the other benefits. The overestimates of costs are at times accompanied by a revived emphasis on the desirability of younger children having full-time care from their mothers (when partnered, at least!) – often a rationalisation when jobs are short.

To be fair to 'MM', the lack of gender neutrality of the changes predicted in the paper is mentioned:

> Clearly the implications of the increasing competitiveness of home production as a means of maintaining living standards could be regarded as reversing trends observed over recent decades. In particular the trend for more women to participate in the money economy may well be reversed if the effects we've outlined become prevalent. It may be this trend is undesirable as it is women predominantly who will be 'condemned' to the home. The propensity for women to be affected by the fall in the real value of money earnings though is a function of their market income levels rather than a function of sex, assuming an equal partnership by adults in the family unit ... What is economically optimal from the family unit's perspective, is that the lower income earner be the one to consider home production as a part-time or full-time alternative to participation in the paid workforce (*ibid.*: 6–7).

However, this simply exemplifies the circular reasoning which reinforces and justifies the status quo in gender earnings differences and divisions of labour within households discussed in the previous chapter. Moreover, the assumption in the penultimate sentence has been found inappropriate, at least in the long term, by many women. What may be a rational allocation of household labour in times of harmony can have long-term adverse implications for women if the partnership does not continue owing to death of the spouse, divorce or separation. There is evidence from overseas that despite Matrimonial Property Acts, women are on average worse off after divorce, and men better off (Funder, 1989; Weitzman, 1985).

Changes to the child support system in New Zealand in 1992, with a new assessment formula for payments by the non-custodial parent, could have reduced this effect slightly. The amount payable is based on the non-custodial parent's earnings, together with the number of children in the original and (where relevant) reconstituted families. In most cases this leads to higher payments than the previous system. Further, they can now be deducted automatically from earnings, increasing the compliance rate. However, the changes were aimed more at reducing government expenditure and increasing enforcement than at improving the situation of the custodial parent and children. Payments due to beneficiary families simply reduce their state support. The system is proving hard to administer, and has given rise to widespread complaints, particularly as no account is taken of the income of the custodial parent. A review is currently under way.

As stated in the previous chapter, more recent economic analyses have considered conflict and its consequences. 'MM', however, takes no direct account of this. It does so indirectly by considering skill maintenance (as investment) and a preference for paid work/job satisfaction (as consumption) as rationales beyond the economic benefit of the family for the second income earner to continue in paid work. The fact that skill investment may also be an essential precaution against the consequences of marriage disharmony and break-up is not mentioned. A further conclusion in 'MM' is that childcare subsidies should not currently be provided, because there is an excess labour supply. There is also a suggestion that superannuitants should (compulsorily?) assist with childcare:

> One of the high direct costs identified in procuring the second family income is the cost of childcare. It seems wasteful that there are numbers of recipients of national superannuation grants who would be quite capable of offering this service to home units. Rather than the present Minister's preference for the taxpayer subsidising the cost of childcare, there must be at least some scope for recipients of the GRI who are capable of having their benefit tailored to provide them an incentive to participate more in the production sector. (*ibid.*: 13)

Apart from the reference to superannuation as a grant and the implied threat to those unwilling or not in a position to participate in childcare, the suggestion that childcare should not be subsidised is disquieting. There has already been a sharp reduction in the real value of the community's contribution to raising children (Thomson, 1991). Further, adequate and affordable childcare has regularly been shown to be the most critical factor in permitting women with family responsibilities to be in paid work. It is cynical, though not unusual, for (hopefully) short-term labour supply considerations to govern such policy. By contrast, longer-term economic arguments favour provisions which allow women's human capital to be fully utilised. This requires adequate childcare, which also provides further employment and leads to positive multiplier effects.

'Mitigating Misery': efficiency in home production

The link from the first to the second major area discussed in 'MM' is shown clearly in the following extract:

> The failure of conventional measures to take proper account of the value of home production has resulted in a system of welfare benefits to be structured in a manner that ignores the necessity of pursuing efficiency in the home production sector ... The formulation of economic policy should recognise that omission of the home production sector from measures of economic welfare will give rise to policies that distort efficiency of investment. For example, depending on amounts involved, taxing the market economy to pay some participants in the home production sector, could effectively be a consumption subsidy, since the recipients work at home productions, consume that output, and then receive taxpayer funding on top of that. ('MM': 13 and 12)

This constitutes an attack on the existence or levels of family support and all other forms of benefit. 'MM' slides quickly from the fairly innocuous-sounding notion that efficiency in home production will be necessary for those on low and declining incomes to the stronger notion that it should be encouraged, with time substituted for money, to the still tougher conclusion that such efficiency should be assumed, with some benefits able to be lowered still further. 'Incentives' for efficiency are a euphemism for cutting benefits. The claim – to be examined – is that hardship would not result if the households involved used their time and money more efficiently.

The intention is not to imply that beneficiaries are managing. Many, especially families, are not, because of debt burdens, high housing costs and a pattern of consumption based on higher cash incomes. What is suggested is that a cultural change to more productive consumption will be forced on them as real incomes fall further, in order to survive ... Apparel comprises principally women's clothing in the expenditure survey. Therefore application to clothes making, which is likely to be a skill still known to many older women, will reap cash savings ... The estimates above suggest that at the low end of the income scale there are significant gains in efficiency that households could capture as a counter to the falls in real market incomes. Further, we expect that it will be necessary for them to do so in order to prevent the income falls producing unnecessary hardship ... If there are substantial fiscal savings that can be made by recognising that present welfare transfers are not properly researched and formulated, but rather the result of some arbitrary political trade-off, then the implications for economic policy are enormous. It means, for example, that government may well be in a position right now to bias its fiscal programme further away from welfare payments. (*ibid.*: 9, 10 and 12)

This might be summarised as follows: 'Expectations of those on low incomes, especially benefits, are too high. They will, can and should have to manage on less by substituting cheaper goods and their labour for purchases, with women reverting to elbow grease, bottling and making the family clothes. Government should have the guts to make them do this by cutting benefits further.' It is not even clear that in all these areas (baking your own bread is another 'MM' example) home production is cheaper than market purchase. Fortunately, even government ministers are not suggesting that benefits should be cut further on the basis of such doubtful and inequitable arguments.

A genuine attempt to assess minimum income for a decent life is to be preferred to rhetoric from the wealthy about how the poor could and should save money. In fact, both 'MM' and Treasury (New Zealand Treasury, 1990) have attempted to assess such minimum necessary incomes. This raises the issue of the use of absolute or relative measures in deciding benefit levels. The criterion of relative income levels and standards of living has been used in setting benefits and judging poverty in the last few decades. Thus, those relying on the welfare system could expect to increase their standards of living in line with general income growth while the economy was expanding. However, economic stagnation, the backlash against high government revenue and expenditure, and the revival of the concept of the welfare state as only a safety net have meant that, among policy-makers at least, the often less generous absolute needs approach has been revived.

Table 2.1 shows the 'MM' and Treasury calculations of minimum needs, and compares them with actual average household expenditures, prevailing benefit rates, and income levels calculated from relative income measures suggested by the 1972 Royal Commission on Social Security. The food budget suggested by Alison Holst (who probably did not envisage use of her budget for essentially political purposes!), mentioned earlier, is used as the basis of necessary expenditure in that area by 'MM'. The figures are halfway between the 'basic' and 'with extras' calculations of Alison Holst in the *Sunday Times* in 1991, scaled for different household structures. Housing costs are the Housing Corporation's guide of 25 per cent of net income, and estimates are made for electricity, clothing, transport and so on. As 'MM' states:

> The budgets are for a basic standard of living, but are not based on simply doing without. They incorporate cash saving made possible through the productive use of at-home time. The food budget requires a great deal of time in food preparation. It does not allow for the purchase of convenience foods. The concept of substituting time for cash impacts throughout the budget. Cleaning materials which are easier to use are out and basic materials requiring elbow grease are in ... Leisure and entertainment focus on simple pleasures. A car is out ... The incorporation of an elderly relative into the home reduces her shelter cost and also offers the opportunity for child care for the family ... For a solo parent, the cost of housing will impel many to seek a sharing arrangement with others. (*ibid.*: 8)

This fairly casual suggestion that the clock may and should be put back 60 years or so, particularly for women, speaks for itself. In fact, real average incomes have risen substantially over this period, even if they have suffered a recent decline. Hence society as a whole should have sufficient resources to make sharp cuts in the standard of living of low-income groups quite unnecessary. Further, there is a larger higher-income group than in the Depression years, and there is no suggestion in 'MM' that they should share in any sacrifices. Government policy does claim to be based on shared sacrifice, although via user pays rather than higher income tax rates. However, the policies of both the National and Labour parties over the last few years have led to lower-income groups experiencing absolute and relative declines in their real incomes.

Table 2.1: **'Measures of Income Adequacy', Benefit levels, and Expenditures**

	Single adult		Sole parent, one child		Two parents, two children	
'Measures of Income Adequacy'						
	(Treasury)	('MM')	(Treasury)	('MM')	(Treasury)	('MM')
Food	30.06	23	42.48	33	63.35	55
Total Household Budget	120.25	133	169.91	173	261.40	271
50% median income	122.11		172.55		265.46	
78.6% Labourers award	138.71		196.00		301.54	
65% average wage	163.22		230.63		354.82	
Benefit Rates						
March 1991						
Unemployed 20+/DPB	143.57		255.14		319.08	
Invalid/sickness	162.26		n.a.		319.08	
April 1991						
Unemployed under 25/DPB	108.17		227.93		293.88	
Unemployed over 25/DPB	129.81		227.93		293.88	
Sickness under 25	129.81		n.a.		309.86	
Sickness over 25	135.22		n.a.		309.86	
Invalid	162.26		n.a.		334.44	
Average expenditures						
	229		358		716	
	(single households not in labour force)		(1 adult, 1 or more children)		(2 adults, 2 children)	

Sources: Based on Infometrics (1991); New Zealand Treasury (1990); Department of Social Welfare benefit rate figures.

Treasury calculations on the absolute needs approach for household expenditures yield similar but even lower results than 'MM' (based on 1990 figures and prices). Treasury's food costs are higher, but its lower figures for other costs give lower totals overall. Treasury's figures for food are based on an Otago University economy food plan, costed and updated, while the differing needs of different sizes of household are allowed for (using a Jensen household equivalence scale). The total budget is grossed up from this with a casualness which takes one's breath away: 'The budget for food can be multiplied by a factor to assess total household expenditure needs. In this case the food budget is multiplied by four. Some sources consider it adequate to multiply food needs by three and others consider five is a more fair figure' (New Zealand Treasury, 1990: 150). 'MM' at least used empirical estimates for non-food expenditures.

Also shown in the table are average expenditures for three different household structures, benefit levels before and after the April 1991 cuts, and some relative income measures produced by Treasury. Relativities to the labourers' basic award rate (78.6 per cent) and the average weekly wage rate (65 per cent) are based on suggestions of the 1972 Royal Commission on Social Security, and illustrate its commitment to the relative concept for assessment of benefits, rather than the absolute needs approach. The lowest of these alternatives is 50 per cent of median household income, which includes total earnings and other incomes of all members of the household, and thus a higher base. However, the smaller fraction used yields the lowest of the three relative measures. For each household structure, this gives an income close to the Treasury's needs budget, which may have been how the 50 per cent figure was selected.

The conclusions drawn from this table will depend on judgements about the reasonableness of the minimum needs budgets for adequate living, on degrees of inequality regarded as acceptable, and on views about economic and fiscal policy generally. With 65 per cent of the average wage as a yardstick, adjusted for household structure, Guaranteed Retirement Income (GRI) and the invalids benefit are the only single-person benefits to meet it. The two adult, two children benefits also fail this test of adequacy, but sole parents have just sufficient by this measure, even after the cuts. However, the table shows that for each household type (two adults, sole parent with one child, two adults with two children) the average expenditure is much higher than benefit rates. For households with two parents and two children average expenditures are well over double the highest benefit rate. This puts the tightness of the benefit levels in perspective.

Some other points made in 'MM' deserve examination.

> The necessary shift of market income towards firms and away from households (we've been paying ourselves too much!) will likely accentuate the differences in material wealth between those households fully participating in the market economy, and those who become more dependent upon home production. While the political and economic ramifications may be significant, it is likely that a dual economy will develop with the behaviour of one group of households driven by market economy forces, while the other group becomes increasingly immune to market cycles. (*ibid.*: 15)

This passage reinforces the prescription suggested earlier in 'MM' that benefits should be reduced, with the savings used to reduce the tax burden from business. It also advocates the line of national development based on a dual economy, with a large low-wage secondary sector rather than the high-skill, high-wage economy which could allow less inequality. Its emphasis on lower wages to produce greater competitiveness also implies reliance on exports instead of, rather than as well as, a growing home market. While the passage talks of 'paying ourselves too much', it rarely appears to be top incomes which are meant. Instead, it is special-interest pleading for business.

As well as the dual economy envisaged in 'MM', contrasts are drawn between the position of low-income, single-earner households and beneficiaries:

> The conclusion we draw is that labour market policy that ignores the value of home production that is potentially available to households, discriminates against non-beneficiary households who are efficient home production units. An example here would be the unpaid spouse in a low market income household baking bread to make ends meet, while a beneficiary household has sufficient income to buy a loaf from the corner dairy. (*ibid.*: 14)

This passage is worrying. First, the low income-earner household should be eligible for family support and/or guaranteed minimum family income. Second, while agreeing that household work should not be undervalued, this emotive passage is of a type which sets one low-income group against another in a way which can suit advocates of current policies.

A final concern about distributive justice and opportunity for all across class, ethnicity and gender is raised by the following passage: 'The relevance of a traditional education may diminish for many, if the market economy is unable to provide paid work for them. For many, such is the case already' (*ibid.*: 11). If this is intended as a critique of the educational system, further development of the argument in terms of the need for continuing education through life, and the development of flexibility and a range of abilities, could be a useful contribution. However, the suspicion is that it is more allied to the dual economy argument, with only the elite given a superior education.

Many will find the arguments and conclusions advanced in 'MM' unconvincing and unacceptable. They do, however, need to be taken seriously. The co-option of feminist ideas has been demonstrated, while the argument supports policy changes in the same direction as recent ones, but even more extreme in nature. Alternatives to the current directions of economic and social policies are being researched and advocated by a number of groups and individuals. Bringing these to full development, building the coalitions of those opposed to current policies and gaining ground in the political process is a major challenge.

Part II

Equal Pay and Pay Equity Struggles

3

The History and Concepts of Equal Pay and Pay Equity in New Zealand

'Equal pay for equal work' is the term for the principle and practice of women and men receiving the same pay for doing the same work (sometimes extended to highly similar work). Worldwide, men were paid more than most women doing the same jobs in the nineteenth and first half of the twentieth century. Occupational segregation by gender also kept women's average pay low: areas of women's work were defined as unskilled, whatever their content. For example, dexterity, caring for people and the ability to undertake repetitive and accurate work were seen as natural to women and they were not rewarded in the same way as the demands of men's jobs, such as heavy lifting. The recent change in emphasis in many areas of work from collective to individualised pay fixing based on performance in the job, not simply the nature of the job, makes the area of equal pay more problematic.

'Equal pay for work of equal value' is a broader concept than equal pay for equal work. In fact three different terms are in common use for this broader concept. The other two are 'comparable worth' and 'pay equity'. Shifts between them have been partly a question of strategy and politics. The equal pay for work of equal value position suggests that work assessed as requiring similar overall levels of skill, responsibility, effort and working conditions (in total, not necessarily on each component separately) should be paid equally. The demand for its implementation is based on the argument that characteristics of female-dominated work are under-valued both by the market and in negotiations, as in the dexterity example.

Opponents argue that there is no real or objective measure of value distinct from the established market-value level of pay on offer. Interventions in the working of the market are claimed to be arbitrary and costly in money and employment terms. However, few labour markets see wages set through a pure auction system. The skills involved, the status of the job, the bargaining process, government actions, individual and/or group performance and historical factors modify supply and demand factors in fixing wages (Deeks and Boxall, 1989). The profitability of the individual firm is also relevant. However, discrimination on the grounds of gender and other variables can be present in almost all these factors and systems. Even in markets for less scarce (or secondary) labour, where wage determination most closely approximates pure supply and demand in action, discrimination is by no means absent.

History

Gender discrimination is clear from New Zealand in the 1880s, when the conditions of sweated labour were appalling. Women were paid less than men and often treated worse: 'A woman collected a load of fabric from a contractor, took it to her home, worked for 12 hours, carried the lot back to work – 151 oatmeal bags – and was paid 8d, the price for a gross' (Sutch, 1974: 73). There were 'the long rows of women in impossible seating, who wrapped rags around their legs as protection from the cold that seeped from the concrete floors' (Coney 1986: 19) and 'the fifteen girl apprentices, aged from 14 to 18 years, working unpaid in the hope that one day it would lead to a pay packet. In reality, it would more likely lead to the sack when the apprenticeship was completed. A skilled woman tailoress might get 26–35s a week, but a tailor would collect 70s' (*ibid.*: 20).

The early days: a strong feminist consciousness

Noting that the Canterbury Board of Education paid 20 per cent less to an assistant master (*sic*) if a female teacher was employed, Kate Sheppard commented that, 'There is no difference in the work to be done. The same standards have to be taught and the same examinations passed ... How manifestly unfair then to have two rates of pay for the same work, merely because one of the workers is a woman' (Sheppard, 1892: 6). In speaking to a resolution in favour of equal pay at the 1900 National Council of Women meeting, Christina Henderson was careful to specify that the work must be carried out as well as by men. 'To avoid any misunderstanding, I must explain that this does not mean that where men and women are engaged on the same work they are necessarily to have the same wages, but that where exactly similar results are expected and obtained, the pay should be the same' (Henderson, 1900). This is resonant of the problem which arises when women have attempted to establish individual discrimination on the basis of gender under the Equal Pay Act 1972, discussed later. The special qualities clause of that legislation allows a defence where some specific factor not involving gender discrimination, such as special qualifications or experience, is shown to be the reason for the pay difference. In practice, the Arbitration Court has made it easy for such a factor to be justified.

The general notion that women do not perform as well as men at work was strongly resisted by early equal pay advocates. 'It is quite as easy to say that women work better than men, and quite as easy to prove it ... Honours, prizes, scholarships are freely carried off by women students ... In business, women clerks are preferred to men clerks, employers universally declaring them to be more careful, faithful and adaptable' (Mackay, 1902). Jessie Mackay countered other stock arguments against equal pay and economic equality for women, including the family wage issue, the contention that women are unfitted to take care of money, the cost effects and the suggestion that the result would be a drop in male wages, with the institution of marriage endangered. She argued that even if male wages were reduced, which was uncertain, so also would their expenses be reduced, because female relatives would be better able to look after themselves. She accepted happily that prostitution and marriages of convenience might become rarer, but she saw no problem for other marriages.

Other arguments used in favour of equal pay (by Stella Henderson, an early holder of the MA and LLB degrees) included economic independence and the promotion of feelings of self-worth in women, which would make them less ready to accept a dependent position within marriage (Sheppard, 1898: 1–2). There was also a clear realisation that women were being used as a cheap source of labour by employers, and that both direct opposition to the employment of women and support for equal pay by some male workers were intended to avoid replacement of male workers by females.

Equal opportunity and pay had also long been on the agenda of overseas campaigners for women's rights. Access to a wider range of work was usually given the higher priority, reasonably enough at a time when opportunity was so restricted. It was also recognised that the occupational crowding which resulted was itself one of the factors in women's pay being so low. In his *Principles of Political Economy*, John Stuart Mill (influenced by Harriet Taylor, as discussed in Part I) gave crowding, prejudice and the family wage principle as the main factors in women's low pay, and argued that women are not less productive than men; indeed, they show greater versatility: 'The varied though petty details which compose the occupation of most women, call forth probably as much of mental ability, as the uniform routine of the pursuits which are the habitual occupation of a large majority of men' (Taylor, [1851], 1983: 28–9). However, Mill and Taylor did not specifically argue for equal pay or discuss whether their proposal of a minimum wage should apply to women (Pujol, 1992). Taylor did, though, discuss the issue of female employment depressing male wages, arguing that 'so long as competition is the general law of human life, it is tyranny to shut out half the competitors' (Taylor, [1851], 1983: 21) and suggesting that remedies would be found. One she put forward herself was that young children should be more rigidly excluded from factory employment.

Barbara Bodichon (1857) and Harriet Martineau also strongly supported equal opportunity, and it can be argued that the latter's equal pay advocacy in an *Edinburgh Review* article extended to the concept of equal pay for work of equal value. Discussing the hard physical work of dairymaids, she suggested that 'such work as this ought at least to be paid as well as the equivalent work of men' (Martineau, 1859: 300, quoted in Yates, 1985: 22).

Equal pay for equal work was adopted as policy by the New Zealand Public Service Association in 1914, and was in the Labour Party platform in 1927 (Corner, 1988). Most unions, however, were concerned with protecting the jobs, status and pay levels of their male members. Their strategies, in addition to direct exclusion or limiting of women's work, in some cases included equal pay, but this was primarily designed to keep the jobs male only. Employers, on the other hand, wanted freedom to employ women wherever convenient and at lower wages. In longstanding areas of work, the Arbitration Court tended to support the status quo for gender divisions of labour. Hence in 1906 it rejected a union demand to pay tailoresses the same wages as tailors, on the basis that equal pay was in fact designed to exclude women from the trade (Robertson, 1991).

The situation of women in terms both of access to employment and of opportunity and pay relative to men has ebbed and flowed with economic conditions. The reserve army of labour treatment has been evident in the Depression, the post-war 'Rosie the Riveter' phenomenon and the rhetoric of young children needing full-time mothering when jobs are short. (*Rosie the Riveter* is an American film, which shows women willingly drafted into a variety of blue-collar trades in wartime, performing admirably but eased or pushed back into the home and/or traditional work 'when the boys came home from war'. Interviews in the film show that some went willingly, albeit encouraged by propaganda, while others were more resistant.)

Technological change has involved both deskilling and reskilling, with ongoing high levels of occupational segregation and lower valuation of women's work but the actual jobs in which women dominate changing. In New Zealand in the 1920s, as in England, women were rooted out of all but low-level public service work. All public servants had reduced conditions in this period of intermittent recession, but women were disproportionately downgraded. In the Post Office in 1921, regulation 8 'placed an arbitrary limit on the salary they could earn, regardless of their seniority, skills and position' (Cook and Matthews, 1990: 173). Women were 16.4 per cent of Post Office employees in 1921, but this had reduced to less than 10 per cent by 1929, with only low-paid, repetitive work available as compared to the higher-skilled postmistress positions filled earlier. During this period (1923–24), there was a lively debate on equal pay in *Katipo*, the journal of the New Zealand Post and Telegraph Officers Association, reviving all the earlier arguments.

Despite their earlier commitment to equal pay, Labour in government in the Depression of the 1930s supported the family wage concept which allowed higher wages for men, irrespective of whether individual men or women actually had dependants. The family wage principle had been enunciated by the Arbitration Court, which in 1922 argued that: 'The material requisites of normal life, for the average adult male, includes provision for his family ... In the case of the wage-earner, this right can be effectuated only through wages; therefore the adult male labourer has a right to a family living wage' (quoted in Iverson, 1987). A minimum wage for women was not set by the court until 1936, and then at only 47 per cent of the male rate. The Clerical Workers Union claimed equal pay for clerks in their first award negotiations in 1937 and regularly thereafter (Hill, 1993), but with no legal underpinning and little bargaining power were unsuccessful.

The 1960s and 1970s: legislation at last

A new campaign led by the Public Service Association (PSA) in the 1950s finally saw public-sector equal pay legislation passed in 1960. Average female factory wages were still only half those of males as late as 1967–68, while for nominal weekly award wage rates across the economy the ratio in that year reached 70.2 per cent. It took 12 years and a commission of inquiry before the public-sector provisions were extended to the private sector. The Equal Pay Act, covering all employment, was passed in 1972, with gradual implementation over the next five years. It covered all remuneration, however determined, and applied to actual rates of pay as well as those prescribed in awards, collective agreements and other formal instruments (Review Committee, 1979).

Compliance with this legislation significantly narrowed the gender gap, with the female–male ratio for average ordinary-time hourly earnings increasing from 72 to 78 per cent during the five-year implementation period. This arose mainly from the elimination of separate rates for women and men in awards and agreements. The ratio has slowly crept up to 81 per cent in the subsequent 17 years. Total weekly and annual earnings show wider gaps, with women predominating in part-time work, and having less access to overtime. Awards and agreements, which until the passing of the 1991 Employment Contracts Act were the main documents establishing basic pay levels, had to provide equal pay for women by 1977. However, low level policing of the Act, based mainly on complaints, and use of discriminatory job titles contributed to evasion of its provisions. Further, placement of individuals on scales, access to promotion and the allocation of above-award payments in a gender-unbiased manner are much harder to enforce. The first two might be considered more matters of unequal opportunity than of lack of equal pay, although the boundaries are unclear. Discrimination in such matters became unlawful under the Human Rights Commission Act 1977.

Another problem arises in the area of female-dominated work, with the 1979 Review Committee believing that this was still an area of concern. The Act had provided for the removal and prevention of discrimination, based on the sex of employees, in the rates of remuneration of males and females in all paid employment. Rates were to contain no element of differentiation based on sex. Section 3(1) sets out the criteria to be applied in determining whether an element of such differentiation based on sex exists for work covered by any instrument. These criteria are:

> (a) For work which is not exclusively or predominantly performed by female employees – (i) The extent to which the work or class of work calls for the same, or substantially similar, degrees of skill, effort, and responsibility; and

(ii) The extent to which the conditions under which the work is to be performed are the same or substantially similar:

(b) For work which is exclusively or predominantly performed by female employees, the rate of remuneration that would be paid to male employees with the same, or substantially similar, skills, responsibility, and service performing the work under the same, or substantially similar, conditions and with the same, or substantially similar, degrees of effort.

This appears to be based on equal pay for work of equal value, rather than just equal pay for identical work. Job classification was required to ensure implementation in predominantly female occupations. The process became known as assessing the 'notional male rate', later changed to the 'equal pay rate' on the recommendation of the Equal Pay Review Committee because a notional rate could be derided as relating to a legal fiction or 'straw man' (Orr, 1986b: 7). However, it was never clear exactly which males (actual or theoretical) could be used for comparison. It was inevitable for employers to look within their own industry. Guidelines published by the Employers Federation for its members in February 1973 suggested consultations to protect their interests and ways of implementing job classification which were as narrow as possible. While job classification or evaluation inevitably involves subjective judgements, a good system opens them to scrutiny and attempts to be gender neutral.

The 1980s and 1990s: towards and after the Employment Equity Act

Ongoing concern in a female-dominated occupation led the Clerical Workers Union to take a case to the Arbitration Court in February 1986 seeking a ruling that employers should be directed to negotiate on a claim for equal pay for work of equal value. The court declined jurisdiction on the basis that if awards had been registered during 1973–77, indicating de facto acceptance that they incorporated equal pay, the question could not be reopened (New Zealand Arbitration Court, 1986). The Arbitration Court decision reinforced pressure for a further review of the Act.

A lack of further progress in narrowing the gap after 1977, the increasing influence of women in trade unions, particularly in female-dominated work, as well as overseas developments contributed to the vigour of the campaign for new legislation before, and more particularly after, the Clerical Workers Union case. It was spearheaded by a new organisation, the Campaign for Equal Value, Equal Pay, which was an alliance of mainly female-dominated unions and women's organisations. It took from 1986 to 1990, two stages of an Equal Pay Study, a Working Group on Equal Opportunities and Equal Pay, and considerable ministerial and bureaucratic debates and delays before the Employment Equity Act was finally passed in 1990. Alex Woodley attributes the success of the campaign to the combination of eight factors. These were: a growing consciousness of the merits of the case; support from women in Parliament and the bureaucracy; support from women's groups and a degree of public support; an informed group of trade union activists; a robust campaign organisation; the neutralisation, for a period, of opposition; and the continuation of pressure. (For further discussion of this period and the politics involved, see Wilson, 1992 and 1993, and Woodley, 1993.) Of course, whether one can really talk of success in passing legislation when it was repealed before it had any labour market impact is a moot point.

The provisions of the 1990 Act, particularly on pay equity, were inevitably a compromise. Cabinet had directed that the new law should not be contrary to the principles and processes of wage fixing built into the industrial relations legislation, including ensuring that it preserved the flexibility and decentralisation of the wage-fixing process. It directed that it should also avoid disruption to economic and labour market activity. Taken strictly, these instructions could mean that any third-party intervention was ruled out, but without it no legislation could be effective. In the end, final-offer arbitration over pay equity claims was contained in the Act.

The pay equity provisions, based on equal value principles, were intended to redress the inequitable impact on women of any current or historical discrimination in respect of their remuneration. A two-stage process was involved. The first stage would have allowed unions representing women in a female-dominated occupation – one with 60 per cent or more women employees – to request a pay equity assessment, suggesting both a definition for that occupation and two male comparator occupations (60 per cent or more male). In some circumstances a group of 20 or more women could have requested an assessment. If the Employment Equity Commissioner had decided to proceed, she would have chosen the definition of the occupation to be assessed and the comparator occupations. These were to display, overall, broadly similar levels of skills, effort and responsibility as the female occupation. The assessment process itself would have considered in more detail these three areas, as well as working conditions, and taken account of differences in remuneration attributable to recruitment and retention differences. The report of the assessment would judge the extent of any gender bias in the remuneration of the female occupation, after allowing for the factors mentioned and considering separately six regions – the five main centres and the rest of the country.

In the second stage, unions representing some or all workers within the female occupation or employers could have made a pay equity claim for a relevant award or agreement. This claim was to be negotiated, but if not settled within 60 days it was to be referred by either party for determination by final-offer arbitration of the Arbitration Commission. The commission would have heard evidence and made a pay equity determination by adopting one or other side's final offer on each provision of the claim, taking into consideration the pay equity report and the submissions and evidence of the parties. It would also have decided on the implementation method and timing, on which matters the Government could be heard.

Some claims were made in the few months of the legislation's existence, but none reached the full assessment stage. As a result of the compromises made in drafting the Act, both proponents and opponents had doubts about its likely effectiveness if it had been allowed to proceed. For the latter group, there were many loopholes to exploit.

Given the problems of the Equal Pay Act, many believe that gender discrimination in pay rates was by no means ended by its implementation or since (for discussion of the 1977–87 period, see Urban Research Associates *et al*, 1987). After repealing the Employment Equity Act, the National Government established a Working Party on Equity in Employment, the terms of reference of which confined it largely to measures to eliminate the barriers facing the groups designated in the equal opportunity part of the repealed legislation. This working party, surprisingly and bravely given its membership and the government to which it was reporting, recommended legislation requiring employers to develop, implement and monitor equal employment opportunities (EEO) programmes. This was the content of Part II of the legislation the government had just repealed. Unsurprisingly, the government rejected the recommendation, preferring voluntary promotion of EEO through a joint private/public sector trust. They would 'in time' review this approach to determine whether it was successful. More innocuous recommendations were accepted.

Proponents of the 1990 legislation on employment equity had deliberately adopted the tactic of putting equal opportunity and pay equity together in the same legislation. This was partly because they were correctly seen as two prongs of an attack on women's disadvantage in the labour market and on the female–male earnings gap. In addition, it was thought that the easier equal opportunity area might allow the more controversial pay equity part to be passed alongside it. The wisdom of this judgement is now a matter of opinion. Whether equal opportunity would have been retained if in separate legislation is a matter of speculation, but it is doubtful in the light of the above. The situation on pay equity after the Employment Contracts Act is discussed in Chapter 8.

The earnings gap between women and men

Table 3.1, based on official survey figures covering the bulk of the labour force other than agriculture and one- or two-person businesses, shows that on average women earn a little less than three-quarters of a man's pay packet, but part of this gap is attributable to a shorter working week. When hourly ordinary-time earnings are compared, the proportion increases to 81 per cent. The pay gap in each case narrowed by about six points during the implementation period between 1973 and 1977. There has been only a slight improvement since then.

Table 3.1: **Average Earnings of Women in New Zealand as Percentage of Male Earnings**

	Ordinary-time earnings		Weekly earnings, including overtime	
	Hourly	Weekly (a)	Gross (b)	Total (a)
Oct 1973	72.1	69.2	57.8	na
Oct 1975	76.4	73.8	60.9	na
Oct 1977	78.5	76.2	63.2	71.1
May 1980	78.2	75.0	62.3	70.4
May 1983	78.6	76.1	na	71.9
May 1985	78.0	75.1	na	70.2
May 1988	79.5	76.1	na	72.2
May 1990	81.0	77.6	na	72.2
May 1993	81.4	77.1	na	74.1

Source: *Labour and Employment Gazette* and *Key Statistics*, various issues.
(a) In calculating these figures, two part-time workers are counted as one full-time equivalent worker: divisor is number of full-time equivalent workers.
(b) In calculating this figure, divisor is the number of workers, irrespective of whether full or part time.

Low pay in female-dominated areas

Department of Labour figures on average wage and salary movements for 1985–86 show that female median earnings were 74.6 per cent of the male median, with 16.7 per cent of women receiving less than 60 per cent of the overall median, as against 6.9 per cent of men (Low Pay Unit, 1986: 2). They also showed that 6.7 per cent of female workers, as against 3.1 per cent of males, earned less than the statutory minimum wage. In 19 industries, covering 18.5 per cent of the total surveyed employment, average ordinary-time weekly earnings were below $250 in 1985 – 84 per cent of the then overall average figure. Women were over-represented in 14 of these industries compared to their share of the labour force, confirming female-dominated industries as low paying. There is also evidence of relatively low male earnings in female-dominated industries. An examination of male earnings in 18 private sector industries showed that average male earnings were under 80 per cent of the male average for all industries. For example, 'the earnings of males in men's and women's hairdressing was approximately 60% of the male average earnings' (Orr, 1986b: 6).

Maori female incomes within broad occupational groups do not lag substantially behind non-Maori levels, but their concentration in the lower-paid occupations means that the overall median income for Maori females is well below the non-Maori equivalent. The tendency to be in the lower-paid, less secure, secondary labour market is particularly pronounced for Maori and Pacific Island women. Compared to Pakeha, they are substantially under-represented in professional, administrative, managerial, clerical and sales occupations, and over-represented in manual work. As a result, in 1986 the proportion of Maori women in the labour force with incomes over $20,000 was only 5.24 per cent and of Pacific Island women 3.22 per cent, as against 11.15 per cent for women overall (National Advisory Council on the Employment of Women, 1990).

The impact of different hours of work

Since each of the measures of relative earning in Table 3.1 is sometimes quoted as 'the' pay gap, it is worth examining the reasons for the differences. Weekly ordinary-time earnings have a female–male earnings ratio about three percentage points wider than the hourly equivalent, because full-time women workers average about 1.5 fewer hours a week than men.

Including overtime widens the gap, because women work on average two hours less overtime each week. Gross weekly earnings (a discontinued series) shows a wider pay gap than total weekly earnings owing to the different treatment of part-time workers. The first series divides total earnings by the total number of workers, whereas the second uses all full-time and half the number of part-time workers in the attempt to construct a full-time equivalent weekly earnings rate.

There is no 'right answer' on average earnings or the female–male ratio. Each measures something slightly different and is relevant to different questions. For actual purchasing power, weekly earnings are more relevant than hourly figures, and the female–male ratio here shows a wider gap. Annual figures would show a wider gap still, as women move in and out of the labour force to a greater extent than men. However, to assess the extent of discrimination, ordinary-time hourly earnings (with the narrowest gap) are often used, since working fewer hours and less overtime may be regarded as a non-discriminatory reason for women's lower average pay. Even then, it should be noted that rather than this being an unconstrained choice many women may have less access to overtime and/or need to work part time because of family commitments. This illustrates that there is room for considerable disagreement over the nature and magnitude of the factors responsible for the earnings gap and the proportion which can be regarded as justified by non-discriminatory factors. Much hinges on how you think wages are set in the market and on definitions of discrimination. Thus, the range of arguments on the issue of how much (if any) of the female–male earnings gap results from discrimination is the subject of the rest of this chapter, starting with a discussion of wage determination in general.

What determines wage levels?

A full analysis of this question at the level of the whole economy, as well as in individual markets, industries and occupations, is beyond the scope of this discussion, but it is important to outline neoclassical and other views.

Standard micro-economic analysis of the wage-setting process starts from supply and demand curves for a particular type of labour, with the price of that labour, or wage rate, determined by where they meet, as in any other market. Shortages of particular types of labour lead to relative wage increases, thus inducing individuals into the occupations concerned. Similarly, oversupply should lead to wage cuts.

The demand for a particular type of labour is derived by adding the amounts each firm would use at a particular wage rate. Firms will employ more labour at a lower wage rate than they would at a higher wage rate. This characteristic is derived from assuming a diminishing 'marginal revenue productivity' of labour. This means that as the amount of labour used increases, with all other inputs into production held constant, the additional output and revenue from each extra unit of labour is assumed to decrease. Adding ever more labour to the same amount of capital and other inputs becomes less productive. This commonsense result is the basis of the supposed wage–employment trade-off, which suggests wage cuts will eliminate unemployment. However, it is open to challenge.

The supply of labour by the individual will depend on his or her relative preference for work (or the spending which remuneration from work allows) and leisure, given the wage rate prevailing for the type of job. Generally it is postulated that a higher wage rate will induce higher labour supply, although for an individual with an adequate living standard it is possible that a wage increase may induce a smaller number of hours to be supplied. This is unlikely, however, in aggregate, so the usual upward-sloping supply curve will be observed, along with the downward-sloping demand curve from marginal productivity. Allowing for unpaid work, as well as paid work and leisure, alters the analysis somewhat, and has gender impacts discussed in Part III.

Different wages among different occupations and industries arise in orthodox analysis from variations in the supply and demand curves. On the demand side, higher levels of skill, training, experience and responsibility are the 'human capital' factors which should increase the productivity of types of labour and hence increase its demand and wage rate. The upsurge in female labour-force participation means that women are on average younger and have less training and years of experience than men in the labour force, which is one factor in women's lower average wages.

In addition, there is a need to recoup the costs of training through increased wages. 'The most important basic component of occupational wage differentials is the return on investment in acquiring skills. If a skilled occupation is to attract new entrants, the private costs of the training needed to enter it must be recouped over the recruit's working life with a rate of return equal to the return on other equally risky investments, or equal to the subjective rate of discount used by entrants in making their decision' (Rees, 1979: 155–6).

Attributes of jobs other than salaries are also relevant to the labour supply at any level. According to orthodoxy, 'the advantages of employment include not only the pay and any perquisites or amenities that go with it, but the prestige in which it is held and the satisfactions of working in it. If an occupation is disagreeable or held in low esteem, its pay must be higher to compensate for this' (*ibid.*: 155). It is here that doubts about both this account and its application to the gender pay gap set in. Do high-prestige occupations, to which recruits are easily attracted, pay less than those involving comparable training but lower prestige, particularly when the number entering many professions is controlled by professional associations, universities and/or governments? There appear to be few accountants or doctors who would switch to manual work, even if they could increase their pay by so doing. People in professional and management jobs often appear to be able to charge almost what they like, within some limits.

It is assumed in Rees's analysis of occupational differentials that skill is an objectively measured variable, whereas there is a growing literature which argues that its evaluation is in part socially determined and is under-assessed in female-dominated occupations. If skills needed in many women-dominated occupations are under-valued, and training acquired in work at home is seen as needing no economic return, then pay in such occupations may be lower than productivity factors would justify. Social conditioning, prejudice, male-designed promotion and training systems, and lack of equal opportunity may also contribute to women's lesser acquisition of pay-related human capital factors.

It is interesting that the literature has plenty of material on the cause and impact of aggregate wage movements, on institutional wage-setting in practice, on rates of return to education and on individual labour markets. By contrast, there is curiously little written on the historical evolution of overall pay structures and relativities, and whether they are reasonable. Perhaps myth prevails in this field because current structures benefit decision-makers, who are still largely white, middle-class men. Clearly skill-level differences and the role of relative scarcity in valuing them are not totally a matter of myth, but they are often exaggerated to widen differentials and benefit powerful groups.

Doubts should also extend to the whole basis of the orthodox demand for labour and marginal productivity theory. It is unclear whether the marginal productivity of labour can be measured except in economists' graphs (Thurow, 1975). Teamwork, the dependence of every type of worker on the work of others, the other inputs that are held constant in the analysis and the quality of management are among factors which blur the picture. Further, marginal productivity can be seen as another of the economists' circular tricks. Analytically, the wage rate must reflect the value to the employer of the extra amount produced (in perfect competition at least). However, only the wage is observed, so it is simply presumed to reflect marginal product. This can persuade people that there is an objectivity to the wage determination process. In service industries there is even less chance of determining the value of output. Much attention is now paid to the principal agent problem, which essentially recognises this issue. In the labour market, employers need to find ways of ensuring they receive the work input for which they are paying. Hence attempts to assess individual or team performance are growing, but they are often crude and subjective, and many of the output measures are open to question.

There have been hints in this discussion that labour markets are not perfectly competitive, and that they never could be. Government deregulation moves are intended to move them closer to perfect competition, by curbing the power of unions and of professional associations over entry limitations and wages. In the past, many historical differentials have been perpetuated through wage negotiations, legislation and procedures in which changes in relativities were regarded as a legitimate source for a catch-up claim. Thus gender-discriminating relativities between occupations could be perpetuated. In theory, therefore, deregulation could reduce differentials and benefit women, but considerable doubts about this remain, as discussed here and in a later chapter.

As stated earlier, labour is not an auction market and will always be different in significant ways from most other markets. 'The employment of labour involves a continuing personal relationship between an employer and an employee, whereas transactions in most other markets are by comparison brief and impersonal' (Rees, 1979: ix). Moreover, adjustment processes are slow, with considerable financial and psychic costs involved in hiring, training and firing. Outcomes depend as much or more on historical, social and power considerations as on economic and productivity-related factors. These features were among the reasons for the development of separate labour laws and protections, some of which have recently been dismantled in New Zealand. Also critical in the development of labour law was a recognition of the possibility of exploitation, the importance of employment to achieving a reasonable standard of living, and the inherent power superiority of employer over employee, except for those with very scarce skills.

Discrimination: alternative views

The general discussion on wage determination has already pointed to a number of issues pertaining to women's wages and the female–male earnings gap. Reasons why women, on average, may have lower levels of human capital and hence productivity have been given, but it has also been suggested that this results from lesser access. Further, the whole area of skill, human capital, and productivity definition and measurement may be imbued with discrimination against female-dominated areas. Within orthodoxy, wage discrimination cannot persist.

> Earnings differentials between workers of the same level of productivity would be expected to be eliminated through the forces of competition. The fact that employers are assumed to have a unisex outlook would imply that differences between the sexes, when workers are of the same level of productivity, would not therefore last, if they ever existed. When we examine the data, however, we find that average earnings of women are well below those of men in every country for which data are available. Within the orthodox theory, persistent wage differences between groups of workers could be the result of three factors: either workers have differing productivities and are not therefore equivalent, or they may have differing supply preferences and choose lower or higher paying jobs as a preference, or the market may have some imperfections or monopoly elements which prevent the wages being equalised. (Dex, 1985: 116)

Human capital theories examined earlier are concerned with productivity differences, while theories of discrimination examine the possibility of paying those with the same productivity differently. In perfect markets, such a 'taste' for discrimination would be hard to perpetuate since employers without such a taste would benefit. However, in imperfectly competitive markets, it can persist; it may indeed persist even in competitive markets when it is in the joint interests of male employers and employees (England, 1993).

So far, discrimination has been discussed without explicit attention to alternative definitions. The first point to make is that discrimination does not have to be deliberate or done through prejudice, even though it may be. It is simply the unfairness of the outcome that defines discrimination, although what counts as unfair is controversial. One helpful distinction is between wage discrimination and other forms that may operate in the labour market. It is implicit in the arguments above that, to the orthodox economist, wage discrimination occurs only when workers of equal productivity to an employer are paid unequally. Of course, this begs the questions of assessing productivity and skill mentioned earlier. Non-wage labour market discrimination can occur with unequal access to jobs, training, promotion and any other human capital-enhancing factors. While any such discrimination against women will lower female wages relative to men's in aggregate, its existence is compatible with an absence of wage discrimination in the narrow sense.

However, to advocates of equal pay for work of equal value, undervaluation of skills in female-dominated work is a reality and constitutes a form of wage discrimination. The existence of non-wage discrimination is fairly widely accepted and requires equal opportunity policies. Wage discrimination against female-dominated work is, however, not accepted by orthodox economists, for whom the conventional analysis applies. The challenges to that analysis made above convince advocates of equal value that market valuation is not objective and inevitable, but that it is instead often discriminatory.

Another useful distinction is between direct and indirect discrimination by gender, race or other factors. The former is simply a wage or non-wage difference in treatment based on the classifying variable, even if it is less straightforward to prove when denied. The latter may be more difficult to detect, arising when a practice which is not needed for efficient operation in a job occurs and has a differentially adverse effect on a particular group. Requiring educational qualifications not actually needed in a position but used as screening devices, in preference to assessing possession of the relevant skills, can indirectly discriminate against Maori or women, for example.

The role of occupational segregation and crowding

One major element of the female–male earnings gap is the obvious fact that women tend to work in different occupations from men, and fewer are in managerial and high-level positions. Horizontal occupational segregation, with women working in different types of jobs from men, is breaking down only very slowly. Women apprentices in areas other than hairdressing are still a rarity, and female-dominated occupations are predominantly low paying. Vertical segregation, with women placed lower in job hierarchies, is beginning to break down, but is not yet reflected in substantial changes to the aggregate statistics.

Segregation, with women in lower-paid jobs, is more evident the more detailed the breakdown of jobs. While about 90 per cent of the membership of the New Zealand Clerical Workers Union covered by the clerical workers award were women, there are certain jobs which are almost exclusively male. 'Women are not in charge of stores, supplies and materials. Nor do they manage offices to the same extent men do. They are heavily over-represented in jobs which require keyboard skills ... A disproportionate percentage of women were in the lower income brackets while men dominated the higher brackets' (New Zealand Federated Clerical, Administrative and Related Workers Industrial Association of Workers, 1986: 43 and 46).

A questionnaire completed in 1982 by 1,156 workers covered by the clerical award, of whom 91 per cent were female, showed that 48 per cent of the men but only 33 per cent of the women were on the top two of the five grades. This meant that men constituted 25 per cent of those in the top grade, though only 9 per cent of the total sample. It gives support to the proposition that even in female-dominated occupations, men are disproportionately represented at high levels – a point also made as men move into occupations such as nursing.

Occupational segregation can lead to lower earnings for women through both supply and demand factors, even within orthodox analysis. If women, by choice or discrimination, are 'crowded' into a narrow range of occupations, their excess supply may lower the marginal productivity and thus the wage rate. Thus, to orthodoxy, non-wage discrimination is present in the constraints on occupational choice but there is no wage discrimination between occupations. However, some empirical studies argue that more of the earnings gap is attributable to a lower payback from education and training rather than to less of such training (Buchele and Aldrich, 1985). These lower returns are found whether women are in male- or female-dominated occupations. In this case there must be a degree of pay discrimination if the results occur within the workforce of a single employer. It is more arguable if the results occur only across employers, since differences both in what is valued by employers and in ability to pay may impact on rates of return to the same amount of measured human capital.

A useful model shows the impact of occupational segregation on pay within a standard supply and demand analysis (Bergmann, 1985). Barbara Bergmann models a simple two-occupation situation in which the needs of the jobs and the preferences of workers for them are the same, and shows that male and female wages in each should be the same, but with women restricted to only one of the jobs they could be paid less. She points out that to conclude that the jobs should be paid the same, it is not necessary to assume that all women should be willing and able to take on the male job.

> Just enough women need to be willing and able to change occupations so that the 'crowding' of labor in the women's occupations would be relieved if employer-enforced segregation were relaxed . . . If that modest number of women were willing to shift, as their current response to limited opportunities to make such a shift demonstrates is the case, then discrimination rather than women's choices is responsible for much of the wage gap between the sexes. The wage-setting process in the present market is tainted by discrimination. And it is that taint that invalidates the common assumption that market wages are sacrosanct. (*ibid.*: 82)

The effect which horizontal occupational and industrial segregation has on pay levels overall and particularly in female-dominated areas is less easy to document unequivocally in New Zealand than the phenomenon itself. However, it was noted earlier that female-dominated industries and occupations in New Zealand are low paying. Vertical segregation is a major factor in the earnings gap.

Earnings functions

Overseas, but not in New Zealand, there are many studies that attempt to identify the extent of various productivity-related elements which may justify female–male earnings differences and to see what remains: this is likely at least partly to reflect discrimination. Using survey or census data, individual observations of earnings classified by various personal and job-related variables are analysed by statistical methods to assess what proportion of the pay gap can be attributed to each identified factor and what proportion remains as an unexplained residual. Generally, the more homogeneous the labour market being considered, the smaller the element of discrimination revealed. But by taking a very narrow group of workers, much of the non-wage discrimination is assumed away. In New Zealand very little analysis of this type has been undertaken, largely because of a lack of adequate earnings data classified by the relevant variables.

There is, however, one micro-level study in which Frances Sutton analysed the earnings of a sample of the executive–clerical class in the public service, covering this group within the Treasury and the Department of Internal Affairs. She found that 28 per cent of the men and only 2.5 per cent of the similar number of women were at grade seven and above, with female earnings averaging about three-quarters of those of males. Higher educational levels and lengths of service accounted for part of the difference, with 40 per cent of men, as against 19 per cent of women, having a degree or equivalent, and 42 per cent, as against 17 per cent, having ten or more years of service at March 1984. Statistical analysis of the data showed each of these factors accounting for about one-third of the pay gap, leaving one-third attributed to discrimination or other unexplained factors (Sutton, 1985).

Earnings function studies do not, of course, yield unchallengeable answers to the extent of even direct wage discrimination, let alone overall discrimination. Some orthodox economists believe that the human capital measures, such as years of education and experience, are too crude to pick up all the productivity differences. Hence the residual may simply reflect unmeasured productivity differences. For pay equity advocates, by contrast, the wage discrimination found in earning functions studies is a minimal estimate of overall discrimination, for reasons stated earlier.

Following discussion on these lines, the *New Zealand Equal Pay Study* summarised the debate as follows:

> There is no consensus in quantitative or conceptual terms as to what elements of the pay gap are justifiable or unjustifiable, discriminatory or non-discriminatory ... Factors, including occupational differences ... and lower experience and seniority levels, certainly contribute to the pay gap but can be interpreted as either discriminatory, non-discriminatory or, more reasonably, as having elements of each. (Urban Research Associates *et al*, 1987)

Other points on equal pay for work of equal value

It is clear that the main arguments in favour of policies to implement equal pay for work of equal value are equity ones. Nevertheless, it can be argued that efficiency requires a degree of equalisation of rates of return to human capital acquisition in order to avoid distortion of career choice decisions by both women and men. The efficiency case for equal employment opportunity is even clearer, with the need to utilise effectively the full range of available talent.

The main arguments of opponents of equal value policies are the desirability of unfettered market valuation, discussed earlier, and the subjectivity of other processes including job evaluation, discussed in the next chapter. They also suggest that there would be excessive costs and employment losses for the women involved or more generally. Such fears were also raised before the 1972 Equal Pay Act was passed and in all similar overseas initiatives. It is argued, just as it is with respect to abolition of special low pay rates for young people or workers with disabilities, that implementation would lead to substitution against that group in the labour market. Thus, it is contended, unemployment levels for that group would increase and the group as a whole (though not those still in employment, who would benefit) would be worse off.

Empirical results show that these fears are exaggerated. The evidence does not support such substitution during the New Zealand equal pay implementation period, when full-time employment of females grew by 19 per cent, as against 8 per cent for males. Only in a few industries which were female dominated, such as textiles, was there some evidence of slower growth of employment than might otherwise have occurred. The Australian evidence from the 1970 to 1975 period, during which the female–male pay gap was substantially narrowed, is similar. One view is that there was virtually no substitution against women, with their share of the total wage bill increasing from 20 per cent to 28 per cent between 1969 and 1976 (Gregory and Duncan, 1981), although other econometric studies suggest a small element of substitution.

The Working Group on Equal Employment Opportunities and Equal Pay (1988) estimated that pay equity legislation would increase the national wage bill by an estimated 0.7 to 2.25 per cent, spread over lengthy implementation. It argued that wage increases arising from pay equity claims would reflect previous underpayment relative to productivity and should not lead to job losses except where firms could survive only by paying wages below those justified by productivity levels. In addition, somewhat paradoxically, occupational segregation is some protection against job loss.

The Employment Equity Act had built-in protections for areas where job loss could be serious. The fact that it was claims-based, rather than automatic, meant that in any area where job losses were feared (for example, an industry both economically vulnerable and where female wages constitute a high proportion of total costs) unions could decide not to request an assessment. Overall, the potential cost and employment effects were exaggerated by the Act's opponents, although it is clearly more advantageous to introduce such legislation at a time of economic expansion rather than during a recession.

This chapter has discussed the main issues with respect to gender pay discrimination, and narrow and broader concepts of equal pay/pay equity. The next chapters explore the job-evaluation processes and the industrial relations environment into which any such policies and processes must fit; they also make some international comparisons and examine the position with regard to pay equity in present-day New Zealand.

4
Job Evaluation and Levels of Industrial Relations Bargaining

Any attempt to implement equal pay for work of equal value depends on the use of a system or systems of job evaluation. While collective bargaining using equal value arguments may occur without a formal system, the underlying rationale will involve analyses of the nature of the work on job evaluation lines. Hence this chapter is intended to take somewhat further than most New Zealand discussions the relationship between the two areas. A discussion of general issues is followed by an examination of schemes used by two particular firms of consultants – Hay, and Price Waterhouse.

Job evaluation: its relationship to equal pay for work of equal value

There are many slightly different definitions of job evaluation. Some go only as far as the provision of a ranking or points score for different jobs, while others also cover the process of converting this to a salary structure. One general (UK) definition and discussion is as follows: 'Job evaluation is a system of comparing different jobs to provide a basis for a grading and pay structure. The aim is to evaluate the job, not the job holder, but it is recognised that to some extent any assessment of a job's total demands relative to another will always be subjective. Moreover, job evaluation is in large part a social mechanism which establishes agreed differentials within organisations' (Equal Opportunities Commission, 1985: 1).

The analysis here will disregard the somewhat primitive non-analytical job evaluation schemes which assess whole jobs rather than subdividing them into relevant components. Thus, it will concentrate on factor point analytical methods. These methods define factors which are important to the jobs and therefore appear to be a legitimate basis for differences in pay. They then score each job on each factor and add the scores (or weight them in some more complex manner) to give a combined total score. Two jobs do not need to be rated identically on each factor to be judged of equal value. Jobs which have the same (or in some cases very close) aggregate scores are deemed to be of equal value. The factors can generally be divided into sub-groups covering types of skills, effort, responsibilities and working conditions.

An article sceptical of the equal value concept summarises the main issues in job evaluation applied to equal value/comparable worth as follows:

> There is one crucial difference between the kind of job evaluation that would be used with comparable worth policies and that typically used by employers: the latter are typically based explicitly on market considerations ... In contrast, some analysts of comparable worth question such a market-oriented approach on the grounds that the wage relationships that currently exist are likely to be distorted by discrimination. Some comparable worth proponents advocate the use of bias-free job evaluations, i.e., ones that are derived independently of the existing wage structure and in which the weights given to the different factors considered would be determined on an a priori – or to put it less charitably, ad hoc – basis. (Killingsworth, 1985: 87)

The contention of equal value advocates is that current wage relationships are distorted by discrimination. It is argued that the skills needed in many female-dominated occupations are under-valued for historical and social reasons: because they are seen as natural to women, being extensions of their work in the home and of their traditional caring roles; because experience rather than formal training courses may have been involved in their acquisition, and/or because they are based on stereotypes. Further, relativities may be established only between low-waged, female-dominated occupations, not with higher status and more highly paid male-dominated areas. One detailed Australian statement of this position includes the following:

> Whilst the criteria appear to be fair and have no inherent sexual bias, the weighting which has traditionally been assigned to the various factors has led to a high importance being placed on aspects of work which are characteristics of male occupations, e.g. bad working conditions, manual labour and responsibility for plant and machinery. Also skills are usually measured by formal apprenticeship or technical training and these programmes have mainly been instituted in industries which are male dominated ... Why should respon-

sibility for machinery, e.g. mechanic, be considered more valuable than responsibility for people, e.g. nurses? It is curious that where women perform work which has been deemed to involve abilities 'natural' to women these abilities have been devalued and jobs requiring such abilities have been deemed unskilled ... The idea that the skills involved in women's work are inherently inferior is deeply entrenched but it is not sacrosanct and work evaluation studies based on the concept of comparable worth are intended to fairly recognise the particular skills that exist as a component of a job. (Women's Legal Resources Group, 1985: 29, 42, 43, 44, 49–50, 75)

A study of the US Department of Labour's *Dictionary of Occupational Titles*, which rates jobs in terms of a skill–complexity code, showed that 'evaluators had overlooked important characteristics of female-dominated jobs, especially those associated with taking care of children. The evaluators did not regard these as job related skills, but rather as qualities intrinsic to being a woman. Because of this, the job evaluators were confusing the content and responsibilities of a paid job with stereotypic notions about the characteristics of the job-holder' (Steinberg and Haignere, 1985: 13).

A further problem which arises in the use of job evaluation is that of inaccurate or incomplete job descriptions. While self-reporting of job content is to be encouraged for obtaining co-operation and confidence in the process and to avoid the biases of supervisors' inaccurate perceptions, there is considerable evidence of the tendency for women to under-describe and men to over-describe their jobs (*ibid.*: 14; Remick, 1979). 'Halo' effects can also occur, where pre-existing notions about the value of jobs or about particular features of such jobs – often based on their current market valuation – colour the view of what they must involve on other factors and thus perpetuate their inflation or undervaluation.

Another general problem with job evaluation systems is one which occurs with any system of combining separate scores. Proposed weightings of different factors will fail to be reflected in realised weightings if the variation in the scores between different jobs is more for some factors than others. Moreover, the tendency to use overlapping or related factors for which job scores are highly correlated means that greater weight may be attached to a group of factors than intended (Gill and Ungerson, 1984: 44–53).

It should be noted that the question of possible revaluation of jobs concerns not only female-dominated occupations. There is also considerable occupational and industrial segregation by race and ethnicity.

Historical differentials, to the extent that they are based on analyses and decisions on skill levels, have therefore been challenged in terms of both gender and race. Generally, it is argued that skill definition and assessment is very largely a social construct, with the skills involved in many jobs undervalued or ignored. There is a growing literature on skill analysis which supports this view (Cockburn, 1983; Hill and Novitz, 1985; Wood, 1985).

Even with the probable prevalence of such gender biases, most job evaluation studies have in fact indicated that women-dominated jobs are relatively underpaid, with the extent of underpayment understated in those which fail to avoid gender bias (Treiman and Hartmann, 1981; Wisconsin Task Force, 1985). Similarly, most statistical studies find that both the base level and incremental salary per job point are higher for men compared with women (Treiman and Hartman, 1981).

It is clear from the discussion that it is mistaken to search for absolute objectivity in job evaluation. However, job evaluation makes explicit and open for discussion the judgements which may otherwise be only implicit. The literature on gender bias in job evaluation schemes now includes welcome attempts to construct improved schemes (Burns and Coleman, 1991; Burton *et al*, 1987; Equal Opportunities Commission, 1985; Hastings, 1991; Steinberg, 1987).

Opponents of the broadening of the concept of equal pay for work of equal value point to the lack of consistency in ranking and scoring of jobs among different studies, and the inevitable subjectivity of job evaluation (Burr, 1986). Another point raised by opponents, and discussed in the previous chapter, is that the market should be the main factor in pay determination. It thus follows that evaluation should be used only to reproduce or justify the current pay structure, or make minor amendments to it, and to slot in new jobs. The contrast between the ad hoc and market approaches to job evaluation is clearly put in the Killingsworth quotation above (p. 102).

Policy capturing studies: the United States experience

In the American literature, these two approaches are often known as 'a priori' and 'policy capturing'. Both have been used in American studies related to comparable worth, one of which describes the latter approach as follows:

> This involves developing a compensation model in which specific job content features needed to perform the job are divided into factors and then these factors are weighted in such a way that they statistically 'predict' the current wage structure. In other words, the weights for each compensable job content characteristic are derived from a statistical model which makes explicit what is currently implicitly valued for compensation purposes within an organisation.
> (Steinberg *et al*, 1986: 9–10)

It might be seen as somewhat surprising that this approach has been used in comparable worth studies, since 'it does not tell an employer what job content should be valued. It requires only that whatever an employer values is valued consistently and systematically across all job titles and not arbitrarily and implicitly as a function of the sex or race/ethnicity of the typical incumbent of a job title' (*ibid*.: 11). Thus, an approach to eliminating pay inequities as suggested by such a study will probably capture only part of what equal value advocates see as discriminatory. If women are paid less than men after standardising for pay differences resulting from all relevant job factors, this can be labelled as direct discrimination (assuming it is not related to assessment of job performance separate from evaluation of the actual job: over a large sample this should not be relevant). However, low or even negative valuation of factors particularly prevalent in female-dominated occupations is not regarded as discriminatory. These valuations will, however, be revealed by such a study. Equal value proponents can then advance arguments that the valuations are inappropriate and biased.

Understanding of the policy capturing approach will be assisted by discussion of a particular case. The New York State Pay Equity Study used a very detailed, self-completed job content questionnaire to sample job characteristics and grading and pay levels for state employees. A high response rate sample of 25,852 usable questionnaires covering 2,582 job titles (from a total of 175,000 employees in 7,350 titles) was gathered in 1985. Eighty job content items were analysed, with 14 factors emerging as important. These were entered as explanatory variables in a statistical model to predict the salary grade of different job titles. Other explanatory variables allowed for whether occupations were female dominated or minority dominated (defined as 67.2 per cent or more female, 30.8 per cent or more minority – which is 40 per cent above the levels of each in the New York State labour force).

Fifteen out of 27 variables were found to be statistically significant, accounting for nearly 90 per cent of the variation in salary grades across jobs. The authors' summary includes the following:

> Our results demonstrate that, for all pay policy lines, education, experience, management, supervision and writing are highly compensated factors in New York State government employment. Moreover, several factors are not valued or are negatively valued. These include unfavourable working conditions, stress, group facilitation, communication with the public, data entry, and autonomy ... With all other job factors held constant, jobs done *entirely* by women are on average two salary grades lower than jobs of equal value to the state done entirely by men. An increase of one salary grade is an increase of approximately five percent in salary ... There is a strong tendency for job titles in the lower salary grades to be more undervalued than job titles in higher salary grades. Particularly among the clerical and health care system job titles it was common to find titles in grade levels 6 and below to be undervalued by four or five salary grades. (Steinberg *et al*, 1986: viii)

The point about which job factors are valued in the New York State system needs further emphasis. The report includes the following extracts:

> It is instructive to note what New York State does not pay for as well as what it does pay for. By and large, the coefficients have the expected sign ... In one case the coefficient was not in the predicted direction. That exception is unfavourable working conditions. Communication with the public is also negatively valued. ... Jobs in New York State requiring contact with difficult clients and jobs involving stress are neither rewarded nor penalized relative to other jobs with similar requirements in all other respects. (*ibid.*: 160)

It goes on to comment that these and other job content characteristics found to be negatively valued or of no value are differentially associated with female-dominated or disproportionately minority job titles, indicating gender and ethnic bias.

Revaluation of characteristics from this point of view did not occur in New York. Only the more minor changes associated with the lower pay of women were made; the previous valuation of job characteristics was otherwise maintained. The senior author of the study later expressed dissatisfaction with this, and went on to work in Philadelphia on a study which allowed more radical changes (Steinberg, 1987: 15–20).

Particular examples of job evaluation

It will be helpful in fleshing out the general discussion above to consider briefly two particular job evaluation systems. Those selected are from two firms of management consultants: Hay, and Price Waterhouse. Like any systems applied to a number of organisations, these are a priori schemes in the terminology discussed above, although they have, of course, been developed and refined over years of use, and some companies are now working with clients on purpose-built systems. In North America, the Hay system had to meet the challenge of comparable worth and to make changes to satisfy the evolving environment (Hay Management Consultants, 1986: 4). The Hay system has been used extensively in New Zealand, so that an understanding of its methodology, assumptions and limitations is important.

In this system, the major factors are know-how (K), problem-solving (P) and accountability (A), each subdivided into more detailed factors in a grid system. The total score is $K + (P\% \text{ of } K) + A$. Under equal value legislation, employers are required to compare all jobs within their organisation in terms of defined factors: 'This means that regardless of differences in job content, the Typist's job would be compared to that of the Inventory Control Clerk, the Secretary to the Machine Operator, the Senior Laboratory Technician to the Junior Engineer, and a Telephone Receptionist to a Truck Driver' (*ibid.*: 1).

The examination and changes Hay had to make to meet the equal pay environment were discussed, in part, as follows: 'Hay re-examined its system to ensure it contained no apparent biases. As a result of this examination, several problems were identified. For instance, Hay found that its system had not recognised the accountability associated with lower level jobs. Nor had it given the proper weighting to mental effort when assessing the nature of working conditions' (*ibid.*: 5). The Hay paper also pointed out other factors affecting individual salaries. 'Job evaluation is the process of determining job size and is the basis for establishing a salary range around the job, not for determining individual salaries. Individuals may be assigned different salary rates within the range based on criteria such as differences in performance, years of service and the like. It is usually agreed that a difference of salary is not discriminatory if it is based on a merit pay system that is free of bias and equally applied to all employees' (*ibid.*: 4).

The Hay paper strongly advocates the view that comparisons must be within the workforce of a single employer, and this is the standard position of most employers. 'The process of a comparison is only applicable within organisations, or to groups of employees of the same employer. Clearly, we do not find in any marketplace analysis that all employers in a given industry will pay to the same marketplace level' (*ibid.*: 4). This will be discussed later.

The contention that the Hay system is now bias free is not accepted by all parties. As in many other systems, managing money and responsibility for heavy equipment receive a higher percentage of overall points than responsibility for clients and human relations skills.

> In the Hay Guide-Chart System, one set of charts is constructed so that the number of points in the 'Managerial Know-How' scale is five times as great as the number of points in the 'Human Relations Know-How' scale. On the same chart, 'Technical Know-How' can receive seven times the number of points as 'Human Relations Know-How.' Human Relations skills are disproportionately found in women's and minorities' jobs. Fiscal responsibility and heavy machinery are disproportionately associated with white male jobs. As a result, the point values contained in the charts may reflect a traditional bias against the content of female and minority jobs. (Steinberg and Haignere, 1985: 19–20)

Other criticisms of the system could be made. For example, the accountability criterion appears to be seen largely in financial terms, neglecting other aspects of possible importance. This is related to the fact that this and similar systems are developed largely for managerial-type jobs and do not seem able to be adapted easily to other areas. Human relations skills are regarded as part of know-how, and the need to exercise them can add on variable numbers of points, increasing with the scientific, technical and practical skills and breadth of management know-how also needed in the job. This means that where scores on the latter are low, the need for human relations skills adds little to the evaluation, and in no case can these skills add as much as one-third to the score provided by the other two elements of the know-how grid.

Turning to a version of the Price Waterhouse system, ten factors are used: education (E), experience (X), complexity (C), scope of work (S), problem solving, supervision received, results of decisions, contacts, authority exercised, and supervisory/managerial responsibility. Complexity and scope are scored in percentage terms, while the remaining factors have a numerical score out of a maximum which varies from 132 for contacts (with other personnel employed and/or the public) to 700 for problem solving and for results of decisions. The total score (T) is calculated as follows: T = (E + X)(C + S) + E + X + F, where F is the sum of the scores on the six last factors listed.

As in the Hay case, questions arise as to the judgements involved in the varying maximum scores on the factors, the criteria in assigning scores and the method of weighting. Results of decisions and the degree of authority exercised are evaluated entirely in financial terms. Education and experience enter the formula both directly and multiplied by the combined percentage assessment of complexity/scope, so they carry double importance.

Despite their reputations and extensive use, schemes such as these are thus not beyond criticism. While two have been selected for examination, this is in no way meant to imply that these schemes are worse than others. All such off-the-shelf schemes have in-built gender biases, with hierarchy heavily emphasised.

Issues with respect to job evaluation

The gender neutrality of some schemes is now being legally challenged in Canada, as discussed in the next chapter. The question of whether any single scheme can be devised for all jobs (at least within the compass of a single employer) is an important one. Clearly the policy capturing method allows for this. An a priori system which attempted to do the same would need to draw on the factors emerging from large cross-occupation policy capturing studies.

A number of researchers studying the application of job evaluation to comparable worth have argued strongly for a single system. 'The goal of pay equity requires the elimination of multiple plan job evaluations within a firm or public jurisdiction ... Comparable worth requires consistent treatment of all job titles in every component of job evaluation' (Steinberg and Haignere, 1985: 12). With multiple job plans, it is argued, the lack of a standardised list of job content features and the use of different factor definitions, evaluations and weightings lead to inconsistencies and difficulty in making comparisons across categories. When different occupational categories, such as clerical, manual labour and managerial jobs, are treated independently and show very different patterns of sex and race profiles, the type of biases discussed earlier can easily emerge.

It has been mentioned that employers argue for within-employer comparisons only, as marketplace factors and differences in values between organisations may account for differences between firms. Even when New Zealand wage settlement was based mainly on awards, above-award payments could differ between firms for many reasons. The Equal Pay Act simply requires that these payments, as with the instruments themselves, not be based on the sex of the employee.

Most activity in the comparable worth area in the United States has been of this within-employer type, and particularly at the level of state and local government employers. A number of factors account for this. Wage-setting mechanisms are more decentralised and mostly a matter of negotiation with individual employers. Government is an easier target for political and pressure group action than private employers, and more likely to feel some responsibility in the area of equal pay. Thus several state governments have instituted pay equity studies on the lines of the New York one discussed earlier, and some have made pay settlements arising from (or even without) such studies. The legislation in Great Britain also relates to individual employers.

By contrast, the systems of pay fixing and of equal pay implementation have until recently been at a more centralised level in Australia and New Zealand. In both countries, many proponents of equal pay for work of equal value have argued that cross-employer equal value claims should therefore be possible, to be tested by job evaluation based on comparing the demands of a female-dominated occupational group with relevant male-dominated occupational groups. Until the late 1980s, at least, this was a greater possibility in New Zealand than in most countries, because of award structures. The short-lived New Zealand Employment Equity Act 1990 did allow this possibility, with some constraints, but the prospect of putting it into practice probably aroused even greater resistance than many other parts of what was controversial legislation. The pay equity section of the Act was also attempting to keep alive industrial relations systems which involved multi-employer bargaining and compulsory final-offer arbitration. This was against the trends of other legislation and policy which was moving towards industry and enterprise-based rather than occupation and craft-based bargaining – contradictions which caused trouble even within the Labour Cabinet which finally passed the legislation. These contradictions, and particularly the interventionist nature of the Act, made its repeal inevitable when National took office later in 1990.

With the repeal of the legislation, job evaluation continues to be used as a management tool, with some increasingly aware employers and employee groups sensitive to the difficulties and attempting to reduce the gender and other biases of a priori schemes. However, firms are usually willing only to make cosmetic and wording changes, to incorporate a wider range of skills, and/or to make sure all aspects of jobs are properly scored on factors. One major constraint to more far-reaching changes is the intention to relate job evaluation scores to market salaries. If the same system is used in a number of firms, the scores can be directly related to the market and to salary levels resulting from surveys.

Policy capturing systems of job evaluation do not fit into the pay settlement framework in New Zealand before or after the recent legislative changes. Nor are many single employers large enough to conduct their own studies on this scale. It would, however, be an interesting and useful exercise, if the data could be acquired, to examine the workforce of the government, of large local government units and some large private firms in this way. Large units with a considerable variety of occupations provide the necessary setting for such an assessment.

Finally it should be reiterated that job evaluation systems must always embody value systems. In these circumstances, in the words of a US study, 'The adoption of any plan depends on its credibility with various groups in the workplace – the pay rates set for jobs must satisfy management, employees, and labor unions. Job evaluation plans instituted in organisations must thus satisfy perceptions of internal equity . . . One implication is that successful implementation may require participation of all the various constituent groups' (Hartmann, Roos and Treiman, 1985: 16–17). This study points out that organisations such as AT & T and the Communications Workers of America have jointly developed job evaluation plans through management and union negotiation.

This approach raises a number of fundamental questions about pay fixing, job evaluation, and the criteria and processes for choosing job factors. Among such questions are:

> Are there potential compensable factors in women's work that are not now recognized as legitimate bases for pay differentials? Are people's judgements about what salaries should be very different from actual salaries? . . . Does adding female tasks (e.g. typing, nurturing, waiting on tables, clerical work) to job descriptions reduce the perceived value of a job? Does the established consensus about the worth of tasks in jobs decline if the number of women entering the field increases? . . . Do men and women value attributes of jobs differently? (*ibid.*: 11, 21, 29 and 30)

Some of these questions have been investigated by psychologists, adding to evidence regarding the undervaluation of female-dominated work. The questions should also be faced by firms using job evaluation. The practical problems of implementing job evaluation and avoiding biases at each stage of the process are considerable, but there is now ample documented experience which can be used – for example, for training purposes (Burton *et al*, 1987, report on the process with respect to Hay in an Australian College of Advanced Education). Only when the lessons of such overseas exercises are learnt and embodied in procedures and practices adopted in New Zealand will a move towards more equitable pay-setting arrangements be possible. The lessons are equally useful, even if a less formal process than job evaluation is used.

Towards decentralisation in industrial relations bargaining

Well before the Employment Contracts Act, legislation (the Labour Relations Act 1987 and State Sector Act 1988) was enacted in New Zealand aimed at directing the wage-fixing system away from national craft and occupational awards and annual wage rounds towards more decentralised bargaining. It was also motivated by the belief that the labour market was particularly inflexible, with a lack of wage flexibility impeding employment growth and a reduction in unemployment. However, a New Zealand Planning Council study cast doubt on the degree of inflexibility in New Zealand relative to other countries, and pointed out that the dispersion in gross real incomes of wage and salary earners has in fact increased since 1976, both pre and post tax (New Zealand Planning Council, 1986).

It is important to distinguish relative and absolute levels of wages, and arguments about flexibility in each. It is relative wage flexibility which was said to be impeded by the wage round system, with minimum-wage legislation and the inability to pay young people a youth 'training' wage preventing creation of new jobs. However, there may be only a weak link in the response of labour supply and demand to wage changes, and with many other intervening factors. The claim that the absolute level of wages is too high, or has been rising too fast from the point of view of international competitiveness, increased growth and employment prospects, is a separate issue.

Another important element of the Labour Relations Act was to eliminate two tiers of bargaining, in which national award settlements yielded minima that were followed by a second round of negotiations at industry or enterprise level, which ratcheted up wages. In the push for greater efficiency in industrial relations matters, the legislation also required larger trade unions, with a 1,000 minimum size for registration. Only 36 per cent of unions exceeded this size in 1986, while about 85 per cent had achieved it by 1990, with a phase-in period before the 1,000 criterion was strictly enforced. In 1990 there were 98 registered unions, with an average size of 6,239, a large increase over the pre-1987 situation. The Employment Contracts Act of course removed this provision, with trade unions totally absent from any mention in legislation. They were replaced by the general term, 'bargaining agent'. This meant the disappearance of the previous requirements for unions to operate democratically and in return receive recognition and some rights.

A major emphasis of the 1980s legislation was a reduction in third-party intervention. Compulsory arbitration was eliminated, with voluntary arbitration available after the agreement by both parties, which rarely occurred. The underlying philosophy was a hands-off approach by government, with responsibility for industrial relations outcomes placed where the costs are incurred, and employers and employees (or their representatives) unable to shift the responsibility. However, this is more rhetoric than reality. Certainly government wished to avoid intervention, directly or through the courts, in individual disputes. But of course the government has set the climate firmly in terms of deregulation and its consequences, so that the balance of power has shifted significantly from employees and unions to employers. This inevitably influences the outcomes in particular directions.

The shift from national occupational awards towards industry and enterprise bargaining was intended to enable settlements more clearly to reflect the particular climate facing an employer, including productivity, profitability and ability to pay, and to incorporate conditions appropriate to the industry or enterprise. It was also hoped that these changes would, together, encourage employers and employees (or their representatives) to move towards a co-operative rather than a conflict situation.

At the aggregate level, there was no equivalent of the Australian Accord between the union movement and government despite much rhetoric during 1986 about a 'Compact'. Shortly before the 1990 election, mainly in forlorn pursuit of re-election, new Labour prime minister Mike Moore made a growth agreement with the Combined Trade Unions (CTU). A guideline of 2 per cent for the wage round was set, well below the prevailing 5 per cent rate of inflation, accompanied by productivity payments negotiable in individual awards and agreements. The expectation was that these would be no more than 1 or 2 per cent, and in some areas zero. Essentially the agreement was an acceptance of realities on the union side. Without it, many unions with low bargaining power would have had to accept no increase at all in wages. The agreement had no legal weight. However, it signalled an attempt to gain simultaneously the advantages of both centralisation and decentralisation in wage negotiations.

There is some international literature which argues from empirical data that systems which are highly decentralised or highly centralised perform best (the Calmors/Driffil thesis: see Boston, 1988). Sweden provides an example of a centralised, corporatist system of wage settlement. New Zealand is argued to have fallen in between the two systems and to have performed badly. What is meant by performing well, however, needs discussion. Indicators such as higher growth, lower inflation and improved international competitiveness are usually used for assessing performance. In practice, it is often assumed that a lower growth of real average wages, and possibly increased differentials, will have a favourable impact on these indicators, and so these outcomes are used to judge the effect of the wage bargaining system. However, lower wage outcomes and increased differentials have their down-side for lower-income groups, in which women and Maori are over-represented.

The distinction between lower growth in average wages and more dispersed wage growth outcomes is sometimes neglected. Centralised systems may deliver low wage growth but entrench existing differentials. Decentralised systems are likely to be more responsive to ability to pay and thus deliver more dispersed wage growth, but not necessarily as low average increases. Whether both results can be obtained by a system trying to use both approaches is uncertain. If so, it implies widening differentials, with low incomes declining.

The 1987 Labour Relations Act made no distinction between occupational, industry or enterprise awards and agreements: its main objectives with regard to wage negotiations were to allow the scope of negotiations to be determined by the parties. However, the further provision that there be a single set of negotiations for wages and conditions rather than two tiers, together with composite procedures, provided encouragement for a shift away from single-union occupation and craft-based documents. Awards involved two or more employer parties, with composite awards or agreements requiring two or more unions. In addition, composite agreements involved a minimum of five unions or at least half the unions involved in the undertaking(s), whichever was the lesser.

The 1990 Labour Relations Amendment Act provided further opportunities for employers to move towards industry or enterprise negotiations. Previously, only unions could initiate separate negotiations at enterprise level. The amendment permitted employers of at least 50 employees at a workplace to initiate an employee ballot for the right to negotiate an enterprise agreement at that workplace (or that and others operated by the same employer). A simple majority allowed the employer to proceed with a notice of claims for an enterprise agreement. This accelerated the significant, if not very rapid, movement towards industry and enterprise agreements. Enterprise agreements were most common in larger manufacturing enterprises. Of 818 documents registered in 1988–89, against 800 in 1984–85, awards were down from 339 to 306, and 32 of the 306 were composites. Agreements were up from 461 to 512, and 53 of the 512 were composites. Eighteen per cent of the 818 documents were across industries.

Enterprise agreements

Among notable enterprise agreements which had wide discussion were those in each of the six car assembly plants, including Nissan and Mitsubishi, a meatworks (Fortex), a whiteware plant (Fisher and Paykel), and New Zealand Steel.

The 1988 Fortex agreement covered the Seafield meatworks. Management secured more efficient use of plant with a double shift through agreement on improved conditions and a co-operative, industrial democracy approach to the employer–union relationship. For example, in the enterprise agreement there was a discussion of the need for a balance between the possible deleterious effects of shiftwork and its economic advantages, and for a sharing of the benefits among the company, workers and farmers. Fortex was widely regarded as a progressive company. Sadly it went into liquidation in 1994. This may have been partly the result of overcapacity in the meat industry, but management problems were also involved, and charges have now been laid against two senior executives.

Car assembly has for some time negotiated partially on an enterprise basis, but reductions in protection gave an impetus to the need for productivity bargaining. The Nissan agreement (like Fisher and Paykel's) was based on Japanese-style systems and incorporated new work practices, including performance pay and a reduced number of occupational classifications, breaking down occupationally based job demarcations. The Engineers Union, in both New Zealand and Australia, was to the fore in promoting changes in industrial structure and initiated a number of enterprise agreements.

This post-Fordist organisation of work involves employees being less tied to one small part of the manufacturing process, allowing more variety in work content and improved career structures. It can reduce hierarchies, encourage the use of individual initiative by all employees and support teamwork. Such workplace reform is thus congenial to many women, Maori and Pacific Islanders, and potentially reduces barriers to their progress. However, it provides both potential for equity policies to be taken seriously, and dangers that women and others often marginalised in the workplace will be even more disadvantaged. One reason for optimism is that efficiency motivations for productive use of all the human resource potential available to organisations may drive equal opportunity and family-friendly policies within the context of an impending decline in numbers entering the labour force. However, the nature of equity policies may need radical change in such a climate. Legislative and cross-employer industrial relations solutions fit less well with the decentralised systems that are evolving.

Several unions were antagonistic to the Nissan agreement, and there was a lengthy strike in 1987. The stores workers led the opposition, and cleaners, clerical and hotel workers also remained outside the agreement, negotiating a separate document. There are differences of opinion about the agreement's success as far as the union side is concerned, with some feeling that it encourages too much competitiveness, setting workers against others for performance pay. However, others argue that group work, pride in work and productivity growth are encouraged, with appropriate monetary recognition for those who respond, and equal opportunity for previously disadvantaged groups of workers.

A reappraisal of the Nissan situation five years on shows that the shop floor workers generally feel positive about the changes (Ryan, 1993). On the basis of semi-structured interviews and discussions with five managers, 23 of 38 supervisors, forepersons and team leaders, and 20 of 70 manufacturing employees, Rose Ryan concluded that the new management style and emphasis on teamwork was removing barriers and thus making it easier for women, Maori and Pacific Island employees to take on supervisory positions. Of the 108 employees, 28 per cent were female, but women made up 48 per cent of team leaders and 33 per cent of forepersons and supervisors. The absence of vertical segregation, with women mainly at the bottom, was attributed by the women themselves 'as being due to the fact that they utilised many of the skills which they had developed in the domestic sphere – organising groups of people, coping with competing demands, coaching people in needed skills, and facilitating group decision-making' (*ibid.*: 22).

Emphasis was on skills, and on training to acquire them, teamwork and problem-solving, rather than formal qualifications. This also suited Pacific Islanders, who made up half of the employees, and Maori, who made up 23 per cent, with substantial numbers of each in supervisory positions, 'allowing Maori women in particular to gain skills and promotion and enhance their earnings' (*ibid.*: 29). Ryan went so far as to say that 'the operation of teamwork has been largely congruent with the cultural values and assumptions of a largely Maori and Pacific Island workforce, and has resulted in an adaptation of "Japanese" working practices as distinctively "Pacific" ones', with Tilly Reedy calling the work organisation 'the Maori way' (*ibid.*: 27 and 29). The benefits of versatility were stressed, although in some cases it amounted more to multi-tasking than to multi-skilling, thus being less portable to other firms. It was generally agreed that efficiency had increased, with the goals of quality and customer satisfaction accepted by the workforce in the teamwork situation that encouraged active involvement. The intensity of work was felt by some, however, to be too great, and thus to threaten quality. Overall, the evaluation by employees and Ryan was very positive, although there were some questions about sustainability, and it was noted that the lack of turnover and acceptability of change at a time when most are happy to have a job at all might be less evident in a more buoyant labour market.

Industry-based composites negotiated in the late 1980s included the freezing, packaging, timber, dairy and contracting industries. In the printing/packaging industry, an award reasonably satisfactory to all parties was obtained, with 100 or so employers combining. There were eleven schedules of employee conditions in the document, covering printers, storepersons, electrical workers, clerical workers, cleaners, tearoom workers, watchmen, drivers and engineers. The process of obtaining the settlement was well planned, through a representative working party, and skill reclassification exercises on similar lines to Australian award restructuring cases were undertaken. The intention was that process workers should have the opportunity through appropriate training to move through all the grades. Company variations in conditions, such as hours, shift arrangements and meal breaks, were permitted by agreement between the parties. The award replaced coverage by 12 occupational awards.

Attitudes and evaluation

Evaluation of different structures needs to recognise the complexity of the issues. Considerable variation is possible within each structure. The Labour Government pushed for a shift from occupational awards, but left the balance between the industry and enterprise level more open than the National Government did. The Business Roundtable and the New Zealand Employers Federation strongly support the enterprise level, and their views are shared by the National Government, so this is the predominant form pushed by the Employment Contracts Act. Individual employers are much more ambivalent. For small employers, industry or occupational negotiations reduce the necessity for an investment of time and expertise in industrial relations activity, and may avoid conflict. Expressions of this view are seen as weak or lazy by these employers' central organisations.

A 1989–90 survey of 92 South Island employers (McAndrew and Hursthouse, 1990) found them to be equally divided in their preference for enterprise bargaining or the award system. The hypothetical system of enterprise bargaining put to the employers included a single union representing the entire workforce. Almost two-thirds of firms indicated that they would use an outside advocate to provide expertise and outside knowledge. More than one-third of employers saw no advantages to enterprise bargaining, with nearly two-thirds seeing advantages. However, only one-seventh saw no disadvantages for enterprise bargaining, with those perceived including additional cost, isolation from other employers, lack of guidelines for pay setting, possible targeting by the union and damage to management–staff working relationships. Interestingly, slightly more employers perceived enterprise bargaining as being better for their employees than for themselves.

Central union leadership in the late 1980s favoured the move from occupational bargaining to industry-based bargaining and the gradual emergence of industry-structured unions. At that stage about half the workforce was unionised, with around 40 per cent of employees in unions affiliated to the CTU, although a far higher proportion of the workforce was affected by union negotiations directly or through flow-on effects. However, not all individual unions accepted the switch to industry bargaining. Some craft and occupation-based unions which had previously achieved favourable pay and conditions structures foresaw an erosion of their members' position. It is neither surprising nor reprehensible that self-interest is the main, if not only, consideration in forming attitudes. Thus enterprise bargaining started early, during a period of economic growth and prosperity, in areas such as car assembly which were protected and in which unions could extract leap-frogging gains.

The preference among union leadership for industry bargaining recognised realities, but also reflected real advantages. Larger unions with greater resources were envisaged, able to push for industrial democracy initiatives and with more chance of avoiding inter-union conflict over demarcation disputes, particularly if a move towards industry-based membership rules could be achieved. With composite agreements, industry documents with separate schedules for different groups of workers ensured transparency, with each group aware of the conditions of others.

Union attitudes to enterprise bargaining compared with industry-level bargaining were largely determined by the specific circumstances, with some concern about particular workplaces being picked off and attempts subsequently being made to level down the whole industry. Career structure change and skill development were seen as best promoted by an industry-level system, perhaps allowing for local variation, as in the packaging example discussed above. The force of this is recognised by the current government, which has supported industry-level training initiatives through the industry training organisations.

Some unions developed criteria for supporting separate enterprise arrangements. The Engineers Union had an assessment system, including the need to reconcile the needs of the specific group against those of the total membership of the parent award. Even where those covered by the parent document were considered not to have their interests compromised, the union's national council would approve a stand-alone document only if certain conditions were met. An economic assessment should indicate a level of stability for the membership with no anticipated down-side economic consequences, and the level of union organisation in the plant/company be such that the group would be generally industrially self-reliant.

Female-dominated work

The movement away from occupational bargaining was of concern in some areas of female-dominated work. Some believed that women had done better in the 1980s when covered by occupational awards, although this was disputed. There was concern that small groups of women, such as clerical workers, could have their interests under-represented in an industrial or enterprise negotiation in which they are a tiny minority. Other groups of workers may have little understanding of their work and of relevant issues, including pay equity. The Clerical Workers Union was for many years one of the leaders in fighting for improvements for women in the labour force, but it was forced to wind up with the pressures of the Employment Contracts Act.

One former employee of the union argues that its demise was inevitable, given that it had had to rely on protective legislation for viability, with a large general award giving a strong membership base. Its federal nature with local associations also caused difficulties. Its scattered membership in small workplaces, and low active participation, made an independent existence impossible in the absence of compulsion for either arbitration or union membership (Franks, 1993). Hence Peter Franks argues that as the structural problems had remained unaddressed, external amalgamations became inevitable. The attempt to operate along industry lines within an occupational union was eventually discarded in favour of disbanding (approved by 92 per cent of those returning ballots), with membership of another union offered to all members.

Female-dominated groups such as clerical workers have little bargaining power. Their wide dispersion in small workplaces which are hard to organise also means that even if strike action is taken it fails to produce substantial disruption. Hence such workers might be better off as a small part of industry or enterprise negotiations, as Franks argues. The clerical workers' national award was one of a number which failed to settle for some time during 1988–90, with employers attempting to extract considerable concessions. Finally, and in order to obtain a settlement rather than see the award lapse, the union had to agree to the removal of a clause which stipulated that those working more than 30 hours per week should be paid a full week's wage. This clause had been seen as a protection against employers expecting a full week's work from those employed for between 30 and 37.5 hours while also regarding them as part time, with reduced pay and coverage in terms of full-time conditions of work. Removal of a similar clause in the retail area had earlier led to rapidly increased casualisation.

Difficulties over settling this and other awards led the Labour Government to include protracted negotiation provisions in the 1990 Labour Relations Amendment Act. These clauses would have restored a measure of arbitration, in the final-offer form, in cases where documents had not been settled for two years and the Arbitration Commission was satisfied that one party was failing to negotiate in good faith. It was repealed post haste by the National Government, along with the Employment Equity Act.

Overall it is unclear whether occupational bargaining through a union whose sole concern is a group of women-dominated workers would serve their interests better or worse than inclusion in a group with a more powerful position but a wider range of groups and concerns. This comparison is more relevant to large work sites, usually of a manufacturing nature, than to the small workplaces which are predominant in New Zealand. It is hard to envisage meaningful enterprise bargaining in most small retail establishments and other small business. Large workplaces will move towards enterprise bargaining, leaving at best inadequate residual occupational or industry-based awards to cover small business.

The level of unionisation among women has never been known with certainty. However, the proportion of the workforce unionised was probably about the same among women as men at its peak. Early evidence of changes under the Employment Contracts Act suggests that the proportion unionised and covered by collective bargaining remains similar to that of men, contrary to expectations of more negative impacts on women. These expectations arise from women's over-representation in small workplaces and in the part-time, casualised and outwork areas which were less likely to be covered by the old awards and agreements, still less current collective contracts. However, women are also over-represented in the largest workplaces and the public service, where collective organisation is greatest, so the two effects act in opposite directions. However, individual contracts have now become more common at both extremes of the workforce. In the disadvantaged area, mentioned above, women are over-represented. By contrast, the increasing use of individual contracts among those in middle management and other senior positions is more concentrated among men. Thus similar levels of coverage overall do not contradict the trend towards a more segmented or dual labour market, with women and Maori over-represented in the secondary market.

Conscious of the possibility of the interests of women in female-dominated work being insufficiently considered in the moves to industry and enterprise bargaining, the National Women's Committee of the CTU developed in the late 1980s a set of principles to help guide those embarking on composite negotiations. These were intended to ensure that the possible gains to women workers, in terms of better relative wages, conditions geared to needs, more varied work and pathways out of occupation ghettos, were achieved. The principles included female representation commensurate with the document's coverage in the union bargaining team, consensus decision-making, and adequate consultation and communication. The document itself should involve some improvement in employment conditions of particular relevance to women, and the development of career structures and training systems for the lower paid. Union negotiators should also attempt to ensure that enterprise agreements include adequate equal employment opportunity provisions for women and other minority groups, whether or not they are in female-dominated work.

The industrial relations changes which a National Government would make were clear, including a return to voluntary unionism. More accurately this meant the replacement of 'voluntary compulsory unionism', in which a majority vote could decide on a closed shop, subject to conscientious objection, by 'compulsory voluntary unionism', in which the decision is entirely at the level of the individual. While the brief earlier flirtation with this change by National did not result in as great a fall-off in union membership as was feared, and some unions such as the Public Service Association have always been voluntary, there remain concerns about free riders and reductions in membership. This is accentuated by the dual market and casualisation process, and is a particular problem for the areas of female concentration in small workplaces.

National also wished to accelerate the trend to enterprise bargaining and to giving employees more freedom to select their own representatives. The Employment Contracts Act 1991 put these changes into place through its general thrust and specific provisions, which signalled an accelerating movement from union/employee to employer power. Employers were given more freedom to choose whether to negotiate with the agents chosen by employees, and strikes and/or lockouts could occur only when new contracts were being negotiated. Industrial agreements were given the status of binding enforceable contracts, while lockouts to achieve employer ends have been more common than strikes. With only a slow economic upturn, these changes have helped produce a widening of the gaps between high- and low-income groups, between men and women, and between Pakeha and Maori.

These measures have, as expected, resulted in a rapid reduction in union coverage and collective bargaining. Continuing dissatisfaction by many employees is reported by Heylen polls. Personal grievance and disputes procedures were one positive aspect of the Employment Contracts Act, in that default options specified within the legislation were made available to all who did not have alternatives spelt out within their contracts. However, the long delays and expense of taking cases to the Employment Tribunals, combined with fears of retribution from the employer, are inhibiting factors. Even if some productivity gain has resulted from the Act – and the extent of this is still disputed – there are negative results for all but the most scarce employees. For many, the Act has meant the widening of pay differentials and an erosion of conditions.

5
International Comparisons: The Earnings Gap and Pay Equity

In the last few decades international variability in both the extent of the average female–male earnings gap and its pattern of change has been considerable. The types of measures adopted, for equity and/or efficiency reasons, to improve the position of women in the paid labour force have also varied. The pervasiveness of horizontal (and, to a slightly lesser extent, vertical) occupational segregation by gender and ethnicity is a more common thread, but the degree to which this is responsible for the earnings gap is less certain.

Average female earnings and incomes are below those of males in all countries, including New Zealand, but the extent of the gap is very variable, and care must be taken with comparisons because of definitional and data differences. Among Australia, Canada, Great Britain, the United States and New Zealand, the gap is widest in the United States and narrowest in Australia. Great Britain is probably closest to the US and New Zealand to Australia; Canada's position is around the middle.

The use of the gap in average earnings and/or its rate of change as an index of gender discrimination is not without problems. The issues discussed in Chapter 3 with respect to earnings functions studies are confounded by averaging over the entire labour force. Narrowing or widening of the average gap can be caused by a corresponding move in an industry or occupation. However, it can also be caused by changes in the workforce such as an increased proportion of women which reduces the average figure for years of work experience for females. Equating pay levels for comparable work in industries and occupations is the target for pay equity initiatives, and successes at this level will narrow the overall gap. So will gradual change and/or equal opportunity initiatives which result in women being employed at higher levels in higher paid, previously male-dominated types of work. Moreover, all the countries considered in this chapter have, along with New Zealand, experienced recessionary conditions in recent years, with cuts in some male wages. This can make relative advances by women seem more important than they really are. Thus, disentangling changes to the average gender earnings gap is complex. Nevertheless the gap is one broad-brush indicator of gender discrimination and is a starting-point for more detailed investigation of the factors contributing to it.

To throw more light on international differences in experience and policy, a thorough examination is needed of the various legal, administrative, industrial relations and ideological frameworks which govern different countries' labour markets, and of their wider economic and social contexts. This chapter takes a small step in this direction by briefly discussing pay equity initiatives in Australia, Canada, Great Britain and the US, all of which can usefully be compared with the New Zealand situation discussed in the previous chapters.

The justification for pay equity within initiatives towards gender equality is itself controversial. Even among feminists, positions depend on perspectives (over-simplistically, liberal, feminist or socialist), and on assessments of which groups of women, if any, may gain to what extent from pay equity successes (Acker, 1989; Bose and Spitze, 1987; Brenner, 1987; Cuneo, 1990; Evans and Nelson, 1989; Hartmann, 1985; Reskin, 1988). To those economists and policy-makers who believe that the labour market either does or can and should be made to work in a competitive manner, pay equity measures are anathema.

As stated earlier, three different terms are in common use for the broader concept beyond equal pay for identical work. 'Equal pay for work of equal value' has been the common one in Great Britain, Australia and New Zealand, while 'comparable worth' has been more common in the United States. Both are now frequently superseded by the deliberately softer and vaguer term, 'pay equity'. The question of whether the first two have the same meaning has been controversial, particularly in Australia. 'In our view the use of the term comparable worth in the Australian context would lead to confusion, and in particular, we believe that it would be inappropriate and confusing to equate the doctrine with the 1972 principle of equal pay for work of equal value' (Australian Conciliation and Arbitration Commission, 1986: 10).

Whether equal pay for work of equal value (or comparable worth) does or should refer to value in terms of worth to the employer or to worth determined by work value comparisons – and whether there is any reality to such a distinction – is also controversial. Advocates of equal pay for work of equal value argue for examination of work content, provided such comparisons are broadly based and properly value all job content. Presumably value to the employer will also include assessment of the value of the productive work but allow for the inclusion of market forces as well. The distinction between the 'worth to the employer' and 'work value' approaches to pay fixing may not be as exclusive as is asserted in the Australian judgement, but where market factors are allowable as part of the process, past discrimination can be perpetuated. The 1986 Australian judgement included the opinion that comparable worth in the United States refers to worth to the employer, presumably based on market factors. This is not the general understanding of comparable worth.

The term 'equal value' has the advantage (or otherwise!) of bringing into the open major controversies, including the question, 'What is value?' Is price or market value the only meaningful concept, as neoclassicists would assert? Is that the same as value to the employer? Is there a different type of value to be established by gender-neutral job evaluation or work value exercises, and to what extent does the market come into this concept? These points have already been discussed.

Initiatives in each country

Australia

According to most commentators, Australia is the country in which equal pay for equal value initiatives have made the most impact on the female–male earnings gap. This has come about through three decisions, in 1969, 1972 and 1974, of the Australian Conciliation and Arbitration Commission. The first required equal pay for equal work; the second that female rates be determined by work value comparisons without regard to gender, and the third set one minimum rate for each classification in an award. The female–male ratio for average weekly earnings for full-time adult non-managerial employees in the private sector narrowed from 59 per cent in 1970 to 81 per cent in 1976, and had reached 83 per cent by 1988 (Australia Federal Department of Employment, Education and Training Women's Bureau, 1987; National Women's Consultative Council, 1990). The strong impact of these decisions on the earnings ratio can be attributed to a number of factors, including the broad coverage and wider influence of commission decisions across the workforce. The combination of heavily centralised wage settlement and comparatively small disparities between male wages in female- and male-dominated work (discussed later) was critical to this impact. Any negative employment effects were small at a time of strong demand, especially for labour in areas of female dominance.

Nevertheless, pay equity advocates consider that a considerable degree of gender discrimination remains. Allowances, over-award and supplementary payments are greater for men. Only 18 per cent of adult female employees in 35 awards received equal pay for work of equal value through the 1972 decision (*ibid.*: 10), few work value exercises were carried out (Women's Legal Resources Group, 1985), and those that were undertaken were on the narrow basis of like work. A number of cases were put to the commission through the 1980s, when wage settlements were subject to principles agreed under the government/trade union Accord. Flat-rate increases during this period have resulted in some relative gains to lower-paid groups, including women. However, whether women benefited sufficiently from the Accord is an open question. Despite flat-rate pay rises, which favour the low paid in percentage terms, access to additional increases based on actual or potential productivity gains is more open to highly organised male-dominated industries with restrictive practices which can be traded off. The female–male earnings ratio thus failed to narrow further.

It has been difficult to take successful pay equity cases outside the main agreements. One exception was successful use of the anomalies principle by nurses in the Australian Capital Territory to gain increases on the basis that the 1972 decision of the Australian Conciliation and Arbitration Commission had not been correctly applied. An Equal Pay Unit was established in 1992 within the federal bureaucracy. The award restructuring process, together with extended coverage of supplementary payments in some awards, offers the prospect of some further improvements, although progress is likely to be slow.

Canada

The federal–provincial structure in Canada has resulted in a more varied approach to pay equity initiatives than in Australia, where pay settlement is more centralised. Complaints-based equal pay for work of equal value principles were introduced into human rights codes in Quebec and at federal level as early as 1977 and 1978, with only minor impacts. In 1990 a federal public service pay study concluded that four out of nine female-dominated job categories were undervalued, with four others already having received pay equity increases. Five years' backpay was to be paid to 70,000 workers in these groups, which included secretary-typists, who would gain a 5.6 per cent increase from a comparison with printers.

Manitoba and Ontario were the first provinces in Canada to introduce, in 1985 and 1987, proactive pay equity legislation, recognising systemic gender discrimination in wage settlement. Manitoba covers only the public service, whereas Ontario covers in addition private-sector employers, on a mandatory basis for those with 100 or more employees, and on a permissive basis for those with 10 to 99 employees. Women are, as elsewhere, over-represented in small firms.

In Ontario, employers and unions are required to negotiate the pay equity plan jointly. For non-unionised employee classes, the employer is obligated to prepare the plan. Complaints about plans can be taken to the Pay Equity Commission, which is responsible for conciliation and mediation, in addition to education, information and research. There is also a Pay Equity Hearings Tribunal to hear unresolved disputes. The plan involves comparisons between female job classes (60 per cent-plus female) and male job classes (70 per cent-plus male) using some form of job evaluation within an establishment. Excluded from the comparisons are differences based on skill shortages and training, as well as pay differences resulting from seniority and merit pay, provided these have been determined without gender bias.

The Ontario government pay equity plan involved increases averaging 10 per cent for 96.5 per cent of 28,500 women in 162 unionised job classes. The increases, paid over three years, were estimated to be 2.5 per cent of total payroll (Symes, 1990). It is too soon to estimate the impact of private-sector increases. Problems which have arisen in the private sector include the availability of suitable comparators, the adequacy of the comparison, and the implementation and maintenance of the plan, which is the responsibility of the employer. Test cases have already occurred over the question of who is the employer, as a narrow definition prevents there being suitable male comparator job classes or keeps comparisons narrow. The Ontario Nurses Association successfully argued that the Regional Municipality of

Haldiman-Norfolk was the employer of the police force, allowing a comparison for nurses with police.

The gender neutrality of major job evaluation systems in particular applications is under challenge from unions. In the first major decision defining the standards for a gender-neutral job comparison, 'the Tribunal held that the Municipality's bargaining practices and proposed job evaluation system prepared by the consulting firm William M. Mercer Limited violated the Act and failed to identify and rectify the systemic discrimination in compensation faced by the Union's Public Health and Homes for the Aged nurses' (Cornish, 1991: 5). The system was held to have failed accurately to describe, value and make visible the work of the nurses, while the employer ignored criticisms of the system and failed to inform itself about the nurses' work. (Cornish gives a detailed analysis of the case, in which she appeared.) A second, similar judgement has recently been released with respect to application of the SKEW (Aitken) system in a nursing setting.

Great Britain

The equal pay law in Great Britain was amended at the beginning of 1984 after a European Economic Community (EC) directive to extend coverage to work of equal value 'in terms of the demands made on a female worker (for instance, under such headings as effort, skill and decision) compared to that of a man in the same employment' (Equal Opportunities Commission, 1984: 11). Previously, a claim could be made for equal pay only for the same or broadly similar work, or where equal value had already been established under a proper job evaluation scheme. The legislation is complaints based, with claims for equal pay within a firm made on an individual basis only, naming a male comparator, and investigated by an independent expert. The Advisory Conciliation and Arbitration Service appoints this expert to investigate the work demands of the claimant and comparator, using a self-designed framework. An industrial tribunal has first to decide if there is a prima facie case, using the expert's evaluation and hearing the arguments of the parties to the case. Some successful individual cases have had extensive flow-ons to broadly based groups within an industry.

In defending a claim, the employer may assert that a 'material factor' accounts for the difference in pay, despite the jobs being of equal value. On the scope of this defence, the Equal Opportunities Commission argued that: 'It is unclear to what extent factors not personal to the two jobholders (for example commercial or business reasons) will be a justifiable defence once it is established that you are employed on work of equal value and, for example, whether pay differences based on skill shortages could be a genuine material factor' (*ibid.*: 17–18).

Since 1984, a considerable number of cases have been through the British tribunals, and the application of the material factor defence appears to have been inconsistent. Progress has been relatively slow, with the commission and many other groups recently pressing for improvements to the legislation to allow group actions and to speed up proceedings. Arguments for a minimum wage have been linked with these proposals. A National Pay Equality Campaign was launched in 1991, and had Labour been elected in 1992 improvements were likely. In the current climate, use of existing legislation will continue to be stepped up. For example, in the electricity supply industry the union, NALGO, has annually and unsuccessfully submitted a national claim for a grading structure reflecting equal value principles. Since privatisation, the plan is to take at least one case against each electricity supply company, targeting clerical positions and making comparisons with industrial grades, in the hope of persuading employers to negotiate. Some large employers in Britain are no longer as opposed to equal value concepts as in the past. Reviews of antiquated pay systems can lead to efficiency gains and better use of all sections of the workforce.

One point that arises from the British experience is a counter to the concern that only higher-paid, semi-professional women are likely to gain from this type of legislation. This does not seem to be an inevitable outcome, as it is largely women in blue-collar trades who have made successful claims. A famous example is the cook at Cammel Lairds shipyard who successfully compared herself with males in a variety of trades, including that of joiner. Her case was finally upheld in the House of Lords. (See *Hayward* v. *Cammel Laird Shipbuilders Ltd* [1988] 2 All FR 257, HL(E).)

While it was EC pressure, based on Article 119 and the Equal Pay Directive, which led to the changes to the law in Great Britain, it appears that practical progress on equal pay for work of equal value has been disappointing elsewhere in the EC, despite the Equal Treatment Directive and the Danfoss case (Prechal and Burrows, 1990).

United States

The most major developments on equal pay for work of equal value in the US have taken place at state and in some cases local government level, often through the use of policy-capturing job evaluation studies. Implementation of plans to rectify the gender biases identified have varied in their completeness. Issues include political and financial horse-trading about the amount and the phasing-in period, the appropriate pay line and protection for other workers. Changes may in some cases remedy only the obvious gender gap, not the other equity and efficiency issues indicated by what has been shown to be valued by the statistical study (Steinberg, 1987).

In the private sector, collective bargaining and restructuring of pay structures by some firms has allowed a degree of progress, with support from the National Committee on Pay Equity, but the legal support provided by the Equal Pay Act and Title VII of the Civil Rights Act is minimal.

Assessment of progress on pay equity

The following classifications are useful in considering the relative importance of different factors in reducing gender labour market discrimination, including but not limited to pay equity initiatives:

A. Climate for progress on pay equity (interrelated factors):
   A1. economic situation;
   A2. occupational and industrial segregation/structure of pay by occupation, industry, enterprise, gender (and ethnicity);
   A3. systems of pay settlement/industrial relations law and practice;
   A4. political climate/philosophy.
B. Differences in pay equity initiatives:
   B1. structures – legislation/industrial tribunal/administrative decision/collective bargaining/individual bargaining;
   B2. breadth of coverage – complaints-based v general/public sector v public plus private (size limit?)/individual v group;
   B3. comparison methods – policy-capturing job evaluation/a priori job evaluation scheme/ad hoc method;
   B4. comparison groups – across employer v within/across what occupation groups/definitions of female, male, mixed occupations/criteria for comparators/issues of lack of comparators.

It is beyond the scope of this chapter to classify in detail Australia, Canada, Great Britain and the US on the climate variables at various times. However, the discussion of the various countries' approaches indicates where each fits on most of the details of initatives. Clearly, the climate affects what is possible and acceptable, and thus both directly and indirectly has greater impact on the results than the details of the initiatives. Further comments on factors influencing female and male earnings, and the gap between them, will add support to this conclusion.

One obvious point, in comparing Australia and New Zealand with the United States (and also Japan), is that countries with lower levels of unionisation and decentralised wage fixing appear to exhibit wider pay gaps, overall and by gender. The impact of the equal value tribunal decisions and centralised pay systems in Australia contrasts with the deregulated market in the United States. An Australian study, using workplace data, concluded that: 'for those concerned with ending wage discrimination, the much smaller differentials in Australia would appear to represent a resounding success for the principle of equal pay applied through the awards system. By implication, any attempt to shift the Australian industrial relations system towards the US model might be expected to increase wage discrimination as the "flexibility" of wage setting by employers increases' (Drago, 1989: 323).

The comment applies equally to New Zealand, which has had high levels of centralised bargaining and unionisation by international standards. This is particularly true for women, and this, combined with strong participation in union affairs, also appears to be correlated with a lower gender pay gap (Curtin, 1991; Saar, 1992). In New Zealand, part-time workers and female-dominated areas of work in small workplaces have been covered by awards and unionised to a greater extent than in most other countries (Hill, 1992). However, this is already eroding, along with the general decline in collective bargaining and in the proportion of the workforce unionised as a result of the Employment Contracts Act (Harbridge, 1993a; Harbridge and Hince, 1993). The pay and conditions of part-time workers is under-researched in New Zealand. It is instructive to note that in Australia in 1986, the average hourly wage rate of part-time workers was 20 per cent above the full-time hourly wage, whereas in the United States part timers in 1987 received hourly wages between 11 per cent and 44 per cent below those of full timers (Hawke, 1992). Given that New Zealand's institutional structure has been fairly similar to that of

Australia in the past, it is likely that New Zealand will move from something close to the first situation towards the second – to the detriment of women who predominate in part-time work.

Another important point concerns the effect which occupational and industrial segregation has on pay levels overall and particularly in female-dominated areas. The effect on pay levels is less easy to document unequivocally than the phenomenon itself (see Hawke, 1991, for a discussion of the statistical complexities). There is considerable evidence that female-dominated occupations tend to be generally low paying, and particularly so for women. Gregory, Daly and Ho (1986) found that female-dominated, male-dominated and mixed occupations had weekly female–male earnings ratios of 73.5 per cent, 80.3 per cent and 74.1 per cent respectively in Britain, and 74.2 per cent, 87.9 per cent and 77.6 per cent in Australia. The overall ratios were 62.9 per cent in Britain and 75.3 per cent in Australia. In both countries the gap was wider in female-dominated occupations, which also yield much lower absolute levels of female earnings. However, there is one important additional difference between the two countries, and that is the very much lower level of male earnings in female-dominated occupations in Britain. This averaged 96.2 per cent of the male overall average in Australia, as against 82.0 per cent in Britain. The higher male wage in female-dominated occupations in Australia helps pull up female wages there, and perhaps elsewhere.

Gregory has also compared Australian and United States experience, applying the returns to human capital factors in each country, estimated from earnings functions, to the human capital statistics of the other. Within each country, human capital factors can account for about half of the female–male earnings gap. However, the much greater reduction and resulting smaller size of the gap in Australia cannot be explained by differences in industry mix or human capital endowments (Gregory *et al*, 1989). Thus it appears that the institutional factors discussed above for Australia, contrasting with the deregulated market in the United States, have been the most important influence. Overall, research, analysis and feminist efforts in pay equity have been most extensive in the US, but have had the least effect, apart from some public-sector jurisdictions.

Of course, these comparisons simply pose more questions about the factors which brought about the structural differences. Another example is the issue of why under a National Government New Zealand has retained minimum wage legislation but not pay equity legislation, when the reverse situation applies in Great Britain with a government of a similar hue.

Despite the conclusion that the climate is more important than the detail of the pay equity measures, some provisions have more widespread results than others. The Ontario legislation, with its proactive nature, provides the most interesting prospect. It is currently being amended to provide for female job classes with no obvious comparators. Other areas needing attention there are non-unionised workplaces and progress on gender-neutral job evaluation.

While collective bargaining and group action may on their own lead to pay equity settlements, some type of job evaluation is involved in most attempts to implement equal pay for work of equal value, as discussed in Chapter 4. An issue of importance in this connection is the breadth and nature of comparisons between jobs allowed under legislation and its administration. If comparisons are possible only between very similar jobs, the undervaluation of traditionally female-dominated occupations cannot be addressed, particularly if male wages in such occupations are depressed close to the low female level. Where there is a large variety of types of work within a single employer's jurisdiction, such as at US state government level, this is automatically secured. In Australia, the relative homogeneity of male wages meant that the need for comparisons across occupations was less crucial in raising female rates.

The lessons from New Zealand experience are salutary. It is easy to lose battles previously won, particularly in a small country with a unitary structure of government, and where total policy reverses led by a small group have few barriers to overcome. The 1990 pay equity legislation may also have been rather too ambitious and complex.

Whether legislative, administrative, policy-capturing, collective bargaining or proactive systems are used singly or in combination to attempt to secure pay equity, appropriate strategies clearly need to fit particular circumstances. The use of job evaluation may well reach a peak and decline in the face of decentralised human resource management of individuals and teams. In that case, monitoring will still be needed to ensure that empowerment extends to all groups in the workforce. Under any system, it is important that the involvement and support of as many as possible of those affected is secured. This is needed both from individual employees within a firm and in terms of general support for the principle. Without it, changing governments can dismantle past gains, at little perceived cost to themselves. It is worth remembering that early equal pay legislation was introduced more to protect men's jobs – by preventing the employment of women – than with any principles of equity in mind. It was seen as an alternative or supplementary strategy to employing women in segregated work at a lower wage. It is similarly claimed that equal pay principles in the EC were introduced largely to prevent 'unfair competition' from any country not adopting the principle. Whatever the motives of government, any opportunities provided by their actions must be grasped, and new ones created.

6
Equal Pay for Women After the Employment Contracts Act

This chapter focuses on discussing the practical value, if any, of the 1972 Equal Pay Act in the 1990s. Earlier discussion of the adverse implications of decentralised bargaining on pay equity for women internationally indicates that the climate is poor for further progress or even for maintaining previous gains. Some general points about the Employment Contracts Act (ECA), labour market deregulation and the implications for women employees are therefore essential to the discussion.

This chapter also outlines the legislation before and after the amendments made at the time of the Employment Contracts Act 1991, then discusses its effectiveness or otherwise and draws some fairly depressing conclusions. Some possibilities for progress are suggested.

Background

The Minister of Women's Affairs, Jenny Shipley, was quoted in the *Dominion* (1 December 1992) as claiming that the ECA 'has done more towards providing equity for working women than any other development for a long time'. She quoted Quarterly Employment Survey (QES) figures showing an increase in average hourly earnings for women of 2.6 per cent between May 1991 and May 1992. (Incidentally, the fact that this data source showed only a 1.6 per cent increase, which is still misleadingly high, for the August year got less publicity!) The minister's comments provoked strong reaction from some quarters. The then deputy leader of the Labour Party, Helen Clark, alluded to a 10 per cent drop in women's overtime earnings, the over-representation of women in the low-paid section of the workforce which had been adversely affected by the Act, and attacks on wages and conditions in female-dominated occupations. The CTU National

Women's Committee convenor, Carol Hicks, called the minister's claims that women were happy with the Act 'outrageous and insulting'.

Commenting on the issue of earnings growth, a number of surveys have quoted 2 per cent to 3 per cent average annual increases for all or parts of the workforce covered. However, considerable caution is needed in interpreting these figures. First, the same group is not covered at the beginning and end of the period: if employment reductions are disproportionately among the lower paid, increases will be exaggerated. Second, coverage generally needs examination: for example, the QES excludes small workplaces while those based on contracts submitted to the Department of Labour may not be representative of all collective contracts covering 20 or more employees, let alone individual and smaller contracts. Third, care needs to be taken that trade-offs of improved basic earnings for reductions in penal and overtime rates are fully reflected. In some cases, allowances have been incorporated into basic pay.

Raymond Harbridge's contract database, which compares the same group over time, shows a very much smaller increase in earnings, and he has amplified the points above, showing why his figures are a truer reflection of reality (Harbridge, 1993c). This illustrates the need for more adequate official data. It is not a matter of chance that it is not available: it comes from government philosophy and policies in the industrial relations area, as well as inadequate research funding, and helps politicians in their misinterpretation of official statistical sources. Harbridge's figures show an annualised average increase of 0.24 per cent during the first 18 months of the Act's operation. However, even this disguises a considerably higher weighted average increase for men (0.37 per cent) compared with women (0.14 per cent). Further, women were less likely to have contracts which attracted overtime or penal rates for inconvenient working hours or weekend days. Only in an area less directly related to take-home pay – that of leave – were female-dominated contracts slightly better than men's, with more providing a fourth week of annual leave and/or better than minimum sick leave (Hammond and Harbridge, 1993).

More generally, the claim that a deregulated labour market benefits women needs critical scrutiny (Novitz, du Plessis and Jaber, 1990). Certainly in terms of numbers employed and unemployed, women have done slightly less badly than men over the recent period of substantial job loss. However, this is largely because of women's over-representation in part-time, casualised and low-wage sections of the labour market, and in service industries or occupations which are under fewer employment pressures. Predictions and some evidence show that the impact of deregulation on those in the casualised secondary sector is strongly negative (Harbridge, 1993c; Sayers, 1991). The labour market flexibility enhancement purpose of the ECA has been claimed by government ministers and the Business Roundtable, among others, potentially to advantage employees in general and women in particular. However, such flexibility is mainly at the behest of and for the benefit of employers. Only the small proportion of women in highly scarce occupations are likely to be able to bargain flexibility gains of their own.

Evidence on the impact of the Act and the accompanying economic situation and policies on unions and their members is now becoming available. In female-dominated and low-paid areas of work, it is far from encouraging. For example, clerical unions lost about 45 per cent of their members before disbanding; cleaners' unions lost about 20 per cent and the Service Workers and Distribution and General Workers Unions each lost around one-third (Hill and du Plessis, 1993). Loss of membership from resignations or lapses, especially in small work sites, as a result of voluntary unionism was not the only factor. It was supplemented by some employers' ceasing automatic deduction of fees, high employment turnover and pressure, real or feared, from employers.

Comparison of the clerical and cleaning areas, both predominantly small worksite jobs, is salutary. The smaller losses, survival of unions and more prevalent continuation of collective contracts in the cleaning area arise partly because the effective number of employers involved is far fewer than the number of sites. Most school cleaners and caretakers are covered by a multi-employer contract agreed between the Service Workers Union and the State Services Commission (SSC), with most school boards of trustees preferring to leave responsibility for negotiation to the SSC, even under bulk funding within the operations grant. Multinational cleaning companies also preferred a collective multi-employer contract covering 80 per cent of contract cleaning in the private sector, fearing that competition in the tendering process could squeeze profit margins harder in the absence of a uniform pay structure (*ibid.*). However, for both clerical and cleaning workers it is the interests of the employers which determined the bargaining and contract structures, with flexibility priorities and deteriorating conditions just as likely in each situation.

A 1993 survey of 962 women members of the Service Workers Union found that 40 per cent had suffered a household income decline in the previous two years (Harbridge, 1993b). Thirty per cent had lower take-home pay, 47 per cent the same, and only 20 per cent higher take-home pay than two years earlier, with a large part of even this small increase coming from longer hours, reported by 15 per cent of respondents. With as many as 32 per cent reporting higher basic pay than before, the lower incidence of higher take-home pay was largely the result of abolition or reduction of overtime, penal, unsocial hours or weekend rates.

Equal pay for work of equal value, the principle underlying the pay equity part of the short-lived Employment Equity Act, no longer has any legal underpinning. The apparently simpler principle of equal pay for identical work was never as simple as it might seem. It becomes even more elusive in a highly deregulated labour market with inter-firm and regional differences for otherwise the same work, and with individualised and performance-based pay increasingly prevalent. Nevertheless, the Equal Pay Act 1972 (EPA) is still on the books, so whether it, and other anti-discriminatory legislation, has any substantial meaning and effect should be examined.

The legislative changes arising from the Employment Contracts Act

Discrimination in employment on the grounds of gender is outlawed by the Human Rights Commission Act 1977 (HRCA), with extensions to include protection for other groups in the Human Rights Act 1993. It is now illegal to discriminate on the grounds of family status, pregnancy, disability, age, health or sexual orientation. Section 15(1)(a) makes unlawful a refusal, on the basis of sex or the other grounds covered, to employ a person on work of any description which is available and for which that person is qualified. Section 15(1)(b) provides that 'No employer shall refuse or omit to offer or afford any person the same terms of employment, conditions of work, fringe benefits, and opportunities for training, promotion, and transfer as are made available for persons of the same or substantially similar qualifications employed in the same or substantially similar circumstances on work of that description' on the basis of the sex (or other grounds covered) of that person.

Until 1991, no complaint referring solely to equal pay was to be dealt with under this legislation (Section 15(12)), but was instead to be referred by the Human Rights Commission to the Secretary of the Department of Labour for consideration under the EPA. Issues such as possible discrimination in placement on scales and access to promotion are on the borderline of equal pay and gender discrimination/equal opportunity, and thus their status was unclear. The Air New Zealand air hostess case, determined by the Equal Opportunities Tribunal in 1988, involved access to promotion among other matters and was taken to a successful conclusion under the HRCA. The Equal Pay Amendment Act 1991, passed alongside the ECA, repealed Section 15(12) of the HRCA, permitting the Human Rights Commission itself to pursue a complaint on equal pay.

The approach of the EPA to the meaning of equal pay was to prohibit differentiation based on sex. The major problems were the criteria for establishing such differentiation and the resulting interpretation and enforcement, almost all of which are exacerbated by the recent labour market and industrial relations legislation changes.

The 1991 Equal Pay Amendment Act sought to ensure that employment contracts must provide equal pay for equal work by adding to the definition of instruments covered by EPA 'an employment contract within the meaning of the Employment Contracts Act 1991'. Other amendments primarily allowed for institutional change, substituting the Employment Tribunal for previous institutions. Also added was Section 2A(1), prohibiting discrimination in terms and conditions on the basis of gender in a similar way to the portion of the HRCA quoted earlier. The ECA, too, has similar wording in the definition of discrimination within the personal grievance provisions.

It appears, therefore, that three alternative procedures are now available for equal pay or opportunity complaints: under the EPA, the HRCA, or the personal grievance procedures of the ECA. Whether any of these is likely to be effective, and in what circumstances, is examined next.

Effectiveness of equal pay legislation under the Employment Contracts Act

There are a number of forms of possible gender discrimination in remuneration, apart from different basic pay levels for the same work with the same job title. Each of those listed below is hard to address:
1. Using separate job titles for the same work, with one job title used for male jobs, the other for female jobs, and the former being paid more.

2. Unequal above-instrument/contract payments based on gender.
3. Unequal application of criteria for starting salaries, placing employees on scales, promotion, etc, based on gender.
4. Unequal application of performance pay, merit pay, etc, based on gender.
5. Unequal pay for individuals or small groups, with some gender element, when remuneration is fixed by individual contracts or collective contracts with only a few workers.
6. Undervaluation of female-dominated types of work.

The possible inequalities in 2 to 5 may or may not be deliberate. If they are unintended, but arise from criteria some or all of which have a differential effect by gender and are not clearly related to productivity on the job, they should still be classified as discriminatory. This is indirect discrimination.

Ongoing problems

Categories 1 and 2 were clearly covered by the EPA, but are hard to police. Categories 3 and 4 can be thought of as a type of category 2, applicable to individuals rather than groups and to the person in the job rather than the job itself. They are on the equal pay/opportunity border. Category 5 can arise from any of the previous four where small groups are involved, or be independent of them. Category 6 refers to the absence of equal pay for work of equal value – and will not be regarded as discriminatory by those who see the market as the sole and non-discriminating measure of value, even though the wording of the EPA appears to be supportive of the equal value principle.

Even in female-dominated work where job classification exercises were undertaken and led to an increase in remuneration, there has been a period of up to 19 years in which relativities may have changed to the detriment of such work. The 1986 clerical workers' case in which the union sought a judgement that the employers must negotiate on equal pay for work of equal value demonstrated this effect. The grade three hourly rate in the Clerical Award, predominantly female, was 69 per cent of the average male hourly wage in 1974. This ratio rose to 79 per cent in 1979 with equal pay implementation, but fell back to 72 per cent by 1985. Its ratio to core carpenters' and journeymen printers' rates had returned by then to the 1973 figure (New Zealand Federated Clerical, Administrative and Related Workers Industrial Association of Workers, 1986).

The judgement in the clerical workers' case in 1986 effectively closed off use of the Act in this area. However, the erosion of the results of job classification exercises undertaken under the EPA with respect to female-dominated work shows the need for change. The Act, as interpreted by the Arbitration Court, does not allow a further job classification exercise to be insisted on by the union to address such possible erosion.

The Equal Pay Review Committee was concerned about each of the problem areas mentioned above, as well as the means of enforcement. Investigation of possible problems in any of the categories 2 to 5 requires detailed assessment of individual or small-group remuneration in comparison with that of a man or men.

Discrimination in individual cases is much harder to establish than separate rates in an award. Individual complainants were covered by the EPA through their instrument coming under Sections 2(1)(e) or 2(1)(f) of the definition. This is critical, because Section 2(2) qualifies just these types of instrument. It provides that nothing in the Act should apply to any agreement or decision 'made in respect of an individual employee, which fixes a rate of remuneration that is special to that employee by reason of special qualifications, experience, or other qualities possessed by that employee and that does not involve any discrimination based on the sex of the employee'. This applies to contracts under ECA which have been added to Section 2(1)(e).

Two problems arise with regard to Section 2(2). The first is the generality of this exemption, since it removes the obligation of the employer to make a collective determination prior to identifying the factors special to individual employees. The requirement not to discriminate on the basis of the sex of the employee is still present, but without such a determination it is almost impossible to establish whether an element of discrimination exists (Review Committee, 1979: 52). The committee feared that this would act as a general escape clause of wider application than intended, and suggested amendments. These were not made.

The second, related problem is the broad interpretation by the Arbitration Court, which seems to make it possible for employers always to find a justifying factor for pay differences. The Review Committee and one of its members, Elizabeth Orr (1986b), expressed disquiet about the judgements in a number of cases, and the arguments made by employers and accepted. Only ten equal pay cases were determined by the court: nine during the period 1973–79, and the clerical workers' case in 1986 which was submitted essentially as a test case on the continuing applicability of the Act and whether it genuinely covered equal pay for work of equal value. The lack of other cases after 1979 reflects both the completion of the implementation period and a belief by unions and the inspectorate that the court was unlikely to interpret the Act sympathetically towards claimants (Orr, 1986b: 11). In only two cases did the court rule in favour of women claimants.

Four of the complaints decided in the 1970s concerned a single woman (or, in one case, a small group) comparing her pay with that of a single man in the workforce of the same employer. Each involved above-award or non-award rates and each was decided against the claimant. They are relevant here because they most closely resemble the likeliest scenario for complaints under the ECA. In each case factors other than gender were found to account for the pay differences. The most crucial, *Inspector* v *D. F. Jones* [1979] AC D.1008 71/2, relates to two accountant-clerks employed in the same firm and location, on work which the judgement states was broadly similar in content. However, in the words of the judgement, 'Mrs Deverick asked for and was granted a salary of $5,000. Mr Robertson would not accept a post for less money than he was receiving at Massey University. His salary was, by agreement also, fixed at $7,200'. Mrs Deverick was slightly superior in initial qualifications and Mr Robertson had more experience in general administration. The court ruled that 'whatever way the matter is looked at and whatever criteria are applied, there has been no element of differentiation based on the sex of Mrs Deverick', and attributed all of the difference to the man's greater experience.

The 1979 Review Committee was unhappy with this decision, believing the situation to be based on a dual labour market, related to the greater job opportunities for men compared with married women in professional areas in Palmerston North: 'In the committee's view the elimination of just such a sex-biased labour market was and is a major aim of the Equal Pay Act' (Review Committee, 1979: 50). It argued that a dual labour market should not be used to justify differential rates and that the court should have set a common rate for the work and then assessed the payment for the two special factors listed, one on each side. It felt that a differential as large as 44 per cent would be hard to justify on experience alone.

In reviewing this and the other cases, the question arises as to what evidence would have been sufficient to convince the court that discrimination had occurred (Orr, 1986a: 11). It is not surprising that after these determinations neither inspectors nor unions brought any more individual cases to court. Instead, the efforts of women's organisations and unions, particularly after the 1986 judgement, were concentrated on securing better legislation. Attempts to use the collective bargaining system to obtain equal pay for work of equal value were also made, but successes have been very limited without legislative or judicial back-up. Industrial action has been used occasionally. In 1974 women supermarket meat-packers struck over the fixing of the notional man's rate at the level previously paid to women. With support from transport unions, strike action remedied the situation (Osborne, 1976: 354). However, in the changed economic and industrial relations climate of the late 1980s and early 1990s, strike action is less likely to succeed.

Increasing problems

The first new issue which arises after the ECA is what types of complaints or cases it is possible to pursue. The EPA makes unlawful gender differentiation in remuneration payable for any work 'under any instrument'; the ECA extends part (e) of the definition of instrument to include contracts under its jurisdiction. It clearly makes unlawful unequal pay based on gender within the same contract. However, it is less clear whether unequal pay based on gender (as defined by the Act and interpreted by the judicial system, and if it could be established) across contracts is unlawful. If not, those on individual contracts would now have no coverage at all. Different legal opinions have been expressed on this issue, and only a court decision would give a definitive answer.

It is to be hoped that a complaint based on an alleged gender pay difference for the same or substantially similar work for the same employer would be entertained, even though the female complainant and male comparator were each on individual contracts. This can be seen as in some ways similar to earlier individual cases (see *Inspector* v *D. F. Jones*, cited earlier). There might also be circumstances in which it would be desirable to investigate whether equal pay and gender discrimination exists among different collective contracts within the workforce of an employer, but this may be ruled out.

A further possibility is that the addition of Section 2A(1) to the EPA prohibiting discriminatory treatment cuts through this issue by allowing at least individual complaints and comparisons within the workforce of the same employer, whatever the contract status. How this section relates to the rest of the Act is not clear and would be resolved only by case law. Doubts exist about whether it can have any real effect in an EPA context, since no complaints procedures or remedies appear to be set down there, unlike the similar provisions in the HRCA and the personal grievance procedures of the ECA.

Even if comparison of individual contracts is possible, the problems of establishing discrimination in individual cases remain. In fact their effects are exacerbated by the combined impact of the ECA and associated changes in economic climate and bargaining levels. First, individual contracts are becoming much more common and remuneration is likely to be more varied by region, industry, firm and other factors. Thus the problems of establishing discrimination in individual cases will apply to a greater proportion of the workforce, and the greater variation will make the isolation of a gender factor even more difficult (or make it easier to cover up). Collective contracts, too, will on average cover fewer workers, and be more locally based.

Second, fewer people are in a position to know what others are paid, and thus whether there is any discrimination. Only collective contracts with more than 20 people covered have to be lodged with the Industrial Relations Service, and access to this information is uncertain. A more general move – for example, in the public service – to privacy of remuneration information, including positions on scales and merit pay, can mask discrimination. Women, especially those in small workplaces, are likely to be reticent about making inquiries and complaints. This may be the result of socialisation and/or of fears, which may be justified, of retaliation or unpleasantness from the employer or male fellow workers and of long delays in securing an outcome. These fears are likely to be greater with high levels of unemployment, a climate in which the employer has more bargaining power, and a six-month stand-down period for a benefit after voluntarily leaving a job or being dismissed.

Third, merit and performance pay are becoming more common, and despite the efficiency and equity cases which can be made in favour of such pay systems, there is evidence of potential for unintended gender discrimination (Burton, 1987, 1988 and 1990). Fourth, support from a union may be less forthcoming than before, thanks to lower levels of union coverage and other priorities in a more difficult economic and bargaining climate. Fifth, enforcement is likely to be even harder than in the past.

Enforcement

The enforcement procedure under the EPA was originally based on a combination of response to complaints and an investigation and inspection system to ensure compliance. Employers and trade unions as parties to instruments had the obligation during the implementation period to ensure that work classifications and rate-change determinations were made in accordance with the Act. Unions and Labour Department inspectors were able to act as agents of individuals in handling complaints. However, a union had to request the Department of Labour to carry out an investigation rather than undertake one on its own initiative, since only the department had access to confidential wage records, through the inspectorate. The inspectorate at that stage also covered occupational safety, health and welfare, minimum conditions, such as under the Holidays Act, and wages and awards, including the EPA. There was no individual specialisation within the inspectors' overall brief. When inspecting factories, shops and offices, all areas were covered.

It is clear that enforcement was consistently inadequate, with insufficient numbers of inspectors and with health and safety given priority, in accord with the background of most inspectors. From March 1975 to March 1979, the inspectorate grew from 114 to 203, but the department in 1979 assessed the desirable establishment at about 320. This was based on the aim of inspecting factories annually, and shops, offices and other units biennially. In 1978 only 44 per cent of factories were inspected, while shops were being visited about every four years and offices at ten-yearly intervals, reflecting the safety priority. Women employees are of course more dominant in shops and offices than in factories. By February 1986 the inspectorate had been reduced to 144 field staff. A former inspector, subsequently a union official and now an Opposition Member of Parliament, stated that the enforcement of equal pay was very low on the department's priorities, and she queried the department's complacency about compliance with the legislation revealed by its annual reports of 1983, 1984 and 1985 (Tennet, 1986: 3–6).

Several factors make enforcement even harder in the new climate. The reduced level of information available to individual employees, unions or other representatives on remuneration levels of groups and individuals makes for difficulty and increased costs in attempting to investigate and enforce rights under the EPA. Between 1987 and 1991, under the Labour Relations Act, unions had the right to inspect wage records and were in theory therefore able, if alerted to problems, to take a more active role than previously. The ECA removed this right, and thus inspectorate enforcement resumed its previous importance.

The inspectorate has now been divided, with separate administration and responsibility for safety and health on the one hand, and the minimum code on the other. This might be welcomed if the latter group had sufficient resources and instructions to enforce equal pay, but this is unlikely to be the case. There are now only seven such inspectors, plus three information officers. Official policy is now to respond to any written complaints but not to make routine inspections. Since 1980 the number of complaints made under the Act has been very small. The Department of Labour has regularly used this fact to conclude that compliance with the Act is satisfactory, and that equal pay has been achieved. For example, it unilaterally cancelled the additional 1982 review recommended by the 1979 Review Committee. It was argued earlier that the scarcity of complaints relates more to lack of success of earlier cases than to full compliance and acceptance by women that this has occurred.

Four complaints have been investigated by the Labour Inspectorate since August 1988. Two appear not to raise important issues in the current context, while one was successfully settled by the female employee with her employer. The fourth was investigated in 1990, following a complaint from the Human Rights Commission that three female employees had been paid salaries lower than a male employed in a similar capacity by the same employer. The employer defended its decision to pay the male a higher rate than one of the females because he had been earning more previously and the higher rate was needed to attract him to the job. The inspectorate did not consider it worth taking this case to court, even though it was hard to substantiate differential skills and experience. Its legal advice was that the court would accept the previously higher salary as a valid non-gender-related reason for a pay difference. This advice was probably correct in the light of the Jones case, but again allows the perpetuation of gender market differences possibly unrelated to productivity.

A second issue relates to the other rationale given by the employer for the male receiving a higher rate. This was that he had the potential to occupy a more senior position which was to be established. Again, the probably correct legal advice was that the court would consider this to be a 'special quality' under Section 2(2). The problem here is that such an assessment of potential may well be vague, unsubstantiated and gender-biased. To count as a valid special quality, such an assessment should require detailed documentation and comparison between the two people involved. Otherwise it is open to the types of gender bias present in recruitment and performance assessment mentioned earlier.

A final point of importance is that it has to be accepted that equal pay complaints are now possible only within the workforce of a single employer, except in the case of the reducing minority of multi-employer collective contracts (Harbridge, 1993c). While this accords with the current climate, the concept of the undervaluation of skills in female-dominated work which underlies equal pay for work of equal value arguments is an occupationally based one. Cross-employer claims were possible under the Employment Equity Act.

In the light of these problems arising from the EPA, and doubts about the likelihood of claims being made and succeeding under personal grievance procedures at the Employment Tribunal, it may be that the Human Rights Commission is now the best of the three options available for pursuing equal pay. In 1992 the commission investigated a complaint involving equal pay as well as other issues, but because it was settled between the parties with commission assistance, its nature, unfortunately in this context, cannot be discussed.

It is possible that any court proceedings under each of the three options would have to be in the Employment Tribunal, since Section 3(1) of the ECA gives that body 'exclusive jurisdiction to hear and determine any proceedings founded on an employment contract'. However, the Human Rights Commission and others consider that complaints made under its legislation can continue to be dealt with, where appropriate, by the Equal Opportunities Tribunal (EOT). These will now include equal pay cases. It is to be hoped that this interpretation is correct, as the EOT is more specialist and has a better understanding of gender issues.

The future: pay equity

The detailed issues discussed here indicate that the EPA may now have little force, even with respect to identical work. In any case, deregulated labour markets, with pay setting at firm and individual level, make the question of what is identical work uncertain. The comparisons with other countries examined earlier add force to the conclusion that in this climate it is likely that the gender earnings gap will widen again, and that discrimination will increase. While more women are progressing up vertical hierarchies, differentials generally are widening, with those employees classified as unskilled (very largely a social construct), among whom women and Maori predominate, relative losers. An effective minimum wage could be some protection for the lower paid, in which women predominate, but the level has been unchanged since February 1990. In Britain, one strand of the current pay equity campaign is to introduce such a minimum wage. Regular increases in the minimum wage, possibly through indexing it to average earnings, is a worthwhile aim. Of course, it is opposed by those convinced of the existence and strength of a wage-employment trade-off.

Overall the prospects for progress on gender equality and pay equity are far from promising. Only on voluntary (and in the state sector, within limits, compulsory) programmes for equal employment opportunity for women and the other groups designated in the State Sector Act is progress reasonably likely.

What else, if anything, can be done towards greater equality of pay and opportunity in this climate? It is clear that the EPA is now unsatisfactory by any standards. It is hard to read; much of it is irrelevant, referring to the implementation period and earlier industrial relations systems, and what remains in operation is not clearly established. Thus a review is long overdue, although it is questionable whether anything would be accomplished by such a process at present. Equal pay is provided for by legislation in most countries, with 107 having ratified ILO Convention 100 by 1986. This convention is concerned with equal pay for work of equal value, although it is not highly prescriptive with respect to the manner of implementation. It was ratified by New Zealand in 1983 on the basis of the EPA, although there is doubt about whether within the current total policy framework the ILO would regard New Zealand as being in compliance, as it has previously.

Probably more in tune than new or revised legislation with the current non-interventionist stance is educational and publicity material on gender neutrality in remuneration systems, aimed at individual employers. This could encompass job evaluation schemes and other systems for deciding comparative worth and salaries within firms, placement on scales, and merit/performance pay. One useful resource is the *Equity at Work* job evaluation scheme (Burns and Coleman, 1991). Such an approach may well fit with the current moves in the area of workplace reorganisation, reform and emphasis on teamwork. These moves offer the opportunity for equity considerations to be blended with efficiency, but there are dangers that the process may ignore the needs and potential of women, Maori and other groups currently less advantaged in the workforce. There are a few overseas precedents of workplace restructuring and collective and individual bargaining incorporating moves towards pay equity, using arguments based on both undervaluation of skills and efficiency.

Concern for gender neutrality and efficiency can be subsumed under the rubric of equal treatment, encompassing both equal pay and equal opportunity (Orr, 1988). It is a reasonable approach in the short term, with voluntary compliance only. Along these lines, the Campaign for Equal Value, Equal Pay is suggesting that remuneration audits within firms examining equity issues could be a useful measure. The work of the rather small and toothless but acceptable Equal Employment Opportunities Trust is cautious, to avoid offending employers, but is a small step in the right direction. Equal treatment within remuneration audits could also be an appropriate approach in the medium to long term, if the cycle of the economy, social factors and philosophies at some stage gives rise to a more interventionist climate. At that point, the Ontario model of compulsion for the formation of plans within enterprises might be worth considering, perhaps broadened from pay equity to equal treatment. Whether third-party intervention of any form will again become acceptable is uncertain, but there is considerable doubt that major improvements will occur without it.

More fundamentally, the philosophy underlying current policy, which gives primacy to individual freedom of contract in the labour market (regarded as just another market), moves away from any third party enforcement of equal opportunity or gender-neutral comparisons (Dawson, 1992). It is even further, except through lip-service and voluntary measures, from securing gender-neutral outcomes or structural change based on feminist perspectives.

The future: other priorities for gender equality at work

This part of the book has focused on equal pay/pay equity between women and men – one of a large number of issues relevant to women's equality with men in paid and unpaid work. In putting this issue in context, it is useful to conclude with brief mention of a number of other areas critical to the achievement of this end.

True equality of opportunity requires the removal of barriers to access to jobs of all types, and at all levels in hierarchies. A substantial number of these remain intact. An even greater challenge is the view that a combination of equity and efficiency considerations requires that all such hierarchies be dismantled to a considerable degree. The teamwork approach of workplace reform suggests a reduction in the number of levels and salary differentials between them. Glass ceilings currently often prevent women reaching the top positions in management, but many women also see the management process as needing radical change along those lines.

One area which could benefit most groups who are disadvantaged in the labour market is an improved minimum floor of conditions, and its adequate enforcement. Erosion of penal, overtime and hours of work conditions are among those frequently reported since the ECA, with take-home pay thereby often reduced. Five days annual paid sick leave was legally required for the first time by the ECA, but many awards had better provisions than this, with ten days or more. In 1994 there was a lock-out at Mitsubishi over the employers' attempt to reduce sick leave days from ten to seven.

The minimum wage for those aged 20 or above has been unchanged since the National Government was elected in 1990, while the disappearance of awards has meant that many young people are unprotected from exploitation. While many awards had contained youth rates below those of adults, they at least provided some minimum levels of pay. In practice, 18- and 19-year-olds now have a minimum wage of around $136 per week, as against the adult rate of $245 for a 40-hour week. This was created in 1991 when the then Minister of Social Welfare, Jenny Shipley, ruled, with no legislation needed, that turning down two job offers $15 or more above the level of unemployment benefit would result in a stand-down period of six months from the benefit; 16- and 17-year-olds lack even this level of protection. In 1994 it was announced that a minimum wage slightly above the $136 level, at 60 per cent of the adult rate, or $147 for a 40-hour week, would be introduced for those under 20. This is probably better than nothing, although comparatively few full-time workers are paid less than this. Those against any minimum are unhappy with the move, while others think it is at too low a level and should be graduated with age. There are also fears of wages levelling down towards this level.

For the growing proportion of workers who are part time, casualised and/or homeworkers, a minimum floor of conditions may be even more crucial than it is for full-time employees, although for such groups legislative requirements are even harder to enforce. The contracting-out of large areas of work has eroded the distinction between employee and self-employed. Only employees or those on contracts of service are covered by most labour legislation, including the EPA. Those who are not actually employees but are on contracts for services have no such protections, so there is an incentive for employers to transfer work to this group. The coincidence of these trends is eroding the simple picture of a labour force with one person, one job, and instead producing a kaleidoscope in which individuals may need several sources of work to survive, moving in and out of a number of them in a comparatively short time. The picture of the labour force produced by surveys based on old definitions is therefore becoming increasingly misleading and our knowledge of what is happening somewhat limited.

Genuine equality of opportunity also requires family-friendly workplaces, with improved domestic and (preferably partly paid) parental leave, as well as a major boost to childcare funding and facilities. These are some of the ways of enabling paid and unpaid work to be combined more easily, by men as well as women, thus reducing the double burden effect on women. Self-employment is another growth area in which women are under-represented but increasing their presence rapidly. With many small businesses being only of short duration and the current growth propelled partly by the shortage of employment opportunities, it is not the solution for all or most of those seeking financially rewarding work. However, it is an empowering option for many, and one in which women may be able to implement feminist principles.

Many of the measures and areas discussed could benefit most men as well as women. Many men are seeking to drop out of the management rat-race, and find trends towards greater teamwork and sharing of responsibility just as satisfying as many women and Maori and Pacific Islanders do. The situation of over-employment for some and unemployment or under-employment for many others is absurdly unbalanced. Over-employment, at a rate of 60 work-hours a week or more, is made possible only by the unpaid work of other family members. Over-employment is partly a phenomenon of those who are highly placed in hierarchies, but it may also be needed to make ends meet for people on low pay with a number of dependants. For the latter group, higher basic pay and/or state support is needed. For the former group, family-friendly philosophies of work would attack over-employment as being unnecessary, undesirable, unfair to dependants and partners, and discriminating against those groups unable or unwilling to avoid unpaid caring commitments.

Finally, many of the measures and areas discussed would also benefit other groups currently disadvantaged in the labour force, as well as women, and particularly women from those groups. For example, occupational segregation by race/ethnicity is every bit as pervasive and discriminatory as occupational segregation by gender. Equal opportunity policies are thus critical for Maori, Pacific Islanders and all ethnic minorities as well as others, including those with disabilities, lesbians and gay men, and younger and older workers. Protection against discrimination in employment has recently been extended to the last three groups, but many equal opportunity policies are confined to gender, ethnicity and disability issues.

Part III

A Modest Safety Net?
Women, the State
and Social Policy

7
The State, Income Maintenance and Economic Independence for Women

The state has a key role in setting the frameworks which help determine economic and social possibilities and outcomes. As argued in Part I, many feminists think it essential for government to have a continuing leading role in helping all New Zealanders achieve social well-being, including a standard of living sufficient for participation and fulfilment in the community.

This was a major message of the 1988 report of the Royal Commission on Social Policy, which was sadly neglected and mocked. Some of the criticisms of the report were valid. For example, it was difficult to find the major threads of argument, and the costing was incomplete. However, the main reason for its neglect was that it was out of tune with government thinking. Yet the report's main message is still endorsed by many New Zealanders. The economic and social ills arising from unemployment and increasing inequality, together with concern about the changes to the health and education systems, were major issues in the 1993 general election. They contributed to the lower share of total votes gained by the National Party, the increasing spread of voting and, with general disillusion with the political system, to the switch to MMP.

The role of the state: alternative views on fairness, equity and justice

The Royal Commission on Social Policy clearly recognised power differences and structural inequalities in the community, with Maori and women particularly disadvantaged. The objectives of social policy in the light of these realities were argued to require tax/income maintenance policies and income redistribution involving more than a simple safety-net attitude to payment of benefits. While individual and group aspirations and responsibility were recognised (in the latter area particularly in the Maori community), equity objectives were seen to require strong state leadership, with continued funding and provision of services in key areas.

The royal commission's discussions of basic concepts are still useful in discussing principles of social policy. It identified two key areas: development of a coherent approach to clarifying the goals, values and principles underlying New Zealand society, present and future, and recognition of the basic nature of the Maori dimension and its implications for social policy.

In the first area, four conclusions were reached by Maxine Barrett's background paper (1988) and endorsed by the commission:

1. All participants in current debates appear to accept that advances made in individual and collective well-being in this century have resulted from the recognition that the responsibility for basic needs in modern industrial societies must be collective rather than an individual matter.
2. Social policy, embracing interventions concerned with promotion of the well-being of the individual and of society as a whole, gives rise to rights which every New Zealander can claim.
3. Well-being is concerned not so much with the treatment of problems or problem people as with identifying their causes in institutions and social structures, and with attacking the problems at their presumed sources.
4. A rights-based approach to social policy recognises that there are claims all human beings ought to be able to make. It follows that taxing all members of the community to finance this entitlement to the basic requirements for well-being cannot be considered coercion. It is simply the requirement to meet an obligation that all have by virtue of being members of the community.

However, the commission admitted that the agreement asserted to exist on the first point may be somewhat illusory. Supporters of the view that the role of the state should be a minimal one see group responsibility only in terms of a safety net for the 'deserving disadvantaged' who are unable to support themselves via market and family support. Others locate disadvantage in a life cycle and structural setting, and thus support the other three principles.

Morris and Batten (1988), in a background paper for the commission, outlined four standard models of the role of the state within the context of a western, mixed-economy society. These are what they term the minimal, instrumentalist, just, and maximal or ethical views of the state, which they associate respectively with the names of Nozick, Hayek, Rawls and Hegel. Endorsement of the four principles outlined above places the royal commission well towards the maximalist end of the spectrum, in contrast to Treasury and other government advisers. For example, the 'taxation as coercion' view rejected by the royal commission has frequently been affirmed by Alan Gibbs, who has been appointed to many key government advisory bodies and positions.

Treasury writing is less outspoken, but *Government Management* states that 'it seems likely that an appropriate role for the state in many areas is to define a clear set of rights for people and to permit individuals to voluntarily transact between one another in order to pursue their own wellbeing' (New Zealand Treasury, 1987: 124). This conclusion was based on individuals being best judges of their own self-interest and particular needs and valuations, and the inability of agencies to predict outcomes. Admittedly, its view is softened by references to inequalities of opportunity and outcome, and a lack of equity in initial allocations and in processes. However, the overall tone of Treasury argument is of the minimalist or, at most, instrumentalist tradition.

Marilyn Waring's critique of all these four models, developed by northern hemisphere men and ignoring sexism, racism and ageism, has been discussed earlier. There is a need for more locally based feminist analyses of women and social policy, and for more women as decision-makers in systems where they form the majority of both consumers and providers. Otherwise feminist values, goals and understandings of institutional sexism and racism will be missing from the policy process (Fenwick, 1988). The opportunity provided by the royal commission was taken for feminist analysis, but a large and fair role in decision-making is further away. The input of women in general and Maori women in particular, many of them feminists, to the deliberations of the commission, as members, staff and producers of submissions, was proportionately far more substantial than in the past or relative to their power in policy-making. It is somewhat sad and not coincidental that the report admirably reflects that change in perspective, but that it was neglected.

What position on fairness or equity follows from the royal commission's endorsement of the principles outlined above? It argues in general terms that a fair and just society 'is one which allows people to have a voice in their future, choice in their lives and a sense of belonging that affirms their dignity and identity' (Royal Commission on Social Policy, 1988: II, 12). Giving specificity to the aim of the maintenance for all of a standard of living sufficient for participation and belonging is more difficult.

The royal commission argued that benefit levels should not be eroded. However, it was less clear about the degree of income redistribution which is desirable. Equity or fairness gives little guidance on the particular level of equality or inequality which is acceptable: 'The distribution of the wealth and resources of the nation must be fair. It need not be equal so long as the inequalities are such as can be justified in a fair society' (*ibid.*: 14). Equity is defined as 'the distribution of resources in accordance with prevailing conceptions of fairness and social justice' (*ibid.*: 792): in practice, 'prevailing conceptions' means falling back onto government assessment, which politicians can, dubiously, claim to be justified through the political process. However, the commission pointed out the high degree of support for most income maintenance policies revealed in its survey of public opinion.

The royal commission also discussed the concept of justice. Again Barrett's paper, which takes account of how women's positions and concerns may differ from men's, is a good starting-point. Justice is defined as to each according to his or her due – but due can be assessed in accordance with rights, deserts or needs. Deserts, if regarded as a reward for skill and effort, will be seen by free-market advocates as best determined by competition in that context. However, Barrett points out that rewards are only partly the result of personal qualities and effort. The results obtained by individual men are dependent also on external circumstances, the efforts of others in an interdependent modern economy and the contribution of the largely unrecognised and unrewarded domestic labour, usually of a spouse. Rewards according only to exchange value omit all domestic and voluntary work. In addition she points out that 'a realistic view of modern society suggests that what in fact determines success in a competitive market is less likely to be due to those features of a person which have some claim to be morally significant, including ability or effort, but rather initial social status, race, gender or sheer luck' (Barrett, 1988: 53).

The selfish motives which are both assumed and rewarded in economic theory and models are not universally regarded as morally praiseworthy. A possible exception is self-reliance. Inevitably the balance between self-reliance, family and whanau, community and iwi interdependence, and voluntary organisation and state responsibility is a matter of degree. So is the extent of state provision in areas such as health, education and housing.

Income maintenance alone is not sufficient for accessibility of essential services. Funding in co-operation with community agencies is appropriate in some areas and direct provision essential in others.

Government's prompt response to the 1988 Picot report on the governance of schools was a telling contrast to its reaction to the royal commission. Devolution of power and responsibilities is an area discussed in both reports, and more simplistically in the one accepted for implementation. There are weighty arguments for devolution, particularly to Maori authorities, and for greater community involvement in decision-making, particularly if accompanied by the provision of adequate resources. However, there are also problems for feminists in decentralisation and the elimination of standardised practices when those in decision-making positions are likely to be mainly white, middle-class men. In addition, if adequate resources are not provided, community provision can simply mean additional unpaid work by women. Paradoxically, despite efforts to measure voluntary and unpaid work with a view to greater recognition of its extent, value and the predominant input of women, current trends may serve only to extend it, rather than sharing it more equally or giving it the economic recognition which it deserves.

Individual, household, family, and community responsibility: units of assessment

The perspective of 'individuals in relation', discussed earlier, can be seen as requiring joint responsibility which ripples outwards from individuals to the whole community in a variety of areas, particularly the upbringing of the next generation. Hence the Royal Commission on Social Policy saw a role for tax-based support of children, including maintenance of a universal element. Its rationale included the recognition of a community responsibility for children, of the valuable caring work involved, and of the costs of raising children to which society in general and those without children in particular should contribute. If only a minority could afford to have children, the community would shrink and become unbalanced. In addition, family benefit was an independent source of income for women and for some their only such source.

In fact the small universal element of family benefit was abolished in 1990. It had been only $6 per week per child, and at abolition would have needed to be about $25 to maintain its original value. This is one of several reductions of entitlement, tighter targeting of benefits and other changes, including more rigorous stand-down periods, which cut government expenditure. Motivated also by a return to the rhetoric of self-reliance, these reductions imply a swing back to individual and family responsibility, and a reduced partnership with the community. Other policy elements are portrayed as helping the partnership, but are at least partly intended to be cost saving and behaviour changing. For example, the new 'parents as first teachers' programme is intended to promote and provide parent education. While this may be worthwhile, there is some suspicion that it is closely linked with a more punitive approach to parental adequacy. The revamped child support scheme is geared mainly at fiscal savings rather than better support for the custodial parent.

The targeted family support to low-income earners and beneficiaries is not particularly generous, so that even for these groups community responsibility is limited. Until late 1993 it was at the rate of $36 per week for the first child and others over 16. The rate was $16 for subsequent children, available in full from 1990–91 where family income was less than $17,500, abating at the relatively low rate of 18 cents in the dollar up to $27,000 and then at 30 cents. The $6 universal child benefit was additional until its abolition, and then added in for those families eligible. The level of payment was not increased from its introduction in October 1986 until October 1993, when the ongoing rate of $42 for the first child was supplemented by a rate of $35 for additional children over 13 and $24 for those under 13. While involving an increase for second and later children under 16, the change is in fact a decrease of $7 per week for second children over 16. Family assistance is one area where levels are higher in Australia than New Zealand, and they are also price indexed in the former. In both countries, direct payments to the mother are seen by women as crucial for ensuring a degree of intra-family equity and independence.

The low level of community support for childcare outside the household, compared with the situation in most European countries, is another aspect of the emphasis on individual responsibility. While per-child subsidies to approved childcare centres increased during the 1980s, the required fee levels are still too high for families in which both parents are in low-paid employment. The other area of government support, a payment to parents using such childcare for up to 30 hours per week, is sharply income targeted. This means that many parents have to use less expensive family or informal care options, or take jobs with little overlap of hours, so that their time together is limited. The parent subsidy was also restricted late in 1993 at the maximum 30-hour level to parents in paid work or approved training. Others, including voluntary workers and beneficiaries likely to meet the income tests, can now receive support only for up to nine hours of such care per week, on the argument that they are available to care for the child themselves.

This seems somewhat counter to the requirement that those among this group receiving unemployment benefit should be actively seeking work. In addition, childcare providers argue that pre-school formal care should be available to all children for the educational and social experience it provides. In response to disquiet about the change, the new Minister of Social Welfare announced in January 1994 a relaxation to the policy so that 30 hours would be available to those who meet the income test but not the work/training requirement, where the child concerned had a disability. This small improvement did not satisfy critics. The overall policy is being reviewed.

A number of other aspects of policies aimed at lowering government expenditure, combined with demographic changes such as New Zealand's ageing society, effectively increase the responsibilities of women in the household and community. There is increasing community responsibility for groups who were previously often institutionalised. However desirable this might be when adequate resources are made available, it implies that female relatives are often responsible for the care of young or old dependants for a large proportion of their lives. Financial pressures on lower-income families disproportionately affect women as the main day-to-day managers of the household budget.

The 'individuals in relation' approach is argued by Nelson (1991) to imply that the marriage licence should be of no relevance. Instead, all situations of economic dependency should be treated alike, where self-support is impossible. This raises practical demarcation issues, but is valuable as a principle. It also recognises the inequity of any regulation that suggests that women should be economically dependent on a male partner rather than having the opportunity for economic independence.

The assumption or requirement of adult financial dependency, which applies to de facto and marital relationships only, can be argued to violate this principle. Eligibility for unemployment, sickness and disability benefits is based on the individual qualifying in the relevant category, but the rate of benefit paid (if any) is based on the couple's income. This system means that the income available to a two-earner household declines sharply if either loses their job. It may be even more inappropriate in many Maori living situations than in Pakeha ones. The Royal Commission on Social Policy recommended that the basis for benefit entitlement should move in the direction of individual entitlement in two-adult families. Recognising the sharp increase in expenditure which would arise if this change was introduced immediately, proposals were made for interim steps, with the invalids' benefit being the first for its introduction. These proposals have not been followed.

The Australian social security system was also reviewed in the second half of the 1980s. This review, too, discussed the unit of assessment. It rejected individual entitlement as too expensive, but suggested ways of avoiding the assumption of spousal dependence and lack of incentive for the (usually female) spouse of an unemployment beneficiary to be in paid work. In 1986 women with unemployed husbands had an unemployment rate of 51 per cent, as against 5.5 per cent for all wives, while the participation rate of this group of women was 31 per cent, compared with 48 per cent for all married women (Cass, 1988a: 231). As in New Zealand, the deterrent arises from high replacement ratios and effective marginal tax rates. These result from stringent joint-income tests with low free areas (amounts that can be earned before the benefit begins to be reduced) and rapid abatement, and from the low incomes which most women in this situation would earn in the labour force.

The Australian review suggested a number of means of ameliorating the disincentives and lack of financial benefit from paid work for spouses of beneficiaries. These included extending the application of the more generous free-area provisions for pensions to benefits, and granting additional flexibility for casual work by allowing the accumulation of credit for unused fortnightly free areas. These recommendations were well received among women's groups making submissions on the issues paper: a strong theme was the need to remove disincentives for women to enter the workforce. There is still a dependent spouse tax rebate in Australia, unlike New Zealand. While the review did not recommend its abolition, many submissions to the 1989 Women's Tax Convention did so, seeing as inappropriate its emphasis on dependence, its disincentive effects and its payment to the paid worker, almost always the male.

Income maintenance and taxation – some issues and gender implications

Both the Australian and New Zealand social security systems incorporate a categorical approach to entitlement for payments, with categories established on the basis of need related to inability to participate fully in the paid labour force owing to family circumstances or other factors. There have been suggestions that the system common in Europe of contributory social insurance might be introduced in New Zealand. It permits benefits at a higher level, since the individual has paid directly towards the payment. However, it is likely that this would mean a net increase in total tax payments for low-income earners when such families can hardly manage at present, even though there would be some compensating reduction in government expenditure. It would also carry over inequality of earnings into the situation where households are similarly placed with respect to needs but are entitled to different payments. There is, of course, an element of social insurance in New Zealand, in the shape of the employee levy which part-funds the accident compensation scheme. This is payable as a proportion of earnings and entitles accident victims to 80 per cent of previous earnings when incapacitated.

Neither the New Zealand nor Australian review of policy suggested altering the categorical approach, although both suggested improvements to the work tests, abatement procedures and other distinctions between benefits, including raising the single rate of unemployment benefit to equal that of other categories. This has not occurred in New Zealand. The director of the Australian Social Security Review, Bettina Cass, saw some advantages in a basic income approach (Cass, 1988b). Such a scheme guarantees an income to all adult citizens, clawed back through the tax system for those on higher incomes. However, apart from the potentially very high cost, the scheme might entrench a section of the population into an underclass without the linkages between income support arrangements and labour market programmes which a well-designed categorical system should promote. Such a scheme should use the categories, Cass argues, to provide the various purpose-built types of programmes which will promote independence for each group. This would be along the lines of Swedish labour market organisation, and should promote higher employment.

A generic benefit system, giving uniformity in terms of provisions such as residency requirements, stand-down periods and income levels, has considerable appeal. The greater stigma which may attach to some types of benefit might be reduced. However, variations in whether and when workforce participation can be expected are justified for different groups such as solo parents, those on invalid benefits, and young and older unemployed, with the consequent need for different work or useful activity tests and different types of assistance towards rejoining the labour market. Hence, to be fair and efficient, a nominally uniform system must allow for these differences.

Levels of benefits

The adequacy or otherwise of benefits is regularly a controversial issue. The requirement that all New Zealanders should belong and participate in society implies defining poverty and benefit levels in relative rather than absolute terms, as mentioned in Part I. It is not sufficient that minimum needs – for example, for shelter and food – are met, but rather that everyone, including low-wage earners and beneficiaries, should share in rising living standards, and by extension share sacrifices if real income is falling. In assessing the extent of poverty, different household structures, different levels of assets and regional variations in costs of living are relevant in addition to income. Attempts to assess the number of people in poverty are dependent on establishing a poverty line (minimum desirable income) for each household structure, using the absolute or relative approach, or subjective methods. Poverty rates can then be established for different types of household, along with poverty gaps which indicate how far below the poverty line households fall, and what total extra amount of income would be needed to eliminate poverty. There is a case for using a minimum necessary expenditure rather than income as the basis for a poverty line, since changes to targeted non-cash benefits are more easily handled.

A good survey of issues involved in measuring poverty concludes that any measure is value-laden, since poverty is partly a subjective concept (Stephens, 1988). However, it suggests that New Zealand should develop a poverty line independent of the current benefit level, since one of its major uses is to assess the adequacy of benefit payments. Such a poverty line should at most be quasi-official to ensure such independence. Bob Stephens suggests that it needs to be supplemented by more complex surveys to assess adequacy of living standards overall. He is one of a team now developing poverty lines.

One New Zealand study uses seven different measures of income adequacy, recognising that income is not a complete measure of poverty (Brashares, 1993). The three absolute measures used are based on the low-cost Otago University food plan mentioned in Part I. The food expenditure allowed is grossed up by a multiplier to give a total expenditure figure, which is then regarded as the minimum income needed. Three different multipliers are used – three, four and five – in recognition of the fact that the desirable relationship of food expenditure to total expenditure is controversial. The four relative measures are based on the ratio of benefits to average earnings and incomes. The results indicate that between $12,500 and $15,000 would have been needed in 1988–89 by two-adult, two-children households. This income band excludes the lowest and highest amounts, regarded as unrealistic. Brashares concludes that the social welfare system has been relatively successful at ensuring adequate incomes. However, Stephens disagrees, suggesting that food expenditure multiplied by five is the minimum needed. He also considers that the normal rather than the low-cost food plan is required, and thus obtains higher poverty rates (Stephens, 1992).

Issues relating to intra-household distribution make difficult the assessment of adequacy of standards of living of dependent adults in multi-adult households and of children in all households. It is clear that for the household as a whole, solo-parent families, most of which are women-headed, are below the poverty line to a much greater extent than any other group in New Zealand, as in Australia, Great Britain and the United States. Family and/or child support policies are less generous in the English-speaking world than in most European countries. In Australia and New Zealand the proportion of those in poverty who are solo and low-income parents and their children has risen, as has the proportion of those groups who are in poverty, with some reduction of poverty among the elderly (Stephens, 1987: 24–37).

The Royal Commission on Social Policy was firm in its view that levels of base benefits relative to other incomes should not be eroded. Married benefit rates were then at about half the level of average weekly earnings. The arguments, discussed earlier, that benefit rates might be too high relative to wages – that is, that 'replacement rates', the ratio of after-tax benefit to after-tax earnings, were too large to provide an incentive for beneficiaries to seek paid work – were rejected. Treasury research indicated that only about 5 per cent of the workforce would have a replacement rate above 70 per cent, so that overlap between household incomes when on wages rather than benefits is rare. Deliberate choice of the benefit option because of this is likely to be even rarer, although a subject for strident headlines. Reducing benefits because of this issue was argued by the royal commission to be misguided. Of the two incentive issues relating benefits to workforce rewards, the high effective marginal rates which arise from abatement of targeted benefits is a far more serious deterrent and problem than the absolute levels of benefit relative to wages.

In New Zealand in 1987, the pre-tax married couple basic benefit rate was 51.9 per cent of average weekly earnings, as against 46.4 per cent in Australia (*ibid*.: 18). This inter-country comparison widens when post-tax relativities are used, since the New Zealand tax rate on average earnings was 23.5 per cent in 1987, against 19.7 per cent in Australia. The resulting post-tax benefit/earnings relativities are 67.8 per cent in New Zealand (71.2 per cent allowing for the post-GST benefit adjustment) and 57.5 per cent in Australia (*ibid*.: 19–20). It should be noted that while benefits in both countries are taxable, there is no tax-free allowance in New Zealand, whereas in Australia those with benefit income only pay no tax. However, Australian average incomes are higher, and more benefits in kind are available, so the comparative advantage of beneficiaries in New Zealand is exaggerated by these comparisons, especially after the 1991 benefit cuts.

The indexing system for benefits was changed in New Zealand in 1989 in a manner which was cost saving. The royal commission proposed that indexation be changed from a price basis to an after-tax wage basis, in line with its views on sharing of living standards, but a mixed system has been adopted. Adjustment by the consumer price index had led to the benefit becoming an increasing proportion of average earnings, owing to falling real incomes. Between 1975 and 1986, the married couple basic benefit had risen from 65 per cent of the net average ordinary time weekly wage to 77.5 per cent. The new system constrained that ratio to within a floor of 65 per cent and a ceiling of 72.5 per cent, with price adjustment within those limits. Since then the relativity of benefits has fallen, with actual cuts and no adjustments in some years reducing their purchasing power relative to earnings.

Other cost-saving measures recommended by the royal commission were implemented, even though its cost-incurring suggestions were not. One such change meant that widows and domestic purpose beneficiaries no longer retain entitlement to the benefit once they cease to have the care of dependent children. Given the aims of the domestic purposes benefit, this seems reasonable, with women in this category encouraged to join or rejoin the paid workforce or, if this is impossible, to move to another benefit, normally unemployment. However, many women in this group have had little previous experience in the labour force, while labour-market conditions remain unfavourable and suitable training is not always available. In addition, greater stigma and a more stringent work test for the unemployment benefit, at least compared to the widows' benefit, means that the change is not as innocent as it appears at first sight.

Another suggestion of the royal commission was the replacement of the single/married rate distinction for benefits by a standard individual rate at half the couple rate, combined with a living-alone allowance of an extra 20 per cent. Since the main justification for the individual payment being higher than half the couple payment is that of increased costs owing to lack of economies of scale from joint living arrangements, this appears reasonable. Some have even argued against a living-alone allowance on the basis that while it increases costs, choosing to live alone is a costly consumption decision like any other. However, some people, including many elderly women, have no viable alternative. These changes were not in fact made.

Another major issue in income maintenance systems is that of universally available benefits against targeting. In addition to the specific arguments for some universal element in child support mentioned earlier, the royal commission cited a more general rationale in recommending a non-income-tested element of national superannuation at age 68. This is the notion of social cohesion, with the likelihood that taxation to allow income transfers will command greater support if some parts of the system are universal, so that most people will gain at various points in their life cycle. A rights-based approach to income support also implies a degree of universality. In addition, too heavy an emphasis on targeting can lock households into the benefit system and a cycle of poverty through abatement regimes which make re-entry to the labour force not worthwhile.

However, fiscal constraints and support for individual responsibility wherever possible demand a balance between universality and selectivity in income-maintenance policies. This is particularly so in the workforce age groups at which the need for income support is usually temporary. Income targeting, in theory at least, allows greater support to those most in need. Clearly, arguments over universality against targeting cannot be resolved independently of the total sums to be allocated and of priorities within them, and the desirable balance will be a regular matter for debate.

Flattening of income tax rates

Both the December 1987 and February 1988 economic packages (the latter cancelling some elements of the former) included substantial flattening of the personal income-tax schedule. This meant a much reduced degree of progressivity and a sharp reduction in top rates. The earlier announcement foreshadowed a totally flat rate of taxation which did not proceed. Reduced scope and fewer incentives for evasion and avoidance were among the arguments used by proponents of the package. The changes involved a widening of the tax base by reduction or removal of many deductions, rebates and other ways of avoiding tax, and considerable decreases in marginal rates on higher incomes. The former increases the tax take and the latter reduces it. Thus, pursuing both together helps balance the budget, unlike simply reducing rates, while the conjunction is more politically acceptable to higher-income groups than widening the base without reducing rates.

Those favouring greater redistribution might, of course, prefer to have seen the base widened and a capital gains or wealth tax introduced without rate reductions. This would yield higher levels of government revenue, permitting greater public expenditure and improvements in universal services. However, such a view runs counter to the conventional wisdom that taxation and government expenditure are too high – wisdom that often seems to ignore the services provided and needs met.

Income tax rates are now 24 per cent up to $30,875 and 33 per cent on income above that level (compared with 15 per cent to $9,500, 30 per cent from $9,501 to $30,000 and 48 per cent above $30,000 prior to 1 October 1988). However, a low income earner rebate means that rates are in reality 15 per cent to $9,500, 28 per cent from this figure to $30,875 and 33 per cent on higher levels of income. This was designed so that those eligible for the rebate pay the same tax as before. However, the benefit of the lower tax rates rises rapidly with increasing incomes, primarily men's. The top company tax rate was reduced to 28 per cent, later adjusted to 33 per cent at higher profit levels.

Incentives to work, as well as to save, invest and innovate, are additional arguments used in support of reductions in marginal tax rates, so that the individual keeps more of every extra dollar earned. However, evidence that low tax rates are necessary at high income levels to encourage effort is sparse. Instead, high-income earners or self-employed people may have a target after-tax income and if the marginal rate is lowered so that this target is reached with less effort they may in fact increase their leisure rather than their work. Motives other than money, including power and job satisfaction, are also relevant. In fact, it is more important to have low marginal tax rates on lower incomes, since it is for this group – primarily women – that the effective tax rate is above the stated rate.

The belief that low company tax rates and low individual rates at high incomes will act as an incentive for the creation of new ventures with employment potential is inspired more by hope and a desired ideological direction than derived from theory or empirical observation. The resumption of positive, though slow, growth since 1992 has been largely export led, with only low levels of job creation, so that unemployment forecasts remain high. Even with about 4 per cent growth in national income, the likely job creation will absorb only the natural growth in the workforce and have little impact on current unemployment.

The fundamental argument for progressive rates of taxation is that those with higher incomes have a greater ability to pay while still maintaining an adequate standard of living. Furthermore, this ability to pay can be argued to increase more than proportionately with income level. Total consensus on what needs are basic, what are necessities and what are luxuries is not essential for agreement that discretionary income will increase rapidly for incomes above those devoted entirely to paying for minimum needs. While ability to pay will be affected by a number of factors in addition to income level, such as household structure, lifecycle stage and permanence of the income level, income is still crucial.

The gradual flattening of tax rates and reduction in the take from direct taxation was accompanied by an increase in the share of indirect tax from 22.5 per cent to 33.2 per cent of government income between 1985–86 and 1987–88 (Snively, 1988: 15), largely as a result of the introduction of GST. The increase in its rate of levy from 10 per cent of all expenditures to 12.5 per cent in 1988 further shifted the burden from direct to indirect taxation. GST is a regressive tax, which takes a larger proportion of the income of those at lower levels who have less opportunity to save than those higher up the scale. While income tax remains progressive, it is much less so than it was before the reductions in top rates. With this sharply reduced progression in the tax system, most of the redistributive role of government comes from income maintenance and family support, which are set at too low a level to perform this role adequately.

The result of tax changes, benefit cuts and widening differentials in earnings is that inequality has increased and disposable real incomes have fallen on average for lower-income groups through the 1980s and early 90s. Inevitably, unemployment, widening differentials and government expenditure cuts hit ethnic minorities, women and lower socio-economic groups the hardest.

Assessing differential gender impacts of policies and systems

It was argued in Part I that greater efforts need to be made by economists and policy-makers to identify gender and other specific effects of particular policies. With respect to taxation and social welfare expenditure, it is possible to identify proportions paid by and to broad groups. This is not to say that it is desirable that every group should receive from the tax/benefit system what it pays in. Redistribution from those with greater ability to pay towards those with lesser ability to pay is the major aim of the transfer system.

Even without subscribing to the notion that the balance sheet should equilibrate, it is worth examining differential impacts of tax and benefits overall, or in particular areas. This applies particularly to groups who are disadvantaged, perhaps even discriminated against, in economic and social systems, such as Maori or women. Maori may be disadvantaged in superannuation policies, for example, because of their shorter life expectancy. Policies which convey some advantage to particular groups, such as affirmative action to compensate for past discrimination, can readily be justified but frequently arouse uninformed adverse comment.

Similar to the resistance to affirmative action is a concern about the supposed concentration on aspects of women's health at the expense of men's as a result of such factors as the Cartwright inquiry into the National Women's Hospital and pressure from women's health groups. Examples given in the media have been the failure to target prostate cancer, compared with government expenditure on cervical and breast cancer prevention and screening programmes. However, this ignores evidence about relative effectiveness. It also concentrates on the area of prevention, ignoring the more expensive, high-technology interventions, including heart transplants and bypasses, in which men are disproportionately represented. Work is needed on developing further the methodology and practice of impact assessment by gender and other important profile variables. A preliminary attempt of this type, with respect to the accident compensation scheme, is undertaken next.

Accident compensation: a case study

The earnings-related nature of payments under the accident compensation scheme results in greater average payments to men than women, owing to the lower labour force participation and average earnings of the latter. This is exacerbated by gender differences in patterns for both work and non-work accidents. In one recent full year (1988–89) the proportion of claims made by women was 29 per cent, while their share of compensation was only 22.5 per cent. For work-related accidents, these proportions were 19.8 and 16.6 per cent; for motor vehicle accidents 29.7 and 22.5 per cent; for sports accidents 24.0 and 18.5 per cent; and even for home accidents 46.3 and 37.2 per cent. All non-work accidents gave rise to claims totalling $264.4 million, with men receiving 72.5 per cent of the compensation for 69 per cent of the accidents.

Five sports accounted for half the expenditure on sports injuries. Four of these – rugby, rugby league, soccer and cricket – are overwhelmingly male dominated, while netball, the only predominantly female sport of the five, accounted for just 10 per cent of the payments total for the five, against rugby's 55 per cent. It is worth noting that despite the shift to a predominantly insurance-based approach to the scheme, sports clubs are still not part of its payment base, although there are measurable and in some cases avoidable risks, and great risk variability among sports and between sporting and other activities. One might wonder whether the difficulties have been exaggerated in the context of political risk in an area dear to many New Zealanders.

One reason for the lower access of women to ACC payments is the lack of entitlement for loss of potential earnings for partnered women with permanent disabilities. This contrasts with the expectation, in changes made in 1991, that women will re-enter the labour force if under 45 at the time of the spouse's accident. Ongoing dependence on a spouse is expected in the first case, since compensation for forgone earnings is not forthcoming, whereas actual compensation is withdrawn in the second. Both assist the balance sheet of the scheme, but are based on contrasting assumptions and expectations about the labour market behaviour of women, to their disadvantage.

The relative payments towards the scheme by women and men are not published and, given that it is partly financed by general taxation, hard to estimate. It is not therefore possible to say whether women as a group contribute more than they receive. Since women's average labour force participation and earnings, and hence tax liability, are still below those of men, their contributions to ACC from this source, as well as their payout, will be less than those of men. However, several of the 1991 changes to the scheme reduce women's share of the payout even further. Both equity and incentive rationales were given for the change to a more insurance-based scheme, with employers bearing only the costs of work-related accidents.

For women, however, the move may be to less rather than greater equity. For example, the abolition of lump-sum payments and payments for pain and suffering, including those arising from sexual abuse, skews further the proportion of compensation payable in favour of men. Similarly, the tightening of the definition of medical misadventure, including exclusion of wrong diagnosis, failure to give treatment, and injuries resulting from drug or clinical trials, disproportionately affects women. The criteria for rarity of occurrence and severity of consequences (causing at least 15 per cent permanent impairment) exclude a number of gynaecological medical misadventures previously covered. The large number of cuts to entitlement and anomalies revealed as the changes have become effective have led to public disquiet and a review of the regulations.

The extent of redistribution

Moving from accident compensation to the tax and income maintenance systems generally, how much can be said about their overall gender implications? Certainly these systems redistribute purchasing power towards lower-income groups, among which women are over-represented relative to their population numbers. With women's greater longevity, they also receive more than half of total national superannuation payments. Redistribution is vital to those with few other resources, and benefit levels are important factors in the level of poverty and its distribution by household type. However, the overall degree of inequality of incomes or living standards is more dependent on the extent of differentials in pre-tax labour market earnings and other market income, including interest, dividends and rents. Modification of these differentials by the redistributive effects of government revenue and expenditure is substantial, but still leaves wide inequalities.

For example, in 1987–88 the top 20 per cent of households by income had command of 47.2 per cent of market income, reduced to 34.3 per cent after allowing for taxation, benefits and the remainder of government expenditure. By contrast, the lowest 20 per cent had 0.4 per cent of market income, increased to 9.9 per cent by government activity. (Snively, 1988, and New Zealand Planning Council Group, 1990, from which these figures are taken, have detailed analyses of the effects of government activity on inequality of income levels and between types of household, and the relative roles of the tax and income maintenance systems in the 1980s.) The overall impact of tax changes and benefit cuts since the mid 1980s has been to widen the degree of inequality, with beneficiary and low-income-earner households losing relatively more than higher-income households (Sunday Forum, 1991).

Allowing not only for direct income maintenance payments but also for government-provided or subsidised services, such as health and education, the top 50 per cent of households by income consumed about that same proportion of government expenditure. They were, however, liable for nearly 75 per cent of the tax bill. Thus it was the tax payment or government revenue side which had the greater impact on raising the disposable income of lower-income groups relative to those on higher incomes. Lower-income households received in total only a very slightly higher fraction of total government expenditure than their numerical proportion in the population. This perhaps surprising fact is explained by the counterbalancing effects of social security benefits, exhibiting the expected progressivity through being targeted mainly to lower-income groups, and other government expenditure, particularly on education, giving greater benefits to higher-income groups. These facts are not well known and, given the negative attitudes of some of the better-off to social welfare expenditure, need wider recognition.

Thus the tax system rather than the expenditure side has been more important in redistribution up to the mid 1980s. However, even redistribution through the tax system has reduced recently, since lower-income groups paid a gradually increasing share of taxes through the 1980s and 1990s. They also received a somewhat increased share of expenditure.

Three major factors account for these trends. On the expenditure side, the main one is the greater degree of targeting of benefit expenditure to lower-income groups away from universal entitlement. On the income side, the change is the result of the flattening of income-tax scales and the shift to regressive indirect tax away from progressive tax. The proportion of the burden of tax falling on low-income groups will have increased even further since 1987–88 with the GST increase and full impact of personal tax cuts. Overall, less redistribution is occurring, with inequality increasing both in market earnings and in final income, and obvious results in increased hardship for beneficiary and other low-income groups.

The studies of redistribution also identify ten household types based on numbers of adults, their ages and numbers of dependent children. Average incomes for these household types before and after allowing for tax and government expenditure show the general impact of redistribution on the groups. The most significant change during the 1980s was the increased average income for two-adult, national superannuation households with the improved national superannuation scheme. Together with above-average use of health services, this took their share of income to slightly above their population share, with adjusted income well above market income. By contrast, in the mid 1980s, redistribution was, as expected, away from younger households with no dependants. Two-adult, non-superannuitant households without children comprised 11.9 per cent of the population and 17.2 per cent of all households, and received 19.4 per cent of market income and 15.7 per cent of adjusted income.

Households with children varied in terms of the redistributive effects, both between different types and over the period studied. In all years, single-adult households with children gained through the government budget, with their position improving slightly over the period, although their share of adjusted income remained below their proportion of population and households. In 1987–88 they comprised 3.6 per cent of the population and 3.9 per cent of households, received only 0.9 per cent of market income and increased their share to 2.9 per cent of adjusted income. However, for two-adult households with children, fewer of which are primarily dependent on benefit income, redistributive effects are small and can be in either direction. Furthermore, their share of adjusted income has fallen during the 1980s to a greater extent than their share of the population.

The degree of disadvantage of women and children relative to men in overall standards of living, and the extent to which it is modified by state activity, is almost impossible to assess. Earnings, income and wealth data of varying quality are available by gender but these do not automatically translate into consumption and living standards, and there is a lack of knowledge about intra-household transfers. Nevertheless, income is the main measure available and used for likely well-being, with some attempts to modify it for numbers of dependants, the distribution of home ownership and the impact of services in kind, especially those provided by government. In some surveys, information on more specific aspects of adequacy/inadequacy have been sought, such as ability to afford sufficient food, heating, clothing and so on (Age Concern, 1990).

Clearly the income needed for a reasonable standard of living, relatively defined as above, will depend on the size and structure of the household and a number of other factors, such as location and assets, as well as whether resources are properly shared in the household. Benefit levels take account of the number of dependent children, but most attempts to construct a 'household equivalence' scale to indicate average cost levels in different types of household lead to the conclusion that current benefits fail to compensate totally for extra costs in families with more than two children.

There are a number of reasons why women may have somewhat lesser average access to material and social well-being than men. Five factors were raised in submissions to the Royal Commission on Social Policy. These were lack of recognition for unpaid work, lack of financial independence, the high cost of caring work, the difficulty of combining paid and unpaid work, and a sense of powerlessness and lack of choice in women's lives (Royal Commission on Social Policy, 1988: III/2, 192).

Women's greater responsibility for unpaid household and caring work, lower labour force participation and lower average earnings than men imply that they continue to have less direct personal access to financial resources, despite some narrowing of the gaps. They are thus still more economically dependent on the state or other people, primarily spouses, than is the case for men. While the tax system is essentially based on the individual unit, much of the income maintenance system is based on household income.

Disparities in income and wealth (although data on the latter are inadequate) between women and men in New Zealand have reduced, but remain fairly wide. The 1991 census gives the female adult median income over the previous year as $11,280, only 58.6 per cent of the male equivalent, with the mean slightly higher at 63.6 per cent. For women in full-time employment, the median increases to 67 per cent and the mean to 75 per cent (Statistics New Zealand, 1993). With regard to wealth, women's share of the total is estimated to have risen from 30.5 per cent in 1980–81 to 38 per cent in 1987–88, partly as a result of more equal sharing of property following divorce (New Zealand Planning Council, 1990). Optimism about this trend should be tempered by noting first that tax considerations have strong effects on nominal holding of property and second that 40 per cent of women's wealth, as against under 25 per cent of men's, is owned by those over 60, reflecting inheritance of spousal or joint property by longer-living wives.

Comparatively little is known about the ways in which the varied patterns of income and expenditure, and control and management of money within households and families, affect the distribution of well-being within New Zealand households. (But see Society for Research on Women, 1981; current cross-ethnic research co-ordinated by Robin McKinlay and Susie Easting should provide more up-to-date data.) British evidence suggests that only a small minority of couples had egalitarian access to resources and shared equally in their management. This was more likely to occur when wives earned as much or almost as much of the household income as their husbands (Vogler and Pahl, 1993). However, most attempts to measure impacts of policies on different groups by family type or income simply assume that observed household income is an adequate indicator of the welfare of the household, and ignore both intra-family distribution issues and non-market household production.

Economic independence for women

Each wave of feminism has challenged conventional wisdom on the role of women. An ongoing theme is the need for women, whether partnered or single, to have the opportunity for economic independence. The principle that a married woman should have a legal right to a part share, in some cases equal share, of her husband's income, on the assumption that he was the sole earner, was argued by the 1890s suffragists. The National Council of Women in 1896 passed this motion: 'That in all cases where a woman elects to superintend her own household and to be the mother of children, there shall be a law attaching a certain just share of her husband's earnings or income for her separate use, payable, if she so desired it, into her separate account' (Sheppard, 1896: 7–8).

All the arguments familiar today were used, even if the language was different. They included recognition of the opportunity costs in forgone income of being a full-time housewife and mother, the fact that unpaid work is real work and that the wife's work frees the husband to be active in the paid workforce, and the concern that many wives had to plead for adequate housekeeping allowances let alone personal money. Kate Sheppard made the case in an 1896 *White Ribbon* editorial and a paper to the National Council of Women (NCW) 1899 meeting. She argued that economic independence for women was just, and necessary for their own and their children's protection, as well as for men's protection from themselves, to improve the position of married women, and to provide them with freedom and justice as 'mothers of the race'.

Of all the NCW resolutions, this one, in Roberta Nicholls' view, frightened people most – as it still would today. It provoked adverse reaction from ministers, mayors and editors, and concentrated on Margaret Sievwright, the original author of the resolution, who replied strongly. The editor of the *Lyttelton Times* said in 1896 that 'it would mean, first of all, the degradation of woman from the position of man's equal to that of paid housekeeper. It would ... mean something a thousand times more revolting ... wives would be paid a price for exercising the sacred function of motherhood' (quoted in Nicholls, 1993: 162).

Humour, analogy and colourful language were common in the NCW arguments.

> To be maintained, however luxuriously, without earning anything over which there is undisputed control is to be, in so far, in the position of a slave. Other conditions may, indeed, be very unlike those of servitude, but such a situation presents its essential features. It will be seen that the married woman is exactly in this position, inasmuch as her work in the home does not procure her independence. She is the working partner in a firm in whose profits she has no share. Her share is only in the labour. Yet her husband imagines he is supporting her! (Caird, 1899, reprinted in Malcolm, 1989: 17)

The need for women to have adequate education and training in case they stayed single or became single through death of the spouse was also recognised. In addition, education could prevent women undertaking or staying in unsatisfactory marriages, and provide them with greater bargaining power within marriage in addition to personal fulfilment through a career. An optimistic view on bargaining power was that: 'Now, if a woman had given up a good salary in order to care for her husband's home and happiness, he would naturally feel that she had a right to half of his income' (Smith, 1893).

When neoclassical economics extended its interest to the family, it treated all women as wives and mothers. 'By implicitly generalising from married women to all women, the existence and the needs of women who are not attached to men are denied, and the norm of women's economic dependence is ideologically reinforced by both new (Mincer, Polachek) or old neoclassical economists (Marshall, Pigou, Edgeworth). One has to look hard to find references to single women, or to no-longer married women, let alone to lesbians – whom economists must never have heard of' (Pujol, 1993: 9).

Although single (other than widowed) women were often seen as an aberration, many suffragists, in addition to fighting for the rights of married women, regarded the single state as an honourable one and an appropriate choice for many. In arguing for equal pay, Jessie Mackay said: 'I do not deny, however, that marriage will be somewhat hindered by economic equality ... The old stigma on an unmarried woman has passed away ... It cannot be too often reiterated that at this stage of our development marriage is not the ordained destiny of every man, and certainly not of every woman. The minority whose duty and happiness lie elsewhere have a perfect right to live and thrive in their own way' (Mackay, 1902: 142). She argued that equal pay and opportunity would prevent women being forced into unwanted, loveless marriage or prostitution. The family wage principle, used to argue for higher pay for men on the basis that they had to support the household, ignored the fact that many men did not have dependants and many women did.

The increasing possibility of education and economic independence was essential for the many women who did not have support from men, because they were single, widowed, deserted or married to men who could not or would not support them. In addition, as envisaged by Jessie Mackay, it enabled those who did not wish to marry and were not of independent means to have other options, single and/or lesbian. This is a major reason for the emergence of a separate lesbian culture and identity (Faderman, 1991). While many women had always preferred their strongest friendships and relationships, including sexual relationships, to be with other women, only some of those from higher classes and with economic independence could previously establish lives separate from men. In turn, the emergence of lesbian politics and community, showing the possibility of independence from men, strengthened the position of heterosexual feminists attempting to change their individual roles in relationships with men and the overall gender-biased structures in society.

When single women are mentioned by economists, it is often to use their earnings to deny that discrimination is a major factor in the female–male pay gap. This is done by comparing the earnings of single men and single women, which show a much narrower gap than any comparison involving all or married men with any group of women. The implication drawn is that if married women did not drop out of the workforce (or, perhaps, were expected to take the double burden of care and thus be less available for advancement at work) they would earn as much as men. For example, in the US in 1979, the median earnings of never-married women aged 45-54 was 89 per cent of those of never-married men of the same age group, as against a ratio of 40 per cent for a similar comparison for those married (Landau, 1992: 59). However, never-married men are rare and disadvantaged, with their median earnings only two-thirds those of their married colleagues, perhaps partly because they do not have all their home needs met. The gap between married and single men is a larger factor in the striking 89/40 per cent contrast than the gap between single and married women, which in any case reduces sharply after controlling for education.

While improvements have occurred in the last 100 years in terms of property ownership and division on dissolution of marriage, the right to half the husband's or household income has not eventuated. Dependence on a spouse and/or the state is an ongoing concern for women, with access to paid work the main way of avoiding it. Such access is affected by ideology and various government policies, as discussed next.

Labour force participation of women: the impact of ideology and policy

Economic and social factors and policies combine with prevailing ideology to influence the cyclical changes which occur alongside longer-term trends. The use of women as a reserve army of labour (the 'Rosie the Riveter' phenomenon noted earlier), alongside the trend to increasing participation, is not entirely in the past. But, in addition, tax, benefit, childcare and retraining policies are designed partly for their role in providing incentives and/or constraints to women's labour force participation. As indicated earlier, a weak labour market has contributed to renewed suggestions that married women with low earning power should return full time to the home.

Partnered women

An obvious example of policies affecting participation arises from the use of the household unit for most benefits and family support, discussed above. Although recent writing in new home economics takes account of separate interests and possible conflict, the joint utility function still prevails in most policy analysis. For example, the distributional effects of tax changes are usually studied using a joint utility function, with consumption (proxied by income from paid work) and leisure the only options for use of time. One study finds that welfare orderings which emerge from labour supply models depend critically on the assumption that non-market time is leisure, and fail to treat housework as analogous to market work. Hence the results of standard analysis may be misleading (Apps, 1991).

Flattening of tax rates can also impact negatively on women's labour force incentives and participation. In practice, they mean high effective marginal rates on lower incomes. This comes about through abatement and/or reduced entitlement in one or more of a number of areas. Currently in New Zealand these include benefits, family support, accommodation supplement, student support and community services cards. Apps's careful analysis of Australian data leads to the conclusion that provision of adequate assistance to low-income families without excessive tax burdens for secondary earners is extremely difficult in the context of much reduced progressivity (Apps, 1988). The flattening of tax rates is largely a transfer from middle- to high-income families and gives rise to equity losses. Since her earlier work questions the claimed efficiency gains of flatter rates, she argues persuasively that tax cuts should be in the form of increases in threshold levels rather than rate cuts.

In New Zealand the abatement rate on benefit income from additional earnings beyond the exempt area of $50 without children and $60 with children is 30 per cent up to $80 per week and 70 per cent thereafter. Thus, some partnered women unable to find well-paid, full-time work have little incentive to enter paid work or to increase part-time work beyond a few weekly hours, even if flexibility of hours is available from employers. This situation has combined with a weak demand for labour to halt the long-term trend to higher female labour force participation.

The effect of high effective marginal tax rates on participation is exacerbated by greater labour supply elasticities for married women compared with men (Killingsworth 1983; Prebble and Rebstock, 1992). This means that married women on average increase their labour market activity in response to a wage increase to a greater extent than men. Low elasticities for men come from a small positive substitution effect of work for leisure following a wage increase, arising from the fact that leisure has become relatively more expensive or has a higher opportunity cost in terms of lost earnings than before. However, this is nearly balanced by a negative income effect, since the wage increase over all hours worked makes the employee better off and thus able to take some of the real income gain in leisure time. The income effects of a wage increase, which imply spending more time on 'leisure', are found to be similar in size for women and men, but the substitution effects are generally larger for women. The rationale for the difference is that unpaid and paid work are much more easily substituted than leisure and paid work, in terms both of their greater similarity in output for the individual or household and of the greater reluctance to give up leisure than unpaid work for paid work. With women doing more of the unpaid work, they will thus on average substitute paid work for the unpaid work/leisure alternatives to a greater extent than men.

Since women's labour supply is more elastic, women's wages should be taxed at a lower rate. 'Marginal rates of tax should be inversely related to wage elasticities . . . Thus, ideally, the tax system would impose a lower tax rate on working women for efficiency reasons and for distributional reasons' (Apps and Savage, 1981: 276). Adding to the disincentive effects of high marginal rates for those on benefits are the low levels of exempt income, unchanged since 1986. Australia has indexed thresholds and an earnings credit of up to $1,000 per year which can be built up where the weekly free earnings are not regularly used, allowing a few weeks of higher-paid work or longer hours of work.

The poverty-trap problems posed by high effective marginal tax rates, low levels of exempt income and rapid abatement have long been recognised. Solutions are not easy, since less rapid abatement would result in reduced benefits still being paid at levels of income comparable with those of many in full-time, low-paid work. This is often regarded as being politically unacceptable. The last attempt to solve this dilemma was foreshadowed in the 1991 Budget in the form of a global system of social assistance with single family income tests and exemptions, and a single abatement rate, with benefits abated one by one as income increases. This would have replaced the current overlapping manner of abatement which produces the high effective marginal tax rates. It was suggested that integrated family accounts based on the 'core family' would facilitate the changes. However, the practical and theoretical problems meant that it was never implemented (St John, 1993).

This has some positive aspects, as the core family approach could have meant even more emphasis than before on the nuclear family, ignoring the realities of social change. It might also have increased the assumption of adult dependency, with the family unit being used for abatement of all benefits, and possibly even extended to the tax system. However, the problem is urgent, particularly as targeting has been extended further, and the new Minister of Social Welfare is proposing another attempt to solve it. Susan St John suggests that the New Zealand system has gone too far towards targeting as against universality of provision, with detrimental effects on the ability of women to become financially independent. She also recommends a return to a more progressive tax system.

There is evidence that tax systems and related policies do indeed have a significant effect on women's labour market participation. In Sweden, women contribute 29 per cent of family income, against 15 per cent in Germany and 12 per cent in the Netherlands, based on respective female labour force participation rates of those with children aged six and under of 81 per cent, 54 per cent and 50 per cent. Sweden has individual taxation and childcare/parental leave/family support policies more supportive to dual-earner families, together with high marginal tax rates for single earners, compared with the other two countries (Gustafsson and Bruyn-Hundt, 1991) and, except for individual tax, compared with New Zealand.

Unpartnered women

The vast majority of people bringing up children on their own are women, although sole fathers increased from 13 per cent to 16 per cent of the total between 1986 and 1991 (New Zealand Department of Social Welfare, 1993). Sole fathers receive attention and an odd mixture of curiosity, admiration and stigma beyond their numbers. Sole-parent families now make up a quarter of all families with children, so they have to be regarded as a normal family situation. Sole fathers are more likely to be in paid work than sole mothers, partly as a result of societal expectations and their greater earning power. Only 6.3 per cent of domestic purposes beneficiaries in New Zealand in 1987 were men, although the rate of sole fatherhood was double this. Similarly male beneficiaries, 5.5 per cent of the total receiving benefit, were estimated to be only 38.8 per cent of all male sole parents in 1987 in Australia, compared with 89.3 per cent of females receiving benefit (Raymond, 1987: 40).

Labour force participation for sole mothers is lower in both countries than it is for women in two-parent families. For all sole parents, the full-time employment rate has declined from 27 per cent in 1986 to 21 per cent in 1991 in New Zealand, with a dramatic fall for sole fathers between 1976 and 1991 from 81 per cent to 44 per cent. The difficult employment situation, high effective marginal tax rates and childcare difficulties are among the factors responsible for this. In Sweden, by contrast, almost 90 per cent of sole parents are in the labour force, thanks to better support policies.

Contrasting with ambivalent attitudes to married women with young children participating in the paid labour force is a punitive approach towards similarly placed, unpartnered women. For this group the current policy standpoint is towards as rapid a re-entry as possible into paid work, with the alternatives of going back to the previous marriage or relationship or of entering a new one. The drive to cut government expenditure has the domestic purposes benefit as a major target. However, difficulties arise for individuals from the effective marginal tax rates mentioned above, the problem of finding full-time work yielding sufficient earnings, childcare needs and the level of unemployment. Most women on the domestic purposes benefit wish to re-enter the paid workforce once their children are old enough; this is not surprising given its fairly modest level, the stigma often applied to recipients and the desire for independence.

In fact, average time on the benefit is surprisingly short, given these labour market realities and the actual participation rates for sole parents in paid work. For those moving into work beyond the earnings limit in 1982–83, the average time on the domestic purposes benefit was only 26 months (Dominick *et al*, 1988). While it may have lengthened with a less buoyant economy, the median time on the benefit for current recipients is still only about 27 months, with a small proportion staying on the benefit for much longer. This puts in perspective the 1993 extension of the Training Opportunities Scheme to allow access to recipients of this benefit for four years, even though not registered as unemployed (the normal qualification). While welcome, it will extend access to only a small minority of sole-parent beneficiaries.

A reasonable feminist perspective seems to be that partnered women should not be pushed out of the paid labour force nor unpartnered women with dependants pushed in, but that instead there should be real choice for each group, with minimal constraints. However, realism dictates that economic independence requires earnings from paid work. As a result of this, it can be argued that encouraging the option of full-time parenting is not in women's interests (Landau, 1992). This does not mean that women should be expected to carry the double burden of paid work as well as most of the unpaid work. Instead, perhaps, more equal sharing of unpaid work in the households of two-parent families should be encouraged through education and removal of any benefits which subsidise men whose wives are not in paid work, and through marriage agreements which recognise opportunity costs of not being in paid work. These need to be supplemented by adequate provision and support for childcare in both one- and two-parent families.

This position recognises the actual or likely consequences for women of dropping out of the labour force for long periods. The incidence of poverty is high among sole parents, and re-entry to quality employment becomes more difficult as time out of the labour force increases. In two-parent families, women who choose to withdraw from the labour force may be taking insufficient account of the possibility of later widowhood or marriage break-up, with similar possible consequences. Reva Landau goes further, arguing that women who drop out hurt not only themselves, but all women. Pointing out the advantages which married men with full-time housewives have in the workforce from the provision of services for them at home, she argues that: 'No women should give men an advantage over other women by providing him with housekeeping and childcare services' (*ibid.*: 62).

While there is considerable force in this overall line of reasoning, it may not be realistic at a time of recession. Further, it is a reasonable strategy only if housing, health, education, family allowances and childcare are seen as involving a significant community involvement, and not largely as a family responsibility. At a time when the trend on these issues is in the reverse direction, an expectation that all women should be in paid work could be used to justify even lower state support for income maintenance and services. If it is also unrealisable in practice owing to high levels of unemployment, even greater poverty for women and children could result. Even in recovery there may not be sufficient paid work for all, necessitating some of the more radical solutions discussed in Part IV.

Regarding increased participation as entirely beneficial should also be tempered by acknowledgement of class differences. Prior to the entry of middle-class women into employment, there was little choice for individual women 'as to whether they would undertake paid employment or not: the poor were compelled to and those in a better financial position, with few exceptions, did not even consider it a possibility' (Gilson, 1969: 183). Only very recently have work hours in the home decreased, despite labour-saving devices. Previously, trends to increased quality and switches from cleaning to intensive childcare were among factors maintaining hours of unpaid work, with only a slightly increasing contribution from the spouses of women in the paid workforce. With this double burden, paid work is not necessarily liberating, especially where it is a financial necessity.

Policies aimed at producing economic incentives to re-enter the labour force frequently appear more realistically to provide severe disincentives or punishments for resisting – for example, in the shape of benefit cuts. This is because they ignore the other problems discussed above. Nevertheless, such economic incentives are supplemented by ideological arguments, supported by selective research results. Thus, renewed emphasis is put on the desirability of having full-time mothering in a child's early years to reinforce the withdrawal of partnered women from the labour force. At the same time the ideology of the nuclear family is reasserted, together with the desirability of children being brought up by both parents – for example, in media discussion (Mannion, 1993: 21) – to discourage sole parenting. This ignores the gender-specific reasons for marriage breakdown, with increasing demands on women's refuges and of applications for non-molestation orders attesting to the high incidence of violence within marriage, perpetrated almost entirely by men.

Thus the very small number of women sole parents under 18 have been denied the domestic purposes benefit, and it is intended that beneficiaries should be 'work ready' and, if possible, return to employment when their youngest child reaches seven. This policy has been deferred while the unemployment situation is adverse, but special retraining schemes are being planned for this group. While this is a desirable initiative, it may be a precursor to more punitive rather than helpful measures. The 1991 accident compensation changes originally included the proposal that similar provisions should apply to those receiving compensation as surviving spouses of accident victims. Publicity with respect to the situation of widows of police killed on duty drew attention to this proposal, and caused adverse reaction and its withdrawal.

However, when the cuts in benefits are combined with the stigmatising of beneficiaries and invasions into the privacy of their relationships, it is not surprising that the number of domestic purposes benefits in force has levelled off, with an increase in the number ceasing to claim benefit (Preston, 1993). This result could be claimed as a success of the 1991 benefit cuts, saving both in quantity and rates. However, such an analysis ignores the costs falling on voluntary agencies, on those affected, especially women and children, and possible indirect costs on government. Neither can it be claimed as a vindication of high replacement rates as a reason for not being in paid work, when only 17 per cent of those moving off the benefit in the year to March 1993 were placed in work, as against 43 per cent changing their marital status, 12 per cent transferring to another benefit and 11 per cent having children who left their care or reaching the maximum age.

The hardship caused to those remaining on benefits has been assessed in a number of studies. Reviewing these results and the demands on food banks and social service agencies, as well as their own survey of 23 Christchurch recipients of the domestic purposes benefit, Christine Dann and Rosemary du Plessis argue that:

> The overall picture gained from the study is of normal people in abnormal circumstances. They utilise all sorts of strategies to survive . . . The people we interviewed are imaginative, resourceful and innovative managers – they budget, they barter, exchange, garden, bottle, freeze, collect driftwood for their fires and research the cheapest places to shop each week . . . The analysis of how income is allocated in these households reveals the extent to which those interviewed are going without essentials in order to survive. Of particular concern are the very low amounts spent on food, and the lack of spending on health care for themselves . . . Why are parents who show so much ingenuity, effort and care for their children often treated as moral pariahs by others? Why are they blamed for the material and moral poverty of Aotearoa/New Zealand when they consume so much less than many others? (Dann and du Plessis, 1991: 1, 65 and 66)

8
Income Adequacy for Older Women

Government policies with major impacts on the living standards of the elderly have changed frequently in recent years. This applies not only to the tax-funded pension but also to the treatment of tax savings prior to retirement and of other income during retirement, and to health and other services. The uncertainty about future policy leads to feelings of insecurity which can be almost as serious a problem as actual income inadequacy (Age Concern, 1991). The recent near agreement between the main political parties on the future directions of policy should reduce this uncertainty. However, it is naive to believe either that superannuation policy can be entirely removed from the political arena or that the actual living standards of the elderly can be any more immune than those of other groups from the economic situation and overall economic policies.

Women are a large majority among the elderly, and have fewer opportunities on average than men to save for their retirement years. As a group, they are therefore particularly affected by these problems. However, in old age as at other times, gender interacts with a number of variables including ethnicity, class, educational opportunities and sexual orientation. These factors and the extent of family responsibilities affect the amount and level of paid work undertaken during an individual woman's working-age years, and her ability to have saved independently or jointly with a partner for retirement. It should be noted, too, that retirement is a misnomer for many women, as their unpaid and caring work will usually continue, and may even increase. Women often find when their husbands retire that they have married them not only for better for worse but also for lunch!

This chapter looks briefly at women's economic position in old age, critiques the 1991 changes to policy in the tax-funded pension and related areas, and discusses some underlying issues which arise.

The economic position of older women

In 1990, women in New Zealand constituted 55.8 per cent of the over-60 age group, and 66.4 per cent of the over-80s. Life expectancy at birth, based on 1985–87 life tables, is 77.1 for women, against 71.1 for men, but only 72 and 67 respectively for Maori. Women in New Zealand who reach 60 can expect to live another 21.4 years (18.3 for Maori women), and men 17.2 (15.2 Maori). Three-quarters of men over 60 are currently married, but only 46.6 per cent of women. (The demographic data in this section are from New Zealand Department of Statistics, 1990, and New Zealand Ministry of Senior Citizens, 1990.) The greater longevity of women and the propensity for men to marry women somewhat younger than themselves results in far more women than men having a period of widowhood. The vast majority of older people – 92.5 per cent of those over 60 – remain able to live in private residences, but this decreases to 63.5 per cent of those over 85. Women are much more likely to live alone, with 51.8 per cent of those aged 75 to 79, compared with 21.1 per cent of men, in that category.

Thus, managing alone is to a much greater extent a woman's experience than a man's. Further, women's average incomes in old age (as at other ages) are less than men's, although the gap narrows, with the state-funded pension becoming a significant proportion of income. This reduction of the gap results from a sharp reduction in the average income of men over 70 compared with earlier ages rather than from a large increase in average female incomes, although the female median income (50 per cent have less than this figure, and 50 per cent more) does rise very slightly beyond age 70. This is partly because of the direct receipt by some women of survivor benefits from occupational and private pensions, when the whole of the base pension would have been paid to the member of the scheme while alive.

Median income for all men over 15 was $15,119 at the 1986 Census. For those aged 60–64, median income was $12,173; at 65–69 $8,502, and at 70–74 $7,692, with little change for higher ages. Median incomes for women of similar ages were $7,545 (50 per cent of the male figure) for 15-plus; $7,125 (59 per cent) at 60–64; $7,087 (83 per cent) at 65–69, and $7,145 (93 per cent) at 70–74. Higher incomes, however, are still mainly the prerogative of men, with 14.5 per cent of men over 60 having incomes of more than $20,000 in 1986, against 3.8 per cent of women (New Zealand Department of Statistics, 1990: 36).

In 1987–88, 65.5 per cent of the average income of $12,860 in single-person households with the occupant over 60 came from national superannuation, with 9.6 per cent from paid work and 16.1 per cent from investments. For households consisting of a couple without children and with the woman over 60, the corresponding proportions were 59 per cent, 18 per cent, and 15.1 per cent, of a total income of $23,930 (New Zealand Planning Council, 1990: 120). These contrasting proportions largely reflect differences in age, gender and labour force participation. Averages can give a misleading impression, with the few wealthy having a substantial effect on the average. About two-thirds of those receiving the state pension have no other income, and women form a large majority of this group.

The median incomes given above, together with a recent survey of older New Zealanders, confirm that incomes fall sharply in old age. In fact about half of those surveyed felt that their standard of living, not just their income, had fallen compared with pre-retirement years (Age Concern, 1990). The two are not identical, since work-related and possibly other expenses will have fallen, with fully paid-off home ownership rates highest among the over-60s. Despite this fall, only 23 per cent of respondents considered their standard of living to be inadequate.

Poverty among the elderly was substantially reduced by the national superannuation scheme, which was at a higher level than previous state tax-funded systems. The married couple rate was originally set at 80 per cent of post-tax average ordinary-time earnings, although this relativity has now been cut. Families with children currently experience poverty to a greater extent than the elderly, with family assistance payments having fallen sharply relative to superannuation. Reduction of poverty among the elderly is of course to be welcomed, although not the increase among children, particularly in sole-parent and other low-income families.

The previous chapter discussed the question of how policy-makers and researchers can reasonably judge adequacy of income when government expenditure cuts are sought. However, if the relative poverty trends are used to reduce further the level of superannuation, poverty among the elderly would re-emerge, with women particularly affected.

Government policy

The major rationale for the July 1991 Budget changes to tax-funded pensions was the need to make substantial savings in government expenditure.

Existing provisions were deemed fiscally unsustainable in the light of the ageing of the population and the economic situation. Fourteen per cent of the population were over 60 in 1981, with that figure predicted to rise to 19 per cent by 2011, and possibly as high as 30 per cent by the middle of the next century. Movement towards private provision for retirement was therefore to be encouraged. Full treatment of the demographic and fiscal arguments is beyond the scope of this chapter. However, it should be said that all the claims are open to challenge, with the total dependency ratio having been almost as high at other periods when children as well as the elderly are included.

In any case, the elderly, like the whole population, have to consume actual goods and services largely out of current production (durable goods, like housing and cars, are a partial exception). Exhorting private provision through saving for retirement, if successful, will result in greater claims on current output by the elderly, but those claims will be able to be fully met only if the past saving has resulted in productive investment and higher output. Inflation may otherwise reduce the amount of goods and services those savings can buy, with the possibility also of inter-generational conflict. However, those currently in paid and unpaid work (including the elderly) must always provide the goods and services for those currently fully or partly dependent.

Each cohort benefits from inter-generational transfer and provides for others at different life stages. It should be recalled that many of the old, especially women, are still providing for others through unpaid caring work. A recent survey showed that 29 per cent of women over 60 regularly cared for another person – mostly for a partner but also for grandchildren. One-third of this group provided constant care. This means that 45,000 older people receive constant care from others in the same age group – double the number of older people in continuing-care facilities (Age Concern, 1991).

Changes to the state pension

The fiscal arguments held sufficient sway for severe cuts to the state pension system to be announced in July 1991, with the resulting outcry causing a partial withdrawal. The main features were:
1. the rapid increase in age of eligibility from 60 to 65;
2. the freezing of the level of payment until 1993;

3. the draconian toughening of the outside income test which abates the payment, with a transfer from an Inland Revenue-operated surcharge to a Department of Social Welfare-administered income test;
4. the movement from the individual to a joint spousal/de facto unit of assessment where relevant for this income test;
5. the introduction of a universal element of half the maximum superannuation payment at age 70, a slight offsetting move to the other four.

The outcry, together with the likely non-workability of some of the changes, resulted in a partial retreat from the third and fourth of these features, with some savings by also removing the fifth.

The previous surcharge rate of 20 cents on each dollar of other income (or half the income in the case of approved superannuation schemes) above about $6,000 each for a married couple and $7,200 for a single person was to be tightened so that abatement started when outside income reached only $4,160 for a married couple or single person and proceeded much more rapidly. Instead of a 48 or 53 per cent effective marginal tax rate (28 per cent on lower and 33 per cent on higher incomes, added to the 20 per cent surcharge), the rate would have become 93 per cent in many cases. Full withdrawal of the state pension previously occurred at about $71,000 of other income for a married couple and $43,300 for a single person. This would have been reduced to $23,700 and $16,200 respectively. Abatement at such a high rate makes saving during working life virtually pointless, with little benefit for couples with between $4,000 and $16,000 other income. Exhortations to save in the face of such a lack of incentive would have been largely fruitless. Inevitably, too, avoidance would have been widespread among those already retired and with a reasonable level of assets, particularly in the absence of an assets test. Those with some savings outside an approved scheme would be harder hit, because all rather than half the resulting income would have been abated. Women are less favourably placed to save significant amounts, particularly in such schemes.

The October 1991 revisions became effective from 1 April 1992, and fell between these two extremes. The surcharge was increased by 5 cents to 25 cents on outside income, with the exempt income still at the low figure of $4,160 for single people but increased to $3,120 each for married couples. This implies that married couples lose all their state pension if between them they have outside income above $54,800; single people are similarly affected from $35,802. (Complexities mean that figures in this section are illustrative only. The division of outside income between partners, part of it coming from approved schemes, changes in circumstances during a year, and living alone or otherwise as a single person all affect the outcome.) The government claimed that about 75 per cent of the elderly would be unaffected by the change in surcharge regime, since for most people outside income is zero or below the new exempt figure, while a few had already lost all their pension owing to very high income.

From the point of view of older women, the abatement issue probably received rather more attention than it deserved relative to other changes. The surcharge even at the slightly higher rate involves a not unreasonable degree of targeting, with continued Inland Revenue administration perhaps involving less stigma than would be perceived with Social Welfare means-testing of state pensions. Thus the increased surcharge, the higher age of eligibility (but see the qualifications below) and the withdrawal of the part-universal pension, which benefited only the most well-off, might be regarded as the least harmful of measures that could be taken if savings had to be made. A large proportion of women have zero or very low levels of outside income, so of greater importance to them is the maintenance of the pension level in order to achieve a minimum standard of living. The freeze until 1993 implied, of course, a cut in real terms, although the low prevailing rates of inflation made this less serious than it would have been in earlier years. Nevertheless, the $10 to $15 per week by which the pension would have increased if indexed to the Consumer Price Index would have been important at the margin for those on lower incomes.

In the medium term, an increase in the age of eligibility to 65 may be a reasonable measure. Combined with the prohibition on age discrimination, including the abolition of compulsory retirement ages, it has merit, although it must be recognised that those in physically demanding jobs may need and wish to retire at an earlier age than 65. Further, the legal requirement of non-discrimination does not guarantee its observance in practice, while employer power may ensure that some employees continue to accept retirement ages below the age of superannuation in contract negotiations. Women who have returned to the full-time labour force after periods in unpaid and/or part-time work may still be at the peak of their powers and energy at 60. The opportunity to continue to use the experience of this age group will be particularly desirable in the medium term, as the youth cohort entering the labour force diminishes.

However, the rapid increase in age of eligibility to 65 is very serious for those forced or planning to retire at 60, or unable to find a job. There is little lead time to make extra savings, even if this was possible, for those in their late 50s. Again this is particularly difficult for women, who still have lower labour force participation rates than men in their 60s. Government recognised in principle the need for interim measures for this group. Already in place was the 55-plus benefit, which has less onerous reporting requirements and does not require active job search, in recognition of the reality that few in this age group would be able to find new work. However, its level, equivalent to unemployment benefit, is well below national superannuation.

From 1 April 1994 there is a somewhat more generous transitional benefit available to those over 60. At $166 per week after tax for single people and $277 for married couples, its level is between that of the unemployment benefit and superannuation. This benefit, income tested in the same way as other social welfare benefits rather than the more generous procedures of the superannuation surcharge, is a compromise resulting from the 1993 three-party talks on superannuation. It is a short-term measure to cushion the rapid increase in the eligibility age, phasing out in 2004.

The number receiving national superannuation peaked at more than 509,000 at March 1992, with a fall each quarter since then as the age of eligibility increases. By March 1993, the number was about 485,000. This decrease will continue until 2001, by which time the eligibility age reaches 65. A significant proportion of ineligible over-60s were, and will continue to be, in receipt of an alternative benefit, such as sickness or invalid. Given that this reduces the savings from the rapid increase in age of eligibility, the cost impact of a more gradual raising of the age might have been relatively minor as well as being more equitable.

Another factor which casts doubt on giving unqualified approval to a gradual raising of the age of entitlement is the lower life expectancy of Maori, noted earlier, and hence their lesser receipt of pensions. Since Maori men and women are over-represented among those unemployed, the importance of the interim arrangements is highlighted.

The most welcome climb-down, from a feminist perspective, was the return to the individual unit for receipt of pension and abatement purposes. This partial retreat from the core family unit towards individual entitlement avoids the problems of total loss of pension by a non-working spouse. This would have made it difficult for the partner of a recipient of superannuation to be in paid work, particularly a younger woman (St John, 1991).

Receipt of an independent income, sometimes for the first time, was regarded as of great importance by many older women in a recent Ministry of Women's Affairs consultation.

Of considerable significance is the perspective which underlies the tax-funded pension scheme. The view is common that a state retirement pension is different in kind from other benefits in the social welfare system. Whether justified in terms of recognition of past and/or present contributions to society, the lack of alternatives for many of the elderly, or the fact that it is permanent in that there will be no return to the paid labour force, entitlement to a pension is frequently viewed as more of an unconditional right than is the case with other benefits. This position is sometimes argued in terms of past tax payments, but this consideration is invalid in a pay-as-you-go system. Nevertheless, the feeling that a reasonable standard of living from the basic state pension is a matter of just deserts is a strong one, which polls show is shared by most of the non-elderly (Royal Commission on Social Policy, 1988).

Three lengthy sets of consultations have taken place on the future of superannuation in recent years. In 1988–89, the Labour Government considered a number of options, including a social insurance system and a compulsory, state-run contribution scheme with a private contracting-out option, before deciding instead to make more minor changes to the existing tax-funded, pay-as-you-go scheme (New Zealand Department of Social Welfare, 1988). Both the options mentioned involve compulsory contributions from taxpayers during their working lives. Social insurance can involve either earnings-related or flat-rate payouts, with a tax-financed top-up for those whose contributions had not entitled them to a minimum level of pension. Contribution schemes are similar to employment-based or personal private schemes, with benefit levels dependent on contribution records. If participation in such a scheme was made compulsory, contributions of about 15 per cent of income would be needed for 40 years by those on average earnings to yield a similar level of pension as that currently provided by national superannuation (*ibid.*: 20). A top-up for those whose paid work experience was too little to accumulate adequate contributions for a minimum-level pension would still be necessary. Such a contributory scheme operated briefly during the term of the Labour Government in the mid 1970s. The implications of contributory schemes for women are discussed below.

The most recent report was by the Ad Hoc Cabinet/Caucus Committee on Private Provision for Retirement, supplemented by the Todd Task Force. This had a brief to consider the full range of issues related to private superannuation schemes, discussed later, together with their interface with state-funded schemes and the macro-economic implications of increased savings. The broad principles for its work were encouragement of greater financial self-reliance among retired people, and the promotion of intergenerational equity, of economic efficiency in resource allocation and of fiscal sustainability. Gender issues were nowhere mentioned in its terms of reference. It canvassed three options: a return to a compulsory savings scheme, the reinstatement of tax incentives to save for retirement, and the status quo, with a few refinements. After lengthy consultations and deliberations, it opted for the last, with encouragement and education to individuals to save, and tightened disclosure rules for saving schemes, to ensure understanding and ease of comparison.

A regular plea from the media and groups speaking for the elderly has been for certainty and stability in superannuation policy, and for agreement between the political parties. While any attempt to take a particular area of policy totally out of the political arena is unrealistic, the three-party talks between National, Labour and the Alliance during 1993 did lead to a measure of agreement, with participants reserving their position in some areas. New Zealand First did not participate, continuing to regard the surcharge as a betrayal. The Alliance had previously opposed the raising of the age of eligibility, but its implementation at the current rate was part of the agreement, together with the transitional retirement benefit mentioned earlier. Other elements of the Todd status quo option were adopted, including disclosure rules, a savings ombudsman and a commissioner to promote retirement income policies. Pensions would be indexed to inflation, with the married rate between 65 per cent and 72.5 per cent of the average wage. The Alliance registered that it still opposed the surcharge, favouring instead a more progressive income tax scale with similar effects on incomes of the better-off elderly but involving higher tax than current levels on the younger wealthy.

Despite the maintenance of a level of superannuation which is still reasonably generous by international standards, the overall aim of policy is to give strong signals that the state role in retirement income should move towards a safety net approach (Shipley, 1991). There are regular exhortations from government that everyone should save for their own retirement, starting at an early age, and concerns expressed by the superannuation industry that this is being largely ignored by all but the highest-income earners. This fails to recognise the difficulties for most lower-income families of reserving money for this purpose, and the particular problems facing women in this respect.

Other forms of superannuation/saving for retirement

The major form of saving for retirement in New Zealand is through the purchase of owner-occupied housing. The home ownership rate of the over-60 population is high (73 per cent unmortgaged for over-65s), although less so for women living on their own. Data on other forms of savings are limited, but membership of formal retirement savings schemes, including those organised by employers, is low by international standards. Government actuary data indicates that in 1987 only 23 per cent of those in employment contributed to occupational schemes, with private and personal scheme membership raising this level to 36 per cent, or 24 per cent of the working-age population (St John and Ashton, 1990: 4). By 1992, 44 per cent of men, as against 29 per cent of women, had some sort of superannuation, although this included life insurance endowment policies. The female–male gap is narrowed somewhat by the fact that more women benefit as surviving partners from schemes in which their husbands are members than vice versa (New Zealand Department of Social Welfare Social Policy Agency, 1992).

Predictably, the groups most likely to contribute to superannuation or mutual funds were professional and managerial, with nearly half of those in these occupations making payments in 1988–89 at an average rate of $31 and $44 per week respectively. Over one-third of those in the clerical, sales and service groups also made contributions, but at a much lower average level (*ibid.*: 17). Less than 25 per cent of women made contributions, as against 30 per cent of men. The contribution rates are in more striking contrast. Men averaged payments of $28 per week, over four times the female rate. Hence women's accumulations in and income from such schemes are much lower than men's, while average male payouts are themselves modest in all but a few schemes, such as the Government Superannuation Fund.

These sharp differences are hardly surprising, given a number of economic and social factors, including the relative earnings structures of men and women, and the effects of the rules of many of the schemes. Firstly, higher-income earners, with men over-represented, can afford to contribute more and have better access to occupational schemes. Second, socialisation and past experience have provided an expectation – decreasing but still significant – that a combination of state and partner provision will ensure an adequate income in old age for many women. The existence of spousal benefits in many schemes is one valid factor in this expectation. Third, a labour force participation pattern with gaps and periods in part-time work is not conducive to membership in and substantial benefits from such schemes. Many schemes are open only to certain groups of employees, with part-time workers often excluded and/or minimum periods of service required before being eligible to join. The rules of most schemes give disproportionately more benefits relative to the level of contributions to employees with long service. Typically, employers make contributions to match those of their employees in occupational schemes, but on withdrawal these contributions may not be fully available. The vesting rules, which govern availability to the employee of the employer contribution on withdrawal, frequently require long service before full vesting, with an increasing proportion available as service increases. New Zealand has no legal requirements with respect to vesting, so the average period required is longer than in most other countries. A 15- to 20-year continuous period of service is common in many older schemes, with 10 to 15 years' service more frequent in newer schemes (Seals and Ormrod, 1991).

This implies that those with fewer years of service, frequently women, cross-subsidise those with longer years of service, mainly men. Women who leave the paid workforce for full-time childcare are in most cases required to cash in their superannuation rights, and may also need to do so for family expenses. However, if they do not have access to full vesting they obtain only partial benefit, as well as losing later pension potential and having to start again on re-entry to the labour force. Thus contributory schemes have features which make them less attractive on average to women. Both their under-representation and their relative disadvantage as members would be ameliorated if the past, albeit slow narrowing of labour force participation and earnings differences between women and men accelerated. However, this requires, for example, greater sharing of childcare and active policies towards equal employment opportunity and pay equity which are unlikely at present.

Some features of contributory schemes could be improved, even given the current different labour force profiles of women and men. These changes are desirable, but politically unlikely to be introduced with respect to voluntary schemes. However, if payment into a contributory scheme was to become compulsory, it would be essential for equity for women that the state scheme and any qualifying private schemes should have to satisfy certain gender-neutral criteria. Although National suggested in its 1990 election manifesto that it might reintroduce tax deductions for superannuation savings, the general government preference has been for a 'level playing field' in the savings area, to avoid distortions. Increases in superannuation as a result of tax deductions could simply constitute a shift from other forms of saving and, if genuinely producing an increase in saving, might further contract the economy. A combination of these arguments and the potential loss of tax revenue was responsible for the decision to maintain the status quo of making payments into schemes out of after-tax income while receiving the payout in retirement on a tax-free basis. Tax incentives also disproportionately favour those on higher incomes, with women under-represented.

A report on gender-neutral superannuation commissioned by the Ministry of Women's Affairs outlined the maximum periods of service for full vesting in a number of countries. These include two years' membership or five years' employment in Canada; two years' pensionable service in the UK, and five years' employment in the US. The report mentioned that full vesting below ten years was not well received by the employers consulted, on the grounds of expense and the staff retention aspect of superannuation provision. It put forward a sample scheme design 'intended to strike a balance between desirable design features, employer acceptance and legislative restriction' (Seals and Ormrod, 1991: 13). This included no vesting until two years of service, with vesting of employer contributions at 20 per cent after two years' membership, increasing by 10 per cent per year with full vesting after ten years. If membership of a scheme had been made compulsory, there would be a strong argument that vesting should be full and immediate.

If the total or major emphasis of contributory schemes is to provide an adequate income on retirement, the vesting provisions lose importance relative to the preservation and portability of scheme benefits. If withdrawal is not permitted until retirement (or a particular age), vesting becomes irrelevant and preservation of benefits from previous service automatic. In that case, to avoid the complications and administrative costs of small amounts in several schemes, total portability between schemes is desirable, and the logic points to a single state scheme. If withdrawal was still allowed, the vesting arguments made above apply. If full vesting did not become mandatory, the ability to 'recapture' previous service and benefits on return to work with the same employer, or preferably any employer, would be of importance to women.

No scheme design alone, however, can give women equal benefits to men so long as they have lower average service and earnings. One approach to the first issue, adopted in some countries with social insurance or other forms of compulsory contributory schemes, is that of tax-funded credits being paid to the individual contributor's account during periods of unpaid caring work. If a compulsory scheme was adopted, this approach would reduce the need for top-up payments at retirement. Both credits and top-ups are financed from taxation, but the former have the important advantage of recognising unpaid caring work as real work and avoiding any stigma which is felt to apply, however unfairly, to the latter.

A further difficulty which women face in providing adequately for their retirement arises from their greater average longevity. Since pensions will have to be paid out to women for a longer period on average, pure actuarially based schemes may charge women more for the same annual income. An increasing proportion of occupational and private schemes are of the defined contribution type discussed earlier, and most give lump-sum benefits. If these lump sums are used to purchase an annuity, women will receive less annual income from the same lump sum than men of the same age. Indicative figures of the order of magnitude involved, based on Australian calculations, show that similar contributions might yield a pension of 50 per cent of final salary for a man but only 41 per cent for a woman (Bywater, 1989: 14).

Insurance and superannuation are exempt from the Human Rights Act prohibition on gender discrimination, provided that differences are based on actuarial data. An early version of the 1993 Human Rights Act removed this exemption, but it was restored after submissions from the industry. Ironically, discrimination on the ground of race in this area is prohibited, despite the fact that in the annuity area (though not with respect to life insurance) Maori should, on actuarial grounds, receive higher pensions for the same lump sum than Pakeha owing to lower longevity. A large number of factors other than gender and ethnicity affect longevity, and these are not normally considered in pension scheme provisions.

Averaging risk is a basic insurance principle. While there is a case for basing premiums on identifiable risk categories where individual behaviour increases risk, this does not apply to gender differences. This is part of the case for removing the exemption. A number of European countries, as well as the United States and Australia, are moving towards outlawing use of gender-based actuarial tables. The industry has successfully argued that actuarial principles more completely apply to the risk difference by gender than by race, and that the slight reduction in price or increase in benefits for women that would result from eliminating gender pricing would be dwarfed by a general increase in costs.

One type of scheme which does not discriminate against women on an actuarial basis is the defined benefit type. The payout here is based on years of contribution and finishing salary, in some cases an average over the last few years of service. The Government Superannuation Fund was the largest of such schemes. It is now closed to new members. While it has this actuarial advantage for women, as well as the rare feature of pensions increasing with the rate of inflation, considerable problems accounted for the low female membership noted earlier. Withdrawal benefits are particularly poor, with the main advantages going to long service. However, the replacements offered by public-sector employers have to be fully funded, defined contribution schemes, with other disadvantages to women enumerated earlier.

Another area of importance to women is that of survivor (spouse) benefits in superannuation schemes. These are provided automatically in a majority of defined benefit schemes, usually at 50 per cent of the member's pension (St John and Ashton, 1990: 28). Such benefits may be ruled unlawful following the passage of the Human Rights Act, 1993. The commission considers that such benefits discriminate against single people under the definitions of the Act. At the time of writing a test case is before the Auckland High Court. The logic of the argument for economic independence for women and individual units of assessment would accept that such benefits should be phased out, in the long term at least. The saving achieved through reducing the cost of payouts could be used for increasing the pension or reducing contributions. In the short term, however, they are badly needed by women who have little or no alternative savings. An alternative non-discriminatory but more expensive option is to provide for a nominated survivor, presumably with limits on the length of payout.

One possible way in which older people may be able to supplement their income or acquire a sum for home maintenance or other purposes is through the use of home equity conversion schemes. These are essentially reverse mortgages whereby some of the equity in the family home is sacrificed for lump sums or annuities. This system has not yet been extensively used in New Zealand, but a one-year pilot in Levin, Auckland and Nelson for housing-related costs only was initiated in 1990 by the Housing Corporation. There were only about 60 recipients of these 'Helping Hand' loans before the National Government ended the scheme. One private-sector scheme providing annuities is being marketed through a life insurance company in Wellington (Davey, 1993). With a home valued at $100,000, someone in their late 60s could receive up to $3,000 per annum; at age 85 such a home could yield $9,000. The maximum available on any property is $12,000.

Home equity conversion schemes raise some concerns about depletion of wealth, reduced ability to benefit from rising house prices and lender default (*ibid.*). The issue of erosion of inheritance is less significant with these schemes than it is with the rest-home subsidy, discussed next. This is because the use of assets to pay for rest-home care is not a choice when the care is essential, whereas use of home equity conversion schemes will presumably always be voluntary. Hence, as long as they remain a free choice for those finding it a useful income or lump-sum supplement, such schemes have a modest role to play.

Another problem for some older women is that their standard of living may be substantially reduced through the costs of long-term care for their spouse. The criteria attaching to rest-home subsidies, which reduce the amount payable towards the total costs of care, have recently been standardised for different forms of long-term permanent care. The subsidy is now both income and asset tested on the combined assets of both partners. Previously, in public hospitals, only the superannuation entitlement was payable towards the cost of care. The decision announced in 1993 was that for a single elderly person only $6,500 of assets could be preserved, the remainder being used to pay for the costs of care – usually around $500 to $1,000 per week in a private rest home or $800 to $1,100 in a public hospital. Similarly, if both partners were in care, only $13,000 was to be exempt, meaning in each case that the family home would have to be sold. This would happen straight away or later, with the amount owing to the state coming out of the estate. With one partner in care and the other at home, the exempted assets were to rise to $20,000, and the family home and car not to be counted. There was also an income limit of only $30,000 for the spouse at home before the subsidy could be reduced on income rather than asset grounds.

A case can be made that the basic policy is reasonable, in that the general taxpayer should not have to subsidise the cost of care where assets exist which are being preserved only for inheritance purposes rather than the needs of the elderly themselves. However, the exempt asset levels were set very low, especially in the light of funeral costs, and in other areas policy has moved in the reverse direction. Death duties have recently been abolished, and there are no wealth or capital gains taxes. Hence, inheritance of accumulated wealth proceeds unmolested except for the comparatively few unlucky enough to finish their lives in residential care. Further, creation of family trusts and investigation of disposal of assets which usually goes back only five years may mean that the wealthiest manage to arrange their affairs to avoid the problem while those with only medium assets do not. Another concern is that pressure may be exerted by likely inheritors to avoid expensive care situations.

Widespread disquiet and protests by the elderly and organisations representing them led to the announcement in March 1994 of some relaxation of the policy. The maximum charge for care was cut to $636 per week, even where actual costs were higher; pre-paid funerals were added to the house and car exemptions from the asset test; and allowable assets for married couples with one in care and one at home were raised to $40,000. However, the single person limit of $6,500 was left untouched.

Even if the policy of income and asset testing is considered reasonable, it is essential that the surviving spouse should not be impoverished. This is of course largely an issue for women, because of their greater longevity. The increase to $40,000 of exempt assets, together with the house and car, is some protection, but further changes are needed. The policy, as it is operated, is contrary to moves towards economic independence for women and reduced assumptions of adult dependence. An improvement would be for assets above the exempt limit, whether nominally joint or individual, to be aggregated and halved, with only the half attributable to the partner in care being subject to the test. Another possibility, earlier suggested by the prime minister, would be to attempt – albeit with difficulty – to separate the medical costs from the residential costs of care. Residential costs only would then be payable and subject to subsidy according to income and assets, with medical hospital costs subsidised by the taxpayer as they are for the rest of the population.

Conclusion

The Ministry of Women's Affairs has consistently supported individual entitlement to a targeted tax-funded pension set at an adequate level, with a more generous targeting regime than applies to other social welfare benefits. This is seen as the best option for women, bearing in mind the problems of defined contribution schemes discussed earlier in this chapter. Women who can afford to save will generate additional retirement income, subject to the surcharge if large enough. So far, the tax-funded option survives, albeit somewhat eroded. However, the ministry has argued for a more gradual increase in the age of entitlement than that implemented, and stressed the importance of an accompanying comprehensive package of services and income supplements on the basis of need. The adequacy of such services in the face of expenditure cuts and changes in the health system is open to considerable doubt.

In current circumstances, it is only responsible to advise those who can make individual provision for their own future to do so. However, the debates on demographic and fiscal sustainability disguise the fact that the majority of the elderly are women with little income beyond the basic pension, and with a long and often ongoing involvement in unpaid caring work. As this will change only slowly, it is essential to continue to argue the case for adequate, basic, tax-funded support. Otherwise the situation will continue in which 'every generation [of women] falls back into dependency and relying on daughters/family for care – so trapping them in the same way' (Age Concern, 1991: 3).

9
Women and Housing Policy

Curiously little attention has been given to women and housing in New Zealand, although the 1980s at last saw the Housing Corporation co-operate with the ministries of Women's Affairs and Maori Affairs on consultations with women and a later report on Maori women's housing needs. In the first exercise, formal submissions were received from 173 individuals and 171 groups; there were also many requests for information and cases raised about particular housing difficulties (Housing Corporation of New Zealand, 1987). Major themes included difficulties following marriage breakdown and access to housing for single women. The report's major overall concluding comment was not a surprise: 'Evidence suggests that women face problems in the housing market both because of their generally disadvantaged social position and because of general housing policies which unintentionally overlook the needs of women' (*ibid.*: 62). A number of detailed suggestions were made, and the Housing Corporation Women's Unit subsequently developed a checklist with which to evaluate impacts of policies on women. Unfortunately, the more-market approach extended since then to housing has swamped any improvements which might have arisen from this exercise.

The housing market and government policy

The problems facing low- or even middle-income groups in finding adequate affordable housing worsened considerably in the 1970s and 1980s. The increase in house prices exactly matched the increase in average weekly earnings over the 14-year period 1969–70 to 1983–84, both exceeding general price increases, but considerable year-to-year fluctuations in the rate of price change made the date of purchase crucial. With many institutions requiring higher deposits in proportional as well as absolute terms than in earlier years, both the deposit gap and the repayment problem put house purchase out of reach of many low-income households.

Rental levels in the private sector were also too high for many to enjoy adequate accommodation; there was a shortage of both private and public rentals. The 1981–84 National Government allowed the selling of public rental houses to their tenants at a faster rate than replacement. This contributed to overcrowding and inadequate housing. The fall in inflation and interest rates of more recent years has made housing more affordable, but does not assist with supply problems at the bottom end of the market. In some areas of the country, house prices have started to rise again.

Philosophy and homelessness

With this background, what responsibility does the government take to ensure that every New Zealander is adequately housed? Labour in the 1980s stated the belief that 'a home is the fundamental right of all New Zealanders'. In government, the main emphasis of Labour's policy was to give more modest-income families the chance to buy or build their own homes and to target resources to help those with the most need. Access to good-quality housing is basic to adequate living standards and well-being, and thus policies to facilitate it are an essential part of all social policy.

However, unlike the right to free or subsidised education and medical services, both of which are also admittedly being eroded, there is no comparable right to housing. Some countries have legislation which defines homelessness and obliges government or local authorities to house homeless people. It is not, of course, clear what constitutes homelessness, from sleeping in the street or under a bridge at one extreme to any housing problem at the other. Between these two there are problems which need external assistance, including severe overcrowding, inadequate housing in places like garages and caravans, and health problems exacerbated by inadequate facilities. Others which particularly affect women include actual or desired movement from the family home owing to violence, incest, sexual harassment or marital breakdown. While the refuge movement and other voluntary agencies have made a highly valuable contribution to assisting women in great distress, they can deal only with short-term problems, and it is clear that lack of viable housing and financial alternatives has driven women back to untenable situations.

Whether a statutory obligation to house the homeless would help is arguable. In Britain, interpretation of the legislation has been so varied in terms of local authorities' value judgements – for example, about whether accommodation is reasonable – as to provide no minimum standard. The presence or lack of a real commitment is probably of greater importance than the presence or lack of a legislative requirement.

The National Housing Commission, in its last five-yearly report before its abolition in 1988, discussed the definition and extent of serious housing need, preferring that term to homelessness. This is probably more useful, as it sees the problem as a continuum of more and less critical problems. Serious need was seen as lasting for more than two months and as encompassing overcrowding and residence in substandard, temporary or unsustainably unaffordable housing. In 1987 the commission asked 104 agencies dealing with housing issues and located in a variety of regions about what housing problems were seen as most serious and how extensive they were. It concluded that some 17,500 households with children in major centres were in serious housing need, with Maori and Pacific Island households and the Auckland region heavily over-represented (National Housing Commission, 1988). To this must be added those in small centres and rural areas, and other types of households. There was overwhelming support from the agencies for a statutory right to housing.

Policies in the 1980s

The general philosophy of recent governments towards freeing up the marketplace and targeting social welfare expenditure accurately to those on lowest incomes has been discussed in earlier chapters. Such general policies have at least as much impact on the housing scene as specific housing policies, and some of the latter are needed simply to mitigate the effects of the former. For example, the accommodation benefit was increased in 1985 and made available to low-income earners as well as those on benefits because of the ending of the rent freeze and the expected increase in rents that would result. At that stage, high interest and inflation rates and deregulation of the financial sector made it extremely difficult to achieve home ownership and maintain payments, and they also led to increased rents. GST drove up prices by virtually the whole 10 per cent (now 12.5 per cent) level of the tax. Second-hand house sales do not attract the tax, but prices caught up as the markets were not separate, and rentals followed.

Labour housing policies between 1984 and 1990 included the purchase or building of more new state houses and a partial moratorium on selling state rentals, with the intention of easing the pressure on waiting lists. Housing Corporation loans for low-income families were increased, as were second-chance and refinancing loans available to individuals or families who had previously had a state loan. This still proved insufficient to meet the demand, which is predominantly from women, especially following marriage breakdown.

Take-up of special accommodation benefits was much less than expected, indicating both the usual problems of feelings of stigma or lack of knowledge preventing those eligible from claiming their entitlement, and criteria that were probably too tight. Income-related interest rates for Housing Corporation loans and income-related rents for state housing were introduced. The emphasis on targeting sharply to those in need brings with it detailed means tests. Such targeting was justified as being necessary partly through stories of wealthy businessmen living in subsidised state housing. While outrage might have been justified if this was widespread, a few isolated cases hardly required a response which saw only the very lowest-income households eligible for state housing. Those with slightly higher incomes, but still finding difficulty in securing private-sector housing, missed out.

The 1980s also saw experimentation with equity sharing and sweat equity schemes. Target groups for equity sharing included first-home owners with incomes slightly above the normal Housing Corporation eligibility limits but insufficient to manage repayments of private-sector loans. Second-chance loans could also be obtained, with women leaving a marriage with some equity from a previous house but insufficient deposit or income for a private-sector loan being eligible. The main attraction of the equity sharing scheme was that payments for the house were simply to be 25 per cent of income (more by choice), making outgoings affordable for most, even allowing for rates and maintenance. The main drawback was the indeterminate length of the loan, with the possibility of the house never being paid off. This arose because the interest of 3 per cent and the annual inflation rate were added to the balance of the loan, while the payments made (25 per cent of income) were subtracted. Essentially the borrower and lender share any capital gain. If income is low and the inflation rate high, this leads to an increasing loan balance. Nevertheless, the deposit – a minimum of 10 per cent of the purchasing price – was protected as a proportion of the purchase price, security of tenure was guaranteed, access to affordable housing ensured and ultimate ownership possible if future income relative to price increases was favourable, so the scheme attracted customers. Sweat equity, under which low-income families rent to purchase and undertake renovation with their own labour input becoming the deposit, was another experimental scheme which saw some lower-income households into their first home.

Ownership versus rental

New Zealand has one of the highest levels of private home ownership in the world. Over 70 per cent of properties are owned by their occupiers, with or without a mortgage. Levels of ownership are of course closely related to income, hence the lower rate among single-parent (especially female-headed) families and even lower rate among the Maori and Pacific Island populations, where the ownership/rental proportions are about equal. Whether the idealised quarter-acre section is really what all New Zealanders aspire to, or whether it is economic conditions which have made home ownership so attractive in the past, is a moot question. It is certainly an area which often appears to illustrate that 'to them that hath shall be given'.

It is possible that renting would be more popular if ownership had not, until recently, been so favoured by economic conditions and tax policies. As mentioned earlier, house price increases until recently exceeded general inflation rates and rates of return on most investments, and they do not attract a capital gains tax when owner-occupied. Interest paid on loans was tax deductible for a time, and the fact that imputed rent on owner-occupied housing is not taxed is a further benefit to owning rather than renting. When these factors are combined with security of tenure under ownership, the drying-up of the rental market and the consequent difficulty of finding cheap rental accommodation, it is not surprising that nearly everyone who can manage to buy a house does so. The fact that home ownership may no longer be economically rational in some circumstances has been pointed out by a number of commentators but has, at least as yet, had little impact on aspirations. Instead, government announced in the 1994 Budget that more Housing Corporation rental accommodation would be sold to their tenants, further reducing the amount of affordable rental housing in the market.

The Residential Tenancies Act was intended to improve conditions in the rental market by providing better disputes procedures, ensuring notice to tenants of at least 90 days (and to landlords 21 days) and requiring 60 days' notice of a rent increase, with levels appealable and being subject to no more than six-monthly increases. However, providing for up to four weeks' rent in the form of a centrally held bond makes entry to a rental property difficult for those on low incomes, and a payment of as much as six weeks' rent is needed at the start. One intention of the legislation was to make landlords feel sufficiently reassured to re-enter the market. However, there are still shortages at the bottom of the market in some locations.

One avenue that has been pursued to only a limited extent is greater flexibility of tenure, with half-way procedures between rents and purchase, and mortgages structured to allow lower payments early on and higher payments later when incomes have often increased and/or family-related expenditure decreased. The equity sharing and sweat equity schemes were moves in that direction, as are variable-rate mortgages, rent-to-buy, and the emergence of a secondary mortgage market. However, neither these, nor co-operative housing, have had a major impact.

The role of local government

Local government's activity in housing has varied among different authorities. Provision of rental pensioner housing, the building of which could be undertaken by the local authority borrowing from the Housing Corporation at 3 per cent interest, was common in the 1970s and early 1980s. Urban renewal was a joint central/local government and private concern, with the Community Housing Improvement Programme (CHIP) a prime example. Under this programme, neighbourhood improvement areas could be designated, with improvement loans on favourable terms available to those renovating their homes. The programme was cancelled in 1983 following doubts about whether loans were going to those in need, and concerns that upgrading and gentrification meant that inner-city housing became expensive and low-income earners driven out to the suburbs. Home improvement loans continue, but have been increased insufficiently to meet inflation.

Other aspects of local authority jurisdiction are building standards, zoning and by-laws. It is argued by some that in certain respects – such as densities, space between houses and path requirements – minimum standards are too high, resulting in new housing being overly expensive.

Income maintenance, vouchers, and direct provision

The purest free marketers, if persuaded that some degree of redistribution is justified, prefer untied income maintenance to specific support for housing. The theoretical advantage of untied income support is that it gives more choice to the individual recipient; however, there is no way of ensuring that any particular proportion will be spent on housing or that adequate housing standards will be ensured. It can be argued that part of such support should be targeted to areas society values highly, such as housing (and health and education), particularly when living standards of children are involved. Even Treasury accepts that a principal agent problem may be involved, with some parents taking insufficient account of the housing needs of their children unless some support is targeted. In addition, as housing costs are highest in the main urban centres where people may have the best chance of obtaining employment, there is a strong continuing case for direct housing assistance, geared to regional differences and actual costs. These considerations favour a voucher system, such as the old accommodation benefit or new accommodation supplement.

However, while such a system theoretically deals with the affordability problem, it does nothing to ensure adequate supply of low-cost housing or to deal with problems of discrimination by landlords or lenders. In addition, overseas evidence gives credence to the claim that subsidies are frequently absorbed by matching price increases. It ignores the fact that a degree of market failure in housing is inevitable, particularly at the low-income end of the market. These points constitute the case for continuing state provision of some housing, in addition to the supplement.

Arguing for continuing state provision does not imply approval of wasteful subsidies. Support was already being targeted much more tightly than before under the Labour Government. For example, 31 per cent of Housing Corporation borrowers under the modest income programme were paying the maximum, low-subsidy interest rate at the end of 1987, as against 1 per cent of clients two years earlier. However, subsidies remain essential for those on the lowest incomes, and that support needs to be delivered in a sensitive manner. This is another reason why the Housing Corporation role has been important. It greatly improved its interaction with clients during the 1980s, attempting to be more sensitive to Maori and Pacific Island needs in terms of both specific schemes and the employment of Maori and Pacific Island workers. There is very little reason to believe that the private sector would display similar sensitivity.

Housing policy under the National Government since 1990

Since 1990 major changes have been made to housing policy, its implementation and associated institutions. A new, small Ministry of Housing conducts research and gives policy advice. Housing New Zealand manages the state rental stock, about 70,000 units, managing the mortgage portfolio and acting as a profit-making business. Subsidised mortgages are being phased out. All rents in the public sector are being raised in stages to the 'fair market rent' (FMR), having previously been income related at 25 per cent of income. This has involved three rent increases for public-sector tenants, some of them very large (Sunday Forum, 1991). Whether rentals are in the public or private sector, all assistance is now based on a unified accommodation supplement. This aims to promote equality of treatment, avoiding the different levels of subsidy to households in similar circumstances which could occur with income-related rents in the public sector and the accommodation benefit in the private sector. However, in pursuit of this equality of treatment, it is likely that the poverty of many lower-income families renting in the private sector will simply be extended to others in the public sector.

The accommodation supplement (AS) is calculated from the formula: $AS = 0.65(FMR - .25\ I)$, where I is net income. Hence the supplement pays 65 per cent of the amount by which the fair market rent exceeds 25 per cent of income, up to a limit which varies by region to reflect different rental levels. Where rents are high, this formula can mean that 50 per cent or more of income goes in rent. Accommodation supplement is both income and asset tested, with the targeting very severe.

Women and housing

Prior to the Housing Corporation consultations with women mentioned earlier, the Society for Research on Women had undertaken two opinion surveys on satisfaction levels with housing. The first was of 24 women in low-cost homes in five outer suburbs of Auckland (Reynolds and Bonny, 1976), and the second involved 139 women in an old (Hataitai) and a new suburb (Whitby) of Wellington (Society for Research on Women, 1983). A number of themes emerged. One was the lack of, and importance of, flexibility in housing design and the resulting need to consult women on the arrangements within a house. Another was the importance of access to transport, shopping and community facilities. Isolation was often a problem for those without private transport and not in the paid workforce, while public transport was just as important to those in part-time or full-time paid work. Young families buying their own homes were often forced into the outer suburbs by the lower prices, and sometimes the associated lower quality, which prevailed there.

Several National Housing Commission research papers also addressed problems of particular concern to women. Judith Davey co-authored two studies on the effects of the Matrimonial Property Act and marriage breakdown on women and housing, while her paper on special housing needs in New Zealand paid attention to people living alone, sole parents and emergency housing, in all of which women predominate. She also drew attention to the needs of large families, ethnic minorities and those with disabilities (Davey, 1979; Davey and Atkin, 1980; Davey and Gray, 1985).

Lessons from the past and objectives

Another area in which housing policy needs to catch up with reality is in the rapidly changing patterns of household formation and modes of living. Most housing policy is geared to nuclear families, which now constitute less than half of all households at any one time. One-person households are increasing rapidly, mainly because of the ageing of the population but also because more younger people are choosing to live alone. Households in which two or more unrelated people are living together (including in de facto relationships) and sole-parent families are also rapidly growing in number, and average household size is decreasing. These trends are frequently not recognised in housing design or policy, though they have accelerated in the 1980s and early 1990s.

What of the objectives of policy, particularly as they concern women? Women should have as much freedom as possible (and certainly as much as men) in their choice of lifestyle and the housing that is part of it. Housing policy alone cannot deal with the many constraints women face as a result of economic and social factors, but it can mitigate some of the problems, pending their solution. For example, the growth of sole-parent families has not been accompanied by sufficient attention to their housing needs, with most housing assistance geared to first-home-owner, nuclear families. Many of the problems facing women alone or heading households are similar to those of any low-income household, in terms of access to affordable housing. Female sole parents and women in marriages or de facto relationships are more likely than men to have childcare responsibilities, sometimes in conjunction with paid work, and some are tied to houses in remote suburbs.

With higher female life expectancy, most women will of necessity face a period of life without a partner (many, of course, do so voluntarily). Thus, older women need to have available the choice of whether to stay in their current home, with appropriate support services where necessary, or to move. A smaller house or a move to a better climate may appeal, particularly if well-planned, co-operative living, providing both privacy and chances to meet others in communal facilities, is available. There should not, however, be pressure placed on women to make such a move. Retirement villages have their enthusiastic supporters and their critics. In any case, most of them require sufficient capital to put them out of the range of a large proportion of the population.

Greater flexibility is needed in the types of individual housing and group living facilities available, with more opportunity for joint purchase or rental, or co-operative housing of different sorts. Many individuals or groups, with or without children, might prefer to share housing, given appropriate design for privacy and communal facilities. Joint purchase by unrelated groups occurs at present, but needs more recognition and acceptance by financial institutions, and co-operative housing experiments could be encouraged. Housing trusts and other groups are already working in this area, but further help for different arrangements, including whanau-based housing, is needed. Women still encounter discrimination, prejudice and paternalism in seeking housing loans, even though discrimination is illegal and the position is improving. Additional discrimination is faced by Maori and other racial minorities, and by lesbians. The preferences of Maori men and women in the housing field have received some attention from governments; one measure of significance was the Multiple Ownership Housing Contract which enabled the Housing Corporation to make loans to Maori families wishing to build on land which is multiply owned.

Another area of importance is the link between housing and other factors. Social welfare benefits, the tax system and housing provisions are administered with little reference to each other. The result can be that there is no incentive to obtain part- or full-time work, as the combination of lack of sufficient tax deductions for childcare, abatements of benefits and housing allowances, and increased tax can lead to very high effective marginal tax rates.

Sole mothers in particular face difficult housing problems. The position of those leaving a marriage depends on the agreement made between the partners or decided by the court under matrimonial property legislation, although this does not cover de facto relationships. Women able to stay in the family home with their children are often in the best position. However, this is not always possible if refinancing is necessary. In the 1980s and 1990s the Housing Corporation has made 'second chance' loans available to those who need to refinance. However, there has never been enough money available to meet demand. Women who have always been in rental accommodation may be in even more difficult circumstances when leaving a marriage with few assets.

Some of the problems facing women in the housing market involve lack of information and questions of where to obtain advice. Solicitors, financial institutions and Housing New Zealand are among groups which can be approached. No overall consumer group exists, but a number of agencies are able to help. Tenants Protection Unions are a mine of information in the rental field, while voluntary agencies, including refuges and Citizens Advice Bureaux, have a major role. The Housing Network, made up largely of community workers involved in housing, works in the political arena and provides support and information.

Housing adequacy is, perhaps, the most important determinant of a satisfactory living situation. Yet women have been even less involved in decision-making on the internal design of houses, the planning of subdivisions and communities, and the financial aspects of housing provision than in any other area. This is paradoxical when the home, on a day-to-day basis, is usually a predominantly female domain. Tenant and community participation in controlling housing is a growing trend in Australia, and there is a crying need for more women to be involved in the planning and decision-making agencies throughout the New Zealand housing area.

Part IV

The Future

10
The Last 100 Years and Prospects for Positive Change

What has been good and bad for women about economic change in the last 100 years? This chapter will summarise longer- and shorter-term trends impacting particularly on women. It will then explore some alternative agendas, one liberal and one more radical, which offer the prospect for positive changes along feminist lines.

The rise of the political and economic new right in the last ten years, here and overseas, has involved a substantial backlash against earlier social and economic gains. Indeed, the assumption of selfishness may be a self-fulfilling prophecy, as less community responsibility forces people to operate against their own beliefs and behave selfishly. For example, many have taken out private health insurance and some refused to give blood when they would prefer to pay higher taxes and support a comprehensive public health system rather than pay part-charges and support private health services and a residual system for the uninsured. With increasing demands on community groups and individual families, it is women who take most of the strain, whether willingly or from necessity. International inequalities continue to widen and environmental issues receive largely token attention, with women often the leaders in global networks seeking real change.

Turning to more cheerful trends, disparities in income and wealth between women and men in New Zealand have certainly narrowed over the century as a whole. This has been assisted by gradual improvements in the law with respect to married women's access to property. The gaps, however, remain wide. In 1987–88 the average income of adult women from all but social welfare transfers was $8,360, only 40 per cent of the male figure. Including social welfare, the proportion increases to 51 per cent. With regard to wealth, women's share of the total is estimated to have risen from 30.5 per cent in 1980–81 to 38 per cent in 1987–88, partly as a result of more equal sharing of property following divorce (New Zealand Planning Council, 1990).

The major source of greater economic independence for at least some groups of women has been improved access to participation in a variety of areas of the paid labour force. Women were about 17 per cent of the labour force at the beginning of the century; the percentage increased slowly, with fluctuations for depression, war and its aftermath, to about 25 per cent in 1945 and 1961, and then took off. Today, women are more than 40 per cent of the full-time labour force and almost half the total. A thorough analysis of this increase in employment is a complex issue. A simplified account is that the long-term trend is partly the result of increased demand for goods and services, and therefore labour, with insufficient men to meet it. On the supply side, technological change affecting both the market and household sectors, reduced average family size, increasing education levels and changes in social attitudes interlink with economic necessity and personal preferences to increase the female labour force pool.

However, increased labour force activity has not meant greatly reduced home and caring work. Only very recently have work hours in the home decreased, despite earlier availability of labour-saving devices. Previously, trends to increased quality and switches from cleaning to intensive childcare were among factors maintaining hours of unpaid work, with only a slightly increasing contribution from the spouses of women in the paid workforce. Women in the paid workforce, while spending fewer hours on work in the home than their counterparts for whom this is a full-time job, still have the longest weeks (Schor, 1991, based on American data: no comprehensive data exist for New Zealand, though the limited figures available suggest similar conclusions). Hence the double burden indicates that paid work is not necessarily liberating, especially where it is a financial necessity. This was certainly so early in the century, when the conditions of sweated labour were disgraceful. Publicity about these conditions and the start of union organisation led, through the 1890 Sweating Commission, to improved occupational safety and health legislation and labour law. We might take heart from these examples about the improvements which have occurred. On the other hand, some of the conditions revealed by the second Sweating Commission in 1990, together with the changes to industrial relations legislation, give pause for thought.

One of the earliest pieces of labour legislation, dating from 1873, raises the issue of the pros and cons of special protection for women. The Employment of Females Act provided for an eight-hour day for women, 'but wages were often so impossibly low that women workers colluded with employers in evading the stipulations' (Coney, 1986: 19). Protections against exploitation, some of them desirable for both women and men, have been used to prevent women receiving equal treatment. Night work was for a long period in this category. At least two other protections – equal access to mining employment and to combat duty in the Armed Forces – remain to this day. The combat issue has been under review for some years. Whatever one's position on defence, the limitation has prevented women advancing in that area.

Technological and social change has led to an increasing range of work being available to women, with domestic work reducing from over one-third of women's jobs to its near disappearance as a live-in occupation during and after the Second World War. Factory, office and professional work of a caring type, at least, became available, although the gender division of labour was as strong as ever. The award system gave some protection for women, with minimum rates, but they 'were not framed with the interest of women workers as the foremost concern. When they regulated the employment of women, awards systematised, structured and sustained the segmentation of the labour force' (Robertson, 1991: 33). In longstanding areas of work, the Arbitration Court tended to support the status quo for gender divisions of labour: in new areas of work, it saw machine work as light, specialised and repetitive, and thereby highly suitable for women – at low wages.

Later in the period, gradually increased access to wider ranges of opportunities occurred for women who were able to pursue higher education, although the greater spread of occupational choice has only marginally reduced quantitative measures of the extent to which men and women work in different jobs (Gwartney-Gibbs, 1988; Van Mourik, Poot and Siegers, 1989). Nevertheless, some occupations, including clerical and keyboarding, became feminised. Such feminisation was usually accompanied by lowering of status, with the occupations 'deskilled'. As argued earlier, skills are largely social constructs, with the labelling of female-dominated work as less skilled being a device to suit male-dominated employers and unions. The trades defined as skilled were even slower to admit women through the apprenticeship system.

As the pool of single females contracted, barriers to married women entering the labour force decreased. Marriage bars vanished, and access to higher-level positions gradually improved. Currently married women constitute well over half the female labour force, up from only 3.7 per cent in 1936. However, access to affordable childcare continues to be inadequate, despite some state support.

A final optimistic point on long-term trends is that at least it is not acceptable for men of influence to make quite as blatant comments (out loud, anyway) as those propagated 80 to 100 years ago. For example, Dr F. C. Batchelor told a 1909 conference: 'From the age of puberty, the education of the two sexes should absolutely diverge ... Entry to a profession or securing some clerkship had become more important than motherhood, a grave error opposed to the most elementary principles of physiology' (quoted in Olssen, 1980). Of course, women hit back at these absurdities. Dr Emily Siedeberg, the first woman medical graduate at Otago University, argued that work in a profession improved women's health and happiness. Her further point that working women made the best wives, able to cope without charity or public assistance if husbands should die or become ill, should appeal to government today.

Where are we heading?

Under current policies we are heading for a dual economy, with accentuated differences between haves and have-nots. Even if the government's economic strategy meets with success on growth and competitiveness indicators, the likelihood of 'trickle down' and worthwhile employment for most seems remote. The social ills of poverty, crime, violence and alienation are likely to worsen, and they cannot be cured by ever-harsher measures. The second Sweating Commission and the People's Select Committee have well documented what is happening to those in the low-paid workforce or out of work, while soup kitchens, refuges and other community groups try to alleviate the resulting poverty and its impacts. Only feminists who can somehow reconcile their beliefs with economic orthodoxy can be happy with the continuation of current policies. Empowerment and success, highlighted by the media, are a reality for some professional and self-employed women. Other women, although less affluent, are active in self-help groups and community initiatives, which can also be empowering. However, these trends do not indicate adequate life possibilities for all, or a satisfactory social policy framework.

Views on desirable directions for change, both generally and in women's position in paid and unpaid work, vary between types of feminism. Liberal feminists may see as sufficient an equal place for women in current systems. Some also argue that with decision-making positions equally spread between women and men, the systems themselves would be transformed in desirable directions. Socialist and Marxist feminists, radical, lesbian and eco-feminists consider more drastic change essential, in tackling the other structural inequalities in addition to gender issues.

A liberal agenda

A liberal approach requires, at a minimum, equality of opportunity, the elimination of discrimination and removal or substantial reduction of the constraints which prevent real choices being available. Most women, particularly those who are primary caregivers, require the availability of adequate, affordable childcare before they can make a true choice about whether to participate in the paid as well as the unpaid workforce.

Another necessary item on the liberal agenda to free up choices for women (and men), and allow reasonable standards of living for all, is the continuation of a real, rather than a minimal safety-net welfare state. Changes in benefit levels, superannuation and accident compensation which do not recognise that women currently still have less chance of achieving economic independence – for example, through saving for retirement – are therefore of concern. So are increased reliance on user pays, and less state provision in the health, education and housing area. Lower direct tax rates on income do not compensate for loss of public universal services if the arguments for greater choice are regarded as largely spurious, as argued above. Further, there are inevitable problems of take-up and stigma with increased targeting of benefits and services.

Still needed on the agenda are measures to improve the position of women in education, training and the paid labour force, for equal pay and opportunity have never become a reality. More equal sharing of household work would assist with this, but experience indicates progress will be very slow. There are of course efficiency as well as equity rationales for equal opportunity for women, Maori and other groups experiencing discrimination in the labour market. Use of all human capital resources makes economic sense. Nevertheless, there is little evidence that free markets with minimal labour laws deliver the goods.

There is enough in the liberal agenda for many lifetimes of work, but for those who seek more radical change it is a blinkered and inadequate agenda. It does little to tackle the reality of structural inequalities in society which encompass ethnic, class and gender differentiation (as well as age, disability, sexual orientation and other areas of discrimination). Hierarchy and status differences based on patriarchy, capitalism, multinational enterprise and colonialism appear to be worsening, rather than the reverse, and suit the interests of power elites. To place gender discrimination at the top of any agenda is to miss the interweaving of different elements of disadvantage and discrimination.

A radical agenda

A more radical agenda must be based on substantially different ways of thinking and behaving from the orthodox economic paradigm and its consequences. Such change may anyway be forced on us, worldwide, by the globalisation of economic activity, technological change and environmental threat discussed earlier. Current orthodoxy is pushing macro- and micro-economic conformity on debtor countries, including New Zealand, with enforcement by the OECD, International Monetary Fund and credit-rating agencies. Yet not all countries can run surpluses, international competitiveness requires a low-cost economy, and increasing productivity squeezes out employment unless ever-new overseas markets can be found. While there is talk of a high-wage, high-employment, high-skill and high-productivity economy, in practice we are moving towards a dual economy, with low costs requiring low wages for all but the elite. The panacea of a better educated and trained labour force appears false when there is unemployment even among that group.

It may be that this round of technological change is, unlike previous ones, more labour displacing than creating. If so, and it is economically viable to adopt that change, worldwide there should be real output sufficient for all, with the problems being more to do with distributing the income than creating it. In that case, full employment in the traditional sense may be a thing of the past. In recognising this possibility I find myself, oddly enough, in some agreement with Infometrics (having criticised some of their other analyses in Chapter 2). However, Infometrics' solution consists of tax deductions to the wealthy to assist them to employ home help for gardening and childcare, or as servants. This would accentuate the dual economy of haves and have-nots. Such tax deductions would also move in the opposite direction from the widening of the tax base and level playing fields advocated by government and usually by Infometrics.

Nevertheless, it is difficult to accept the possibility that full employment might never be restored. Paid employment is important not only as a source of income for the worker and of goods and services for the community, but also for the opportunity to develop and use abilities, talents and skills. It provides a time framework, interest and communication with other adults, although some dead-end work can be boring and unsatisfying, undertaken almost entirely as an essential provider of earnings. Unemployment is one source of a variety of negative social consequences. Hence any acceptance that paid employment cannot be achieved for all must ensure that most of its positive aspects are still available.

This may require radically different ways of organising society, based on sustainable development, recognition of the value of all useful activity, and a distribution which provides adequate living standards for all. Many writers, some of them with a specific feminist approach, have common themes in their calls for a major rethink and a repudiation of standard economics (for example, Daly and Cobb, 1989; Henderson, 1978 and 1981; Mies, 1986; Tickner, 1991). These themes include: small is beautiful; appropriate technology; decentralisation of activity and decision-making; self-sufficiency (industry to agriculture, fewer consumer goods and less energy-intensive production); transformed gender division of labour; think global, act local; questioning of the scarcity/market exchange model as imposed when a plenty/gift exchange model may be possible. Intermediate steps suggested include: a consumer liberation movement (boycott unnecessary luxuries and multinationals exploitative of the consumer, of third world producers and/or of animals); employee control of production and marketing; women's coalitions, power bases and networks to organise economic activity and fight for major change.

The notion of short- and long-term changes, or intermediate and more major steps, analogous to liberal and radical agendas, is common to many writers in these areas. A case study of equal opportunity in four British organisations outlines some short agendas, which are minimum initiatives supported by those in management open to some change, and the longer agendas needed for real change (Cockburn, 1991). For example, removing the most obvious sex biases in recruitment, training and promotion may be supported by management. However, these small moves may leave unchanged many organisational practices which continue to discourage women from reaching and/or achieving in top positions. Many women will want to be in top positions only if a substantial change of climate occurs. 'They do not want to be the ones who do all the adapting, but to be active subjects in transforming the organization itself ... They welcome the idea of transformative change that could improve things, they believe, for both women and men' (*ibid.*: 216). Similarly, Cynthia Cockburn argues that management may support some degree of flexibility and support for childcare and maternity leave to enable women to combine work with domestic responsibilities, but not policies that would enable and encourage men to do the same.

Some feminists looking at economics from the outside have a refreshingly trenchant analysis of its inadequacies. 'The drive for economic growth can now be seen as a crucial vehicle for oppression, domination and exploitation, not only of women by men by assigning them the unpaid, low-paid, or low-status work of society, but its accompanying economic reasoning, which abets the subordination of minorities in all countries by designating vital work as less productive' (Henderson, 1981: 367–8). Inspired by Fritz Schumacher's visions of small is beautiful, Hazel Henderson confides that, 'I used to say merely that economics was getting in the way of citizens' talking to each other about what is valuable under drastically changed conditions. After knowing Fritz, I have had the courage to say simply that economics is a form of brain damage' (*ibid.*: 181).

Hazel Henderson sees patriarchy and the nation state as inevitably close to destruction, given a lack of will to make the industrial, technological, energy and cultural changes necessary for global human interdependence on a crowded planet. She sees recycling, more frugal lifestyles, and the decentralising and restructuring of patriarchal institutions as desirable but deeply threatening to those who benefit at present. 'Crucial relationships exist (often denied and rationalised) between culture and ethics and all economic/technical systems. Value systems and ethics, far from being peripheral, are the dominant, driving variables in all economic and technological systems ... Similarly all science is value-based' (*ibid.*: 376). Thus, she argues, the task facing industrial societies is to face the unsustainability of their entire value systems.

These ideas involve a retreat from growth and competitiveness as central concerns, towards sustainability and sharing. Carried into action they have the potential to reduce conflict, violence, crime and unemployment as currently defined, allowing reductions in defence and other expenditure in response to those social ills. Also necessary is the giving of genuine value to all worthwhile activity. This includes household, voluntary and caring work, art, craft, sharing skills and community activities, as well as paid work. This could mean, for example, having a positive rather than negative attitude to young people who wish to spend time surfing. Encouragement to join life-saving clubs and give time to patrolling beaches, and acquiring fitness, communication and other skills in addition to the specific ones needed, would allow a combination of leisure and useful activity. Encouraging and valuing all worthwhile activity involves greatly reduced dichotomies between paid and unpaid work in terms of status, identity and entitlements. It can be assisted by a basic income scheme, which involves universal adult entitlement to a minimum living amount, as discussed in Part III.

Instead of being entitled to income support through belonging to a particular, usually disadvantaged category, such as being unemployed, sick or disabled, all adults would be entitled to such a basic income. This could reduce stigmatisation and the feelings of reduced self-worth and morale experienced by many people currently dependent on benefits. A basic income scheme, clawed back through the tax system for those on higher incomes, allows simplicity, adequacy (including augmentation of low earnings) and removal of the conception of the deserving and undeserving poor. It could help in the quest for a less divided, more decent society for both women and men. Rankin (1991) has some New Zealand calculations on one possible variant. (See also Cass, 1988b; Paulus, 1991, for overseas discussion.) A basic income scheme, combined with a climate of encouragement for skills acquisition, could sharply reduce the hopelessness and destroyed self-esteem of those currently unemployed and labelled as such, as well as the associated personal and social costs. Support for childcare would be needed to supplement the basic income.

Many community initiatives which build on some of the ideas outlined above are already occurring, in New Zealand as elsewhere, with excellent results. These range from Green Dollar schemes, resource centres and other forms of barter and sharing, through investment funds promoting environmentally sound and worthwhile activity, to low-cost community education for adults. Co-operative activity can mean greater autonomy and control over one's own life. Socially responsible investment agencies in the third and first worlds support micro lending and micro enterprise, with the Grameen Bank in Bangladesh a well-known pioneer. Another example comes from Ahmedabad in India, where a social worker helped organise 6,000 female street vendors into an economically viable group. They accumulated a small fund from contributions from each woman, and these were deposited in a bank, allowing low-interest loans and a new economic power and status in the family (Leghorn and Parker, 1981). Although many of these developments arose from economic necessity, they may well be a pattern for the future, empowering individuals and communities.

Feminist and other networks, such as Development Alternatives with Women for a New Era (DAWN), the Prometheus Foundation and The Other Economic Summit, promote and discuss such developments. There are other groups, such as the Ms Foundation Institute on Women and Economic Development, working to achieve economic self-determination for low-income women in developed countries (Blakely, 1992). Some lesbian and feminist initiatives are avowedly separatist, seeing this option as a political statement as well as an important survival mechanism in a hostile world (Hoagland and Penelope, 1988).

These and other feminist, co-operative, environmentally conscious, barter and 'small is beautiful'-inspired projects may be seen as progressive, retrogressive, palliative or marginal, depending on the position of the viewer. They have not, as yet, transformed society in general, but they have had that effect on many individuals and groups. Perhaps it is a combination of 'bottom up' and 'top down' change which will really improve opportunities for an enhanced quality of life for all, with the former pushing the latter.

As invisible as feminist critiques in orthodox economic debates are those of indigenous peoples. The invasion and stealing of lives and land by colonialists also involved the near destruction of some social and economic systems from which there is much to learn. My understanding of Maori culture is limited, but notions of reciprocity, symbolic exchange and the gift economy (utu, hau) have parallels in some feminist writing, and demand respect and attention. Property rights are those of a guardian rather than of an owner allowed rights of disposal, with communality of ownership and intergenerational responsibility the key features (Cross *et al*, 1991). This direction seems much more promising than environmental economists' ideas about finding ways of spreading even wider the domain of property rights and markets into public good/environmentally sensitive situations. That solution addresses only resource allocation on a narrow efficiency basis, not distribution or sustainability (Eckersley, 1992). 'For all the iwi of Aotearoa the discount rate was zero ... The mana of an iwi, hapu or whanau was linked to its resources and to its ability to conserve them. The concept of takitoru is fundamental to Maori. It embodies the inseparability of wairua (spirituality) and oranga (the continuity of existence) from land and illustrates the inseparability of the spiritual value of land from its economic value' (Cross *et al*, 1991: 182).

The gift exchange is of course not totally foreign to economists, with labour contracts having been characterised as partially representing such a process (Akerlof, 1982). Unpaid household and caring work can be characterised as gift labour (although there may be exchange for commodities purchased with the income from paid labour), with the gift and exchange systems seen by some feminists as a contrast between a non-competitive, nurturing, feminine paradigm and a competitive, ego-oriented, masculine one (Vaughan, 1991). Genevieve Vaughan argues that scarcity is both integral to the exchange paradigm and artificially created, so that basing society on giving and orientation towards others is the only hope for the future. Gift systems which are based on the requirement of return might be argued by those wedded to exchange to be more similar than would be implied by two separate paradigms. However, underlying beliefs and structures may be very different.

The circulation of Maori taonga involves reciprocation, but is a matter of honour, not barter, and there is no bargaining over the value of such gifts.

> Gift-exchange can be as cruel as any competitive market ... [but] the market institution, although purporting to eschew violence through giving favoured place to the contractual form, namely voluntary exchanges in the marketplace, actually just veneers over and perpetrates the same violence under other forms ... The gift-exchange sensibility places on centre-stage an awareness of latent violence in all economic life, as something needing to be acknowledged and resolved socially. (O'Connor, 1991:166-8)

Suggesting that simple western notions of equality and liberty are something of a fraud, O'Connor argues that: 'Equality has to be understood, not in the sense of "equal rights" privately held and the inviolable "property" of each individual, but in the sense of a real – material and symbolic – reciprocation between participants in the new society, that upholds the mana of each' (*ibid.*).

For real change we have to listen to the analyses and priorities of all groups, particularly those less empowered by the structures of society. Strategic alliances are needed between all groups striving for change. These need to acknowledge and affirm differences, and be built on theory that explains the complex power relationships in society arising from race, gender, class and other dimensions. They are not easy to achieve, as we have to recognise that almost all of us benefit from power on some dimension and we must listen to the analyses of the less powerful. However, feminism has taught us that power is not all negative. 'Women and other subordinated groups are potentially able to recognize and use power not as domination but as capacity' (Cockburn, 1991: 241). We have to recognise both individual and group identity, with democracy based not on the 'will of the majority, but the enabling of many voices in negotiation' (*ibid.*).

Lisa Leghorn and Katherine Parker pull no punches in asserting that female values are different and better than male ones, and in arguing for a matriarchal society and economy, integrating public and private spheres. They too see a feminist or matriarchal concept of power as having more to do with 'creativity and cooperation, the power to change that comes from the caring for others, than with coercion or control' (Leghorn and Parker, 1981: 287). Divisions of labour would be structured horizontally, with equal decision-making and access to resources: barter might well be more common than monetary exchange and decisions decentralised. They see a transition as involving the building of matriarchal institutions while transforming or eliminating patriarchal ones, similar to the bottom up/top down approach.

A feminist perspective is crucial in helping analyse and solve the complex problems of intranational and international conflicts and inequalities, and environmental crises. It can help us understand 'how the global economy affects those on the fringes of the market, the state or in households as we attempt to build a more secure world where inequalities based on gender and other forms of discrimination are eliminated' (Tickner, 1991: 206). In the process, it also needs to transform the academic discipline of economics; indeed, that might wither away altogether.

References

Acker, J. (1989), *Doing Comparable Worth – Gender, Class, and Pay Equity*, Philadelphia: Temple University Press.

Age Concern (1990), *The 1990 Age Concern/National Mutual Study on the Lifestyle and Well Being of New Zealand Over 60s*, undertaken by Colman Brunton Research, Wellington: Age Concern.

___ (1991), *Equals and Allies? The Status of Older Women in New Zealand*, Wellington: Ministry of Women's Affairs.

Aimer, P. (1993), 'Was There a Gender Gap in New Zealand in 1990?' in H. Catt and E. McLeay (eds), *Women and Politics in New Zealand*, Wellington: Victoria University Press, pp. 63–78.

Akerlof, G. (1982), 'Labor Contracts as Partial Gift Exchange', *Quarterly Journal of Economics* 97, 4, pp. 936–45.

Apps, P. (1988), *Family Policy and Tax-transfer Options*, Canberra: Australian National University Centre for Economic Policy Research Discussion Paper No. 195.

___ (1991), *Labour Supply and Welfare: Some Effects of Neglecting Housework and Intra Family Inequality*, Canberra: Australian National University Centre for Economic Policy Research Discussion Paper No. 240.

Apps, P. and Savage, E. (1981), 'Tax Discrimination by Dependent Spouse Rebates or Joint Taxation', *Australian Quarterly* 53, 3, pp. 262–79.

Armstrong, N. (1992), 'Handling the Hydra: Feminist Analyses of the State' in R. du Plessis *et al*, pp. 224–38.

Australia Department of the Prime Minister and Cabinet, Office of the Status of Women (1987), *Women's Budget Statement: An Assessment of the Impact on Women of the 1987/8 Budget*, Canberra: AGPS.

Australia Federal Department of Employment, Education and Training Women's Bureau (1987), *Pay Equity – A Survey of 7 OECD Countries*, Canberra: DEETWB Information Paper No. 5.

Australian Bureau of Statistics (1990), *Measuring Unpaid Household Work: Issues and Experimental Estimates*, Canberra: ABS.

Australian Conciliation and Arbitration Commission (1986), *Judgement by Mr Justice Madden, President*, PO55CR M.S. 067/86MD Print G 2250, Canberra: AGPS.

Barrett, M. (1988), 'Standards and Foundations for Social Policy' in *The April Report III/1*, Wellington: Royal Commission on Social Policy, pp. 43–78.

Bartlett, R. (1989), *Economics and Power – An Enquiry into Human Relations and Markets*, Cambridge: Cambridge University Press.

Beaglehole, A. (1988), *A Small Price to Pay: Refugees from Hitler in New Zealand, 1936–46*, Wellington: Allen and Unwin.

Becker, G. (1974), 'A Theory of Marriage' in T. Schultz (ed), *Economics of the Family: Marriage, Children and Human Capital*, Chicago: National Bureau for Economic Research/University of Chicago Press, pp. 299–344.

___ (1976), *The Economic Approach to Human Behaviour*, Chicago: University of Chicago Press.

___ (1985), *An Economic Analysis of the Family*, Dublin: Economic and Social Research Institute of Ireland 17th Geary lecture.

Bergmann, B. R. (1981), 'The Economic Risks of being a Housewife', *American Economic Review Papers and Proceedings* 71, 2, pp. 81–5.

___ (1985), 'The Economic Case for Comparable Worth' in H. I. Hartmann (ed), *Comparable Worth: New Directions for Research*, Washington, D.C.: National Academy Press.

Bertram, G. (1988), 'Middle Class Capture' in *The April Report III/2*, Wellington: Royal Commission on Social Policy, pp. 107–70.

Blakely, M. K. (1992), 'Quilting New Networks', *Ms* II/5, pp. 19–23.

Blau, F. and Ferber, M. (1986), *The Economics of Women, Men and Work*, New Jersey: Prentice-Hall.

Blaug, M. (1988), *Economics through the Looking Glass*, London: Institute of Economics Affairs.

Bodichon, B. (1857), *Women and Work*, London: Bosworth and Harrison.

Bordo, S. (1986), 'The Cartesian Masculinisation of Thought', *Signs* 11, 3, pp. 439–56.

Bose, C. and Spitze, G. (eds) (1987), *Ingredients for Women's Employment Policy*, New York: State University of New York Press.

Boston, J. (1988), 'The State, Wage-fixing and Labour Market Reform: Some International Perspectives', *New Zealand Journal of Industrial Research* 13, 2, pp. 121–42.

Brashares, E. (1993), 'Assessing Income Adequacy in New Zealand', *New Zealand Economic Papers* 27, 2, pp. 185–207.

Brenner, J. (1987), 'Feminist Political Discourses: Radical Versus Liberal Approaches to the Feminization of Poverty and Comparable Worth', *Gender and Society* 1, 4, pp. 447–65.

Brosnan, P., Wilson, M. and Wong, D. (1989), 'Welfare Benefits and Labour Supply: a Review of the Empirical Evidence', *New Zealand Journal of Industrial Relations* 14, 1, pp. 17–35.

Bryson, L. (1992), *Welfare and the State – Who Benefits?*, Basingstoke: MacMillan.

Buchele, R. and Aldrich, M. (1985), 'How Much Difference Would Comparable Worth Make?', *Industrial Relations* 24, 2, pp. 222–33.

Burns, J. and Coleman, M. (1991), *Equity at Work – An Approach to Gender Neutral Job Evaluation*, Wellington: State Services Commission and Department of Labour.

Burr, R. (1986), *Are Comparable Worth Systems Truly Comparable?*, St. Louis: Center for the Study of American Business, Washington University.

Burton, C. (1987), 'Merit and Gender: Organisations and the Mobilisation of Masculine Bias', *Australian Journal of Social Issues* 22, 2, pp. 424–35.

___ (1988), *Redefining Merit*, Canberra: Commonwealth of Australia Affirmative Action Agency Monograph No. 2.

___ (1990), 'Report on Gender Bias in the Performance Appraisal Process', unpublished paper.

Burton, C. with Hag, R. and Thompson, G. (1987), *Women's Worth – Pay Equity and Job Evaluation in Australia*, Canberra: AGPS.

Busch, R., Lapsley, H. and Robertson, N. (1992), *Domestic Violence and the Justice System: A Study of Breaches of Protection Orders*, Hamilton: report to Victims Task Force of New Zealand Department of Justice.

Bywater, M. (1989), *Income Security for Older Women*, Wellington: Ministry of Women's Affairs.

Caird, M. (1899), *Motherhood Under Conditions of Dependence* quoted in paper by K. Sheppard, 'The Economic Independence of Married Women', delivered to National Council of Women 1899 meeting, reprinted in Malcolm (1989).

Cass, B. (1988a), *Income Support for the Unemployed in Australia: Towards a More Active System*, Canberra: Social Security Review Issues Paper No. 4.

___ (1988b) 'Combatting Poverty and Vulnerability: New Directions for the Distribution of Work and Income Support', paper delivered to 10th Annual Conference of the Australian Society of Labor Lawyers.

Cockburn, C. (1983), *Brothers – Male Dominance and Technological Change*, London: Pluto Press.

___ (1991), *In the Way of Women – Men's Resistance to Sex Equality in Organisations*, Ithaca, New York: International Labor Relations Press.

Colander, D. (1989), 'Research on the Economics Profession', *Journal of Economic Perspectives* 3, 4, pp. 137–48.

___ (1991), *Why Aren't Economists as Important as Garbagemen? Essays on the State of Economics*, Armonk, New York: M.E. Sharpe.

Colander, D. and Klamer, A. (1987), 'The Making of an Economist', *Journal of Economic Perspectives* 1, 2, pp. 95–111.

Coleman, W. (1992), 'Concord and Discord amongst New Zealand Economists: The Results of an Opinion Survey', *New Zealand Economic Papers* 26, 1, pp. 47–81.

Coney, S. (1986), *Every Girl: A Social History of Women and the Y.W.C.A. in Auckland 1885-1985*, Auckland: YWCA.

Conrad, C. A. (1992), 'Evaluating Undergraduate Courses on Women in the Economy', *American Economic Association Papers and Proceedings* 82, 2, pp. 565–9.

Cook, M. and Matthews, J. (1990), 'Separate Spheres: Ideology at Work in 1920s New Zealand – Letters to the Katipo 1923/4', *Women's Studies Journal* 6, 1/2, pp. 168–93.

Corner, M. (1988), *No Easy Victory – Towards Equal Pay for Women in the Government Service 1890-1960*, Wellington: New Zealand Public Service Association.

Cornish, M. (1991), 'Standards for Making Visible and Positively Valuing Women's Work – Review of Jurisprudence under Ontario's Pay Equity Act', paper delivered to Conference on Pay Equity, London.

Cross, Tu., Wilson, M., Earle, D., Scott, G., Kilby, C. and Chan, S. (1991), 'Iwi and Whanau Economic Development: Social Problems and Policy Implications' in J. Whitwell and M. A. Thompson (eds), *Society and Culture: Economic Perspectives*, Wellington: Proceedings of Sesquicentennial Conference of New Zealand Association of Economists 1990, 1, pp. 180–90.

Cuneo, C. (1990), *Pay Equity – The Labour-Feminist Challenge*, Toronto: Oxford University Press.

Curtin, J. (1991), 'Women, Trade Unions and Equal Pay' in *Proceedings of Union/Tertiary Research Conference* 4, pp. 154–72.

Dann, C. and du Plessis, R. (1991), *After the Cuts: Surviving on the Domestic Purposes Benefit*, Christchurch: University of Canterbury Department of Sociology Working Paper 12.

Daly, H. E. and Cobb, J. B. Jr. (1989), *For the Common Good – Redirecting the Economy towards Community, the Environment and a Sustainable Future*, Boston: Beacon Press.

Davey, J. A. (1979), *Special Housing Needs in New Zealand*, Wellington: National Housing Commission Research Paper 80, 2.

___ (1993), 'Asset Rich and Income Poor: Home Equity Conversion as an Option for Older Women', *Women's Studies Journal* 9, 2, pp. 148–59.

Davey, J. A. and Atken, W. R. (1980), *Housing and the Matrimonial Property Act 1976*, Wellington: National Housing Commission Research Paper 81, 1.

Davey, J. A. and Gray, A. (1985), *Marriage Breakdown and its Effect on Housing*, Wellington: National Housing Commission Research Paper 85, 2.

Dawson, J. (1992), 'Sex Equality and the Law of Employment', *New Zealand Journal of Industrial Relations* 17, 2, pp. 149–60.

Deeks, J. and Boxall, P. (1989), *Labour Relations in New Zealand*, Auckland: Longman Paul.

Dex, S. (1985), *The Sexual Division of Work: on Conceptual Revolutions in the Social Sciences*, Brighton: Wheatsheaf.

Dominick, C. H., Rochford, M. W. and Robb, C. H. (1988), *Solo Parents, Benefits and Employment*, Wellington: Department of Social Welfare Research Series 5.

Drago, R. (1989), 'The Extent of Wage Discrimination in Australia', *Australian Bulletin of Labour* 15, 4, pp. 313–25.

Du Plessis, R. (1992), 'Stating the Contradictions: The Case of Women's Employment' in R. du Plessis *et al*, pp. 209–23.

Du Plessis, R. with P. Bunkle, K. Irwin, A. Laurie and S. Middleton (eds) (1992), *Feminist Voices: a Women's Studies Text for Aotearoa*, Auckland: Oxford University Press.

Easton, B. (1988), 'From Reaganomics to Rogernomics' in A. Bollard (ed), *The Influence of United States Economics on New Zealand*, Wellington: New Zealand Institute of Economic Research Monograph 42.

___ (1989), 'Notes towards the Distributional Consequences of Policy Changes' in P. Saunders and A. Jamrozik (eds), *Social Policy in Australia and New Zealand, Proceedings of Joint Conference with the New Zealand Planning Council*, Sydney: University of New South Wales Social Welfare Research Centre Reports and Proceedings 78, pp. 171–94.

Eckersley, R. (1992), 'Free Market Environmentalism: Friend or Foe?' in A. Marston (ed), *The Other Economy – Economics Nature Can Live With*, Auckland: Learn by Doing Publishers, pp. 173–94.

Eisner, R. (1988), 'Extended Accounts for National Income and Product', *Journal of Economic Literature* XXVI, pp. 1611–84.

Elliot, H. S. R. (1910), *The Letters of John Stuart Mill*, London: Longmans, Green and Co.

Else, A. (1992), 'The State, the New Right and the Family' in R. du Plessis *et al*, pp. 239–51.

Elson, D. (1991), *Male Bias in the Development Process*, Manchester: Manchester University Press.

England, P. (1993), 'The Separative Self: Androcentric Bias in Neoclassical Assumptions' in M. A. Ferber and J. A. Nelson (eds), pp. 37–53.

Equal Opportunities Commission (1984), *Equal Pay for Work of Equal Value – A Guide to the Amended Equal Pay Act*, Manchester: EOC.

___ (1985), *Job Evaluation Schemes Free of Sex Bias*, Manchester: EOC.

Etzioni, A. (1988a), *The Moral Dimension: Toward a New Economics*, New York: Free Press.

___ (1988b), 'Toward a New Paradigm' in P. Albanese (ed), *Psychological Foundations of Economic Behaviour*, New York: Praegar, pp. 165–72.

Evans, S. and Nelson, B. (1989), *Wage Justice: Comparable Worth and the Paradox of Technocratic Reform*, Chicago: University of Chicago Press.

Faderman, L. (1991), *Odd Girls and Twilight Lovers: A History of Lesbian Life in Twentieth Century America*, New York: Columbia University Press.

Feiner, S. F. (1993), 'Reading Neoclassical Economics: Toward an Erotic Economy of Sharing', paper delivered to International Conference Out of the Margin: Feminist Perspectives on Economic Theory, Amsterdam.

Feiner, S. F. and Morgan, B. A. (1987), 'Women and Minorities in Introductory Economics Textbooks: 1974 to 1984', *Journal of Economic Education* 14, 4, pp. 376–92.

Feiner, S. F. and Roberts, B. R. (1990), 'Hidden by the Invisible Hand: Neoclassical Economic Theory and the Textbook Treatment of Race and Gender', *Gender and Society* 4, 2, pp. 159–81.

Fenwick, P. (1988), 'Royal Commissions Can be Good for Women', *Women's Studies Journal* 3, 2, pp. 85–94.

Ferber, M. A. and Nelson, J. A. (eds) (1993), *Beyond Economic Man – Feminist Theory and Economics*, Chicago: University of Chicago Press.

Ferguson, A. (1991), *Sexual Democracy – Women, Oppression and Revolution*, Boulder, Colorado: Westview Press.

Folbre, N. (1993a), 'How Does She Know? Feminist Theories of Gender Bias in Economics', *History of Political Economy* 25, 1, pp. 167–84.

—— (1993b), 'Socialism, Feminist and Scientific' in M. A. Ferber and J. A. Nelson, pp. 94–110.

Folbre, N. and Hartmann, H. (1988), 'The Rhetoric of Self-Interest: Ideology and Gender in Economic Theory' in A. Klamer, D. N. McCloskey and R. M. Solow (eds), *The Consequences of Economic Rhetoric*, Cambridge/New York: Cambridge University Press, pp. 184–203.

Frank, R. H., Gilovich, T. and Regan, D. T. (1993), 'Does Studying Economics Inhibit Cooperation?', *Journal of Economic Perspectives* 7, 2, pp. 159–71.

Franks, P. (1993), 'The Employment Contracts Act and the Demise of the NZ Clerical Workers Union', paper to Victoria University of Wellington Industrial Relations Centre seminar, Wellington.

Funder, K. (1989), 'The Value of Work in Marriage' in D. Ironmonger (ed), *Households Work*, Sydney: Allen and Unwin, pp. 173–89.

Gill, D. and Ungerson, B. (1984), *Equal Pay – The Challenge of Equal Value*, London: Institute of Personnel Management.

Gilligan, C. (1982), *In a Different Voice: Psychological Theory and Women's Development*, Cambridge, Mass: Harvard University Press.

Gilson, M. M. (1969), 'Women in Employment' in J. Forster (ed), *Social Process in New Zealand*, Auckland: Longman Paul, pp. 183–98.

Goldfinch, S. (1990), 'The Ideology of Treasury Economic Advice', paper delivered to Sociological Association of Aotearoa Conference, Christchurch.

Goldschmidt-Clermont, L. (1972), *Unpaid Work in the Household: a Review of Economic Evaluation Methods*, Geneva: International Labour Office.

___ (1983), 'Does Housework Pay? A Product-Related Microeconomic Approach', *Signs* 9, 1, pp. 108–19.

Grappard, U. (1993), 'How to See the Invisible Hand, or From the Benevolence of the Butcher's Wife', paper delivered to International Conference Out of the Margin: Feminist Perspectives on Economic Theory, Amsterdam.

Gregory, R. G., Anstie, R., Daly, A., and Ho, V. (1989), 'Women's Pay in Australia, Britain and the United States: The Role of Laws, Regulations and Human Capital' in R. T. Michael, H. I. Hartmann and B. O'Farrell (eds), *Pay Equity – Empirical Inquiries*, Washington: National Academy Press pp. 222–42.

Gregory, R. G., Daly, A. and Ho, V. (1986), *A Tale of Two Countries: Equal Pay for Women in Australia and Britain*, Canberra: Australian National University Centre for Economic Policy Research Discussion Paper 147.

Gregory, R. G. and Duncan, R. C. (1981), 'Segmented Labour Market Theories of the Australian Experience of Equal Pay for Women', *Journal of Post Keynesian Economics* III, 3, pp. 403–28.

Gustafsson, S. and Bruyn-Hundt, M. (1991), 'Incentives for Women to Work: A Comparison Between The Netherlands, Sweden and West Germany', *Journal of Economic Studies* 18, 5/6, pp. 30–55.

Guy, C., Jones, A. and Simpkin, G. (1990), 'From Piha to Post-Feminism: Radical Feminism in New Zealand', *Sites* 20, pp. 7–19.

Gwartney-Gibbs, P. (1988), 'Sex Segregation in the Paid Workforce: The New Zealand Case', *Australia and New Zealand Journal of Sociology* 24, 2, pp. 264–78.

Hacker, S. (1989), *Pleasure, Power and Technology – Some Tales of Gender, Engineering and the Cooperative Workplace*, Boston: Unwin Hyman.

Hahn, F. and Hollis, M. (eds) (1979), *Philosophy and Economic Theory*, Oxford/New York: Oxford Readings in Economics.

Hammond, S. and Harbridge, R. (1993), 'The Impact of the Employment Contracts Act on Women at Work', *New Zealand Journal of Industrial Relations* 18, 1, pp. 15–30.

Harbridge, R. (1993a), 'Bargaining and the Employment Contracts Act: an Overview' in R. Harbridge (ed), *Employment Contracts: New Zealand Experiences*, Wellington: Victoria University Press, pp. 31–52.

___ (1993b), *Service Workers Union Women Members Survey*, Report to SWU.

___ (1993c), 'The Employment Contracts Act: An Assessment of the Impact of the Legislation on Bargaining Arrangements', paper to AIRAANZ Conference, Auckland.

Harbridge, R. and Hince, K. (1993), 'Organising Workers: The Effects of the Act on the Union Membership and Organisation' in R. Harbridge (ed), *Employment Contracts: New Zealand Experiences*, Wellington: Victoria University Press, pp. 224–36.

Harding, S. (1991), *Whose Science? Whose Knowledge? Thinking from Women's Lives*, Ithaca, New York: Cornell University Press.

Hartmann, H. (ed) (1985), *Comparable Worth: New Directions for Research*, Washington, D.C.: National Academy Press.

Hartmann, H. I., Roos, P. A. and Treiman, D. J. (1985), 'An Agenda for Basic Research on Comparable Worth' in *Comparable Worth: New Directions for Research*, Washington, D.C.: National Academy Press.

Hartsock, N. C. M. (1983), *Money, Sex and Power: Toward a Feminist Historical Materialism*, New York: Longman.

Hastings, S. (1991), *Developing a Less Discriminatory Job Evaluation Scheme*, Oxford: Trade Union Research Unit, Ruskin College Technical Note 109.

Hawke, A. (1991), *Male-Female Wage Differentials: How Important is Occupational Segregation?*, Canberra: Australian National University Centre for Economic Policy Research Discussion Paper 256.

—— (1992), *How Do Australian Part-time Workers Compare with their United States Counterparts?*, Canberra: Australian National University Centre for Economic Policy Research Discussion Paper 273.

Hay Management Consultants (1986), 'The Role of Job Evaluation in Promoting Equal Pay for Work of Equal Value' in *Proceedings of Seminar on Equal Pay*, Wellington: Centre for Continuing Education, Victoria University.

Hayek, F. A. (1951), *John Stuart Mill and Harriet Taylor – Their Correspondence and Subsequent Marriage*, London: Routledge and Kegan Paul.

Henderson, C. (1900), 'The Ethics of Wage Earning', paper delivered to 1900 National Council of Women meeting, reprinted in Lovell-Smith, pp. 132–7.

Henderson, H. (1978), *Creating Alternative Futures – the End of Economics*, New York: Berkeley Publishing Corporation.

—— (1981), *The Politics of the Solar Age: Alternatives to Economics*, Garden City, New York: Anchor Press/Doubleday.

Hickerson, S. (1988), 'Instrumental Valuation: The Normative Compass of Institutional Economics' in M. Tool (ed), *Evolutionary Economics 1*, Armonk, New York: M.E. Sharpe Inc, pp. 167–93.

Hill, L. (1992), 'Review of Out of the Chorus Line: The Progress of Women in New Zealand Unions', *Women's Studies Association Newsletter* 13, 2, pp. 28–9.

—— (1993), '100 Years of the Vote: 80 Percent of the Pay: the Politics of Pay Equity', *Women's Studies Journal* 9, 2, pp. 87–113.

Hill, L. and du Plessis, R. (1993), 'Tracing the Similarities, Identifying the

Differences: Women and the Employment Contracts Act', *New Zealand Journal of Industrial Relations* 18, 1, pp. 31–43.

Hill, R. and Novitz, R. (1985), 'Class, Gender and Technological Change', paper delivered to New Zealand Sociological Association Conference.

Hoagland, S. L. (1988), *Lesbian Ethics – Toward New Value*, Palo Alto: Institute of Lesbian Studies.

Hoagland, S. L. and Penelope, J. (eds) (1988), *For Lesbians Only: a Separatist Anthology*, London: Onlywomen Press.

Housing Corporation of New Zealand (1987), *Women's Views on Housing*, Wellington: HCNZ Policy and Research Division.

Infometrics Business Services Limited (1991), 'Mitigating Misery: A Preliminary Assessment of New Zealanders' Capacity to Absorb Cuts in Real Incomes', unpublished paper.

International Confederation of Free Trade Unions Asian and Pacific Regional Organisation (ICFTU-APRO) (1992), *Regional Seminar on Structural Adjustment and Women – Report*, Mahukari, Japan: ICFTU-APRO.

Ironmonger, D. (1989), 'Households and the Household Economy' in D. Ironmonger (ed), *Households Work*, Sydney: Allen and Unwin, pp. 3–13.

Iverson, S. (1987), 'Why Women Get Paid Less', *Broadsheet* 146, pp. 38–40.

Jennings, A. L. (1993), 'Public or Private? Institutional Economics and Feminism' in M. A. Ferber and J. A. Nelson, pp. 111–29.

Jesson, B. (1987), *Behind the Mirror Glass*, Auckland: Penguin.

Johnson, L. C. (1987), 'Feminist Spaces Down Under', *New Zealand Geographer* 143, pp. 141–5.

Jones, D. (1993), 'Feminism/Postmodernism: A Beginner's Guide', *Women's Studies Association Newsletter* 14, 1, pp. 22–4.

Kelsey, J. (1993), *Rolling Back the State: Privatisation of Power in Aotearoa/New Zealand*, Wellington: Bridget Williams Books.

Killingsworth, M. (1983), *Labour Supply*, Cambridge/New York: Cambridge University Press.

___ (1985), 'The Economics of Comparable Worth: Analytical, Empirical and Policy Questions' in H. Hartmann (ed), *Comparable Worth: New Directions for Research*, Washington, D.C.: National Academy Press.

Klamer, A. (1990), 'The Textbook Presentation of Economic Discourse' in W. J. Samuels (ed), *Economics as Discourse – an Analysis of the Language of Economists*, Boston: Kluwer Academic Publishers, pp. 129–54.

___ (1991), 'On Interpretative and Feminist Economics' in G. K. Shaw (ed), *Economics, Culture and Education*, Aldershot: Edward Elgar, pp. 133–41.

Klein, P. (1988), 'Power and Economic Performance: the Institutionalist View' in M. Tool (ed), *Evolutionary Economics Vol I*, Armonk, New York: M.E. Sharpe, pp. 389–425.

Landau, R. (1992), 'On Making "Choices" ', *Feminist Issues* 12, pp. 47–72.

Lane, R. E. (1991), *The Market Experience*, Cambridge/New York: Cambridge University Press.

Leghorn, L. and Parker, K. (1981), *Woman's Worth – Sexual Economics and the World of Women*, Boston: Routledge and Kegan Paul.

Lewenhak, S. (1992), *The Revaluation of Women's Work*, London: Earthscan Publications.

Lovell-Smith, M. (ed) (1992), *The Woman Question: Writings by the Women Who Won the Vote*, Auckland: New Women's Press.

Low Pay Unit (1986), *Profile of Wage and Salary Earners*, Wellington: New Zealand Department of Labour.

Lutz, M. A. and Lux, K. (1988), *Humanistic Economics – the New Challenge*, New York: Bootstrap Press.

McAndrew, I. and Hursthouse, P. (1990), 'Southern Employers on Enterprise Bargaining', *New Zealand Journal of Industrial Relations* 15, 2, pp. 117–28.

McCloskey, D. N. (1985), *The Rhetoric of Economics*, Madison: University of Wisconsin Press.

___ (1993), 'Some Consequences of a Conjective Economics' in Ferber and Nelson, pp. 69–93.

McCrate, E. (1987), 'Trade, Merger and Employment: Economic Theory on Marriage', *Review of Radical Political Economy* 19, 1, pp. 73–89.

McDonald, E. (1993), 'Provocation, Sexuality and the Actions of "Thoroughly Decent Men" ', *Women's Studies Journal* 9, 2, pp. 126–47.

MacDonald, M. (1981), 'Implications of Understanding Women in the Labour Market Segmentation Analysis – The Unanswered Questions', paper delivered to SSHRC Workshop on Women in the Canadian Labour Force, Vancouver.

___ (1993), 'The Empirical Challenges of Feminist Economics: The Example of Economic Restructuring', paper delivered to International Conference Out of the Margin: Feminist Perspectives on Economic Theory, Amsterdam.

Mackay, J. (1902), 'Equal Pay for Equal Work', paper delivered to 1902 National Council of Women meeting, reprinted in Lovell-Smith, pp. 139–43.

McKinlay, R. (1990), 'Feminists in the Bureaucracy', *Women's Studies Journal* 6, 1/2, pp. 72–95.

Maital, S. (1988), 'Novelty, Comfort and Pleasure: Inside the Utility-function Black

Box' in P. Albanese (ed), *Psychological Foundations of Economic Behaviour*, New York: Praeger, pp. 1–27.

Malcolm, T. (1989), 'Kate Sheppard: Economic Independence of Married Women' introduction, *Women's Studies Journal* 5, 1, pp. 3–24.

Mannion, R. (1993), 'Breaking Up is Hard to Do', *Sunday Times* 25 July, p. 21.

Martineau, H. (1859), 'Female Industry', *Edinburgh Review* 222.

Marwell, G. and Ames, R. (1981), 'Economists Free Ride, Does Anyone Else?', *Journal of Public Economics* 15, pp. 295–310.

Matthaei, J. (1991), 'Marxist-Feminist Contributions to Radical Economics' in B. Roberts and S. Feiner (eds), *Radical Economics*, Boston: Kluwer Academic Publishers, pp. 117–44.

Meekosha, H. and Pettman, J. (1991), 'Beyond Category Politics', *Hecate* XVII, II, pp. 75–92.

Mies, M. (1986), *Patriarchy and Accumulation on a World Scale – Women and the International Division of Labour*, London: Zed Books.

Mill, J. S. (1924), *Autobiography* (ed) J. J. Coss, New York: Columbia University Press.

Morris, M. and Batten, D. (1988), 'Theories of the State: A Background Paper' in *The Role of the State: Five Perspectives*, Wellington: Royal Commission on Social Policy.

National Advisory Council on the Employment of Women (1990), *Beyond the Barriers: the State, the Economy and Women's Employment 1984–1990*, Wellington: New Zealand Department of Labour.

National Housing Commission (1988), *Housing New Zealand – Provision and Policy at the Crossroads*, Wellington: NHC.

National Women's Consultative Council (1990), *Pay Equity for Women in Australia*, Melbourne: Labour Research Centre.

Nell, E. (1972), 'Economics: The Revival of Political Economy' in R. Blackburn (ed), *Ideology in Social Science*, London: Fontana, pp. 76–95.

Nelson, J. A. (1991), 'Tax Reform and Feminist Theory in the United States: Incorporating Human Connection', *Journal of Economic Studies* 18, 5/6, pp. 11–29.

—— (1992), 'Gender, Metaphor, and the Definition of Economics', *Economics and Philosophy* 8, pp. 103–25.

—— (1993a), 'Value-Free or Valueless? Notes on the Pursuit of Detachment in Economics', *History of Political Economy* 25, 1, pp. 121–45.

—— (1993b), 'The Study of Choice or the Study of Provisioning? Gender and the Definition of Economics' in Ferber and Nelson, pp. 23–36.

—— (1993c), 'Feminist Economics: What Might It Look Like?', paper delivered to International Conference Out of the Margin: Feminist Perspectives on Economic Theory, Amsterdam.

___ (1994), 'Gender and Economic Ideologies', *Review of Social Economy*, forthcoming.
New Zealand Arbitration Court (1986), *Oral decision of the Court delivered by Finnigan, J.* (A.C. 24/86 D.I. 176/85): Wellington.
New Zealand Department of Social Welfare (1988), *Income Security for the Elderly – a discussion paper*, Wellington: Department of Social Welfare.
___ (1993), *A Profile of Sole Parents from the 1991 Census*, Wellington: NZDSW.
New Zealand Department of Social Welfare Social Policy Agency (1992), *A Survey of Retirement Provision*, Wellington: NZDSWSPA Research Unit.
New Zealand Department of Statistics (1990), *Elderly Population of New Zealand*, Wellington: Department of Statistics.
New Zealand Federated Clerical, Administrative and Related Workers Industrial Association of Workers (1986), *Submissions to the Arbitration Court on Equal Pay and the Equal Pay Act 1972 in the case with Farmers Trading Company Limited and Others*, Wellington: NZFCARWIAW.
New Zealand Ministry of Senior Citizens (1990), *Senior Citizens in New Zealand – 1st Post Election Briefing*, Wellington: Ministry of Senior Citizens.
New Zealand Planning Council (1986), *Labour Market Flexibility*, Wellington: NZPC Economic Monitoring Group.
___ (1990), *Who Gets What? The Distribution of Income and Wealth in New Zealand*, Wellington: NZPC Income Distribution Group.
New Zealand Treasury (1987), *Government Management*, Wellington: NZ Treasury.
___ (1990), *Briefing to the Incoming Government*, Wellington: NZ Treasury.
Nicholls, R. (1993), 'The Collapse of the Early National Council of Women of New Zealand 1896-1906', *New Zealand Journal of History* 27, 2, pp. 157-72.
Novitz, R., du Plessis, R. and Jaber, N. (1990), 'Pay Equity, The "Free" Market and State Intervention', *New Zealand Journal of Industrial Relations* 15, 3, pp. 251-62.
NZCTU Women's Conference (1993), *Ask the Women! A Survey of Women's Opinions on Economic, Social and Industrial Policy*, Wellington: New Zealand Council of Trade Unions.

O'Brien, M. and Wilkes, C. (1993), *The Tragedy of the Market: A Social Experiment in New Zealand*, Palmerston North: Dunmore Press.
O'Connor, M. (1991), 'Honour the Treaty? Property Rights and Symbolic Exchange' in J. Whitwell and M. A. Thompson (eds), *Society and Culture: Economic Perspectives*, Wellington: Proceedings of Sesquicentennial Conference of New Zealand Association of Economists 1990, 1, pp. 138-79.
Olssen, E. (1980), 'Women, Work and Family: 1880-1926' in P. Bunkle and B. Hughes (eds), *Women in New Zealand Society*, Sydney: Allen and Unwin, pp. 159-83.

Orr, E. (1986a), 'The Arbitration Court's Role in Supervising the Equal Pay Act 1972' in *Proceedings of Seminar on Equal Pay*, Wellington: Centre for Continuing Education, Victoria University.
___ (1986b), 'The Equal Pay Scene Revisited', unpublished paper.
___ (1988), 'Some Reflections and Proposals on Legislation to Promote Equal Pay for Work of Equal Value and Equal Opportunity', unpublished paper.
Osborne, R. (1976), 'Equal Pay for Equal Work: A Study of Legislation in the United States, Canada, the United Kingdom and New Zealand', Doctor of Law thesis, Cornell University.

Paulus, A. T. G. (1991), 'A Negative Income Tax in the Netherlands? A General and Emancipatory Point of View', *Journal of Economic Studies* 18, 5/6, pp. 105–19.
Pollak, R. (1985), 'A Transaction Cost Approach to Families and Households', *Journal of Economic Literature* XXIII, pp. 581–608.
Polanyi L. and Strassmann D. (1993), 'The Economist as Storyteller: What the Texts Reveal', paper delivered to International Conference Out of the Margin: Feminist Perspectives on Economic Theory, Amsterdam.
Power, M., Outhwaite, S. and Rosewarne, S. (1988), 'Writing Women out of the Economy', paper delivered to ANZAAS Congress, Sydney.
Prebble, M. and Rebstock, P. (eds) (1992), *Incentives and Labour Supply: Modelling Taxes and Benefits*, Wellington: Institute of Policy Studies, Victoria University of Wellington.
Prechal, S. and Burrows, N. (1990), *Gender Discrimination Law of the European Community*, Aldershot: Dartmouth Press.
Preston, D. (1993), 'The 1990/91 Benefit Changes', unpublished paper.
Pujol, M. A. (1992), *Feminism and Anti-feminism in Early Economic Thought*, Aldershot: Edward Elgar.
___ (1993), 'Feminism, Anti-feminism and Early Neo-classical Economics', paper delivered to International Conference Out of the Margin: Feminist Perspectives on Economic Theory, Amsterdam.

Rankin, K. (1991), *The Universal Welfare State Incorporating Proposals for a Universal Basic Income*, Auckland: University of Auckland Department of Economics Discussion Paper 12.
Raymond, J. (1987), *Bringing Up The Children Alone: Policies for Sole Parents*, Canberra: Australian Social Security Review Issues Paper 3.
Rees, A. (1979), *The Economics of Work and Pay* 2nd edn, New York: Harper and Row.
Remick, H. (ed) (1979), 'Strategies for Creating Sound Bias-free Job Evaluation Schemes' in *Job Evaluation and EEO: the Emerging Issues*, New York: Industrial Relations Counselors Inc., pp 85–112.

Reskin, B. (1988), 'Bringing the Men Back In: Sex Differentiation and the Devaluation of Women's Work', *Gender and Society* 2, 1, pp. 58–81.

Review Committee on Equal Pay (1979), *Equal Pay Implementation in New Zealand*, Wellington: Department of Labour.

Reynolds, M. and Bonny, S. (1976), *Women's World: Houses and Suburbs*, Auckland: Society for Research on Women in New Zealand Auckland Branch.

Robbins, L. (1976), *Political Economy: Past and Present*, London: Macmillan.

Robertson, S. (1991), 'Women Workers and the New Zealand Arbitration Court, 1894–1920' in R. Frances and B. Scates (eds), *Women, Work and the Labour Movement in Australia and Aotearoa/New Zealand*, Sydney: Australian Society for the Study of Labour History, pp. 30–41.

Robinson, J. (1971), *Freedom and Necessity*, London: Vintage/Random House.

Rosenberg, W. (1993), *New Zealand Can Be Different and Better: Why Deregulation Does Not Work*, Christchurch: New Zealand Monthly Review Society Inc.

Rosetti, J. (1992), 'Deconstruction, Rhetoric and Economics' in N. de Marchi (ed), *Post-Popperian Methodology of Economics*, Boston: Kluwer Academic Publishers, pp. 211–34.

Rossi, A. (1970), 'Sentiment and Intellect – The Story of John Stuart Mill and Harriet Taylor Mill' in Alice S. Rossi (ed), *Essays in Sex Equality by John Stuart Mill and Harriet Taylor Mill*, Chicago: University of Chicago Press, pp. 3–63.

Royal Commission on Social Policy (1988), *The April Report – Report of the RCSP*, Wellington: RCSP.

Ryan, R. (1993), *Japanisation: or a 'New Zealand Way'? Five Years on at Nissan New Zealand*, Wellington: Victoria University of Wellington Industrial Relations Centre Working Paper 5/93.

Saar, P. (1992), *Out of the Chorus Line – The Progress of Women in New Zealand Unions*, Wellington: NZ Council of Trade Unions.

Sawhill, I. (1977), 'Economic Perspectives on the Family', *Daedelus* 106, 2, pp. 115–25.

Sayers, J. (1991), 'Women, the Employment Contracts Act and Bargaining: A Discussion Paper', *New Zealand Journal of Industrial Relations* 16, 2, pp. 159–66.

Schmookler, A. B. (1993), *The Illusion of Choice – How the Market Economy Shapes our Destiny*, New York: State University of New York Press.

Schor, J. B. (1991), *The Overworked American – the Unexpected Decline of Leisure*, New York: Basic Books.

Scitovsky, T. (1976), *The Joyless Economy*, New York: Oxford University Press.

—— (1986), *Human Desire and Economic Satisfaction – Essays on the Frontiers of Economics*, Brighton: Wheatsheaf.

Seals, B. and Ormrod, C. (1991), *Gender-neutral Superannuation*, Wellington: Ministry

Women's Affairs and State Services Commission.
Seiz, J. A. (1990), 'Comment on Klamer's Paper' in W. J. Samuels (ed), *Economics as Discourse – an Analysis of the Language of Economists*, Boston: Kluwer Academic Publishers, pp. 155–65.
___ (1991), 'The Bargaining Approach and Feminist Methodology', *Review of Radical Political Economics* 23, 1/2, pp. 22–9.
___ (1992), 'Gender and Economic Research' in N. de Marchi (ed), *Post-Popperian Methodology of Economics*, Boston: Kluwer Academic Publishers, pp. 273–319.
___ (1993), 'Feminism and the History of Economic Thought', *History of Political Economy* 25, 1, pp. 185–201.
Sen, A. K. (1984), *Resources, Values and Development*, Cambridge, Mass: Harvard University Press.
___ (1990), 'Gender and Cooperative Conflicts' in I. Tinker (ed), *Persistent Inequalities – Women and World Development*, New York: Oxford University Press, pp. 123–49.
Sharp, R. and Broomhill, R. (1988), *Short Changed: Women and Economic Policies*, Sydney: Allen and Unwin.
Sheppard, K. (1892), 'Economics', *Canterbury Times* 15 December 1892, p. 6, reprinted in Lovell-Smith, pp. 106–9.
___ (1896), 'Economic Independence of Married Women', *White Ribbon*, pp. 7–8, reprinted in Lovell-Smith, pp. 152–3.
___ (1898), 'Interview with Stella Henderson', *White Ribbon*, June, pp. 1–2, reprinted in Lovell-Smith, pp. 125–9.
Shipley, Hon. J. (1991), *Social Assistance – Welfare that Works: A Statement of Government Policy on Social Assistance*, Wellington: Government Budget Document.
Smith, L. (1893), 'The Economic Independence of Women', *Canterbury Times*, 2 March 1893, p. 7, reprinted in Lovell-Smith, p. 110.
Snively, S. (1988), *The Government Budget and Social Policy*, Wellington: Royal Commission on Social Policy.
Society for Research on Women (1983), *House or Home*, Wellington: SROW Wellington Branch.
Sonius, E. (1989), *Time for Kids? The Impact of Children on Household Production*, University of Melbourne Department of Architecture and Building, Centre for Applied Research on the Future, Research Discussion Paper 7.
Soper, K. (1983), 'New Introduction' in Harriet Taylor Mill, *'Enfranchisement of Women' and John Stuart Mill, 'The Subjection of Women'*, London: Virago, pp. i–xvi.
Statistics New Zealand (1993), *Incomes Statistics 1992*, Wellington: Statistics NZ.
Steinberg, R. J. (1987), 'Dilemmas of Advocacy Research: Experiences with Comparable Worth', paper delivered to plenary panel of Social Science Research and Law Reform, Law and Society Association.

Steinberg, R. J. and Haignere, L. (1985), 'Equitable Compensation: Methodological Criteria for Comparable Worth' in C. Bose and G. Spitze (eds), *Ingredients for Women's Employment Policy*, Albany, New York: State University of New York Press, pp. 159-82.

Steinberg, R. J., Haignere, L., Possin, C., Chertos, C. H. and Treiman, D. (1986), *The New York Pay Equity Study: A Research Report*, Albany, New York: Center for Women in Government.

Stephens, R. (1987), *Social Welfare in Australia: A View from the East*, Melbourne: University of Melbourne Department of Economics Research Paper 169.

___ (1988), *Issues in the Measurement of Poverty and Standards of Living*, Wellington: Victoria University of Wellington Department of Economics Discussion Paper 48.

___ (1992), 'Budgeting with the Benefit Cuts' in J. Boston and P. Dalziel (eds), *The Decent Society? Essays in Response to National's Economic and Social Policy*, Auckland: Oxford University Press.

Stilwell, F. (1988), 'Contemporary Political Economy: Common and Contested Terrain', *Economic Record* 64, 184, pp. 14-25.

St John, S. (1991), 'The Core Family Unit – the Implications of the 1991 Budget for Women', *Women's Studies Journal* 7, 2, pp. 1-13.

___ (1993), 'The Tax/Benefit Interface' in C. Scott (ed), *Women and Taxation*, Wellington: Victoria University of Wellington Institute of Policy Studies, pp. 132-46.

St John, S. and Ashton, T. (1990), *Private Pensions in New Zealand – Country Report for the OECD*, Wellington: Victoria University of Wellington Institute of Policy Studies.

Strassman, D. (1993a), 'The Stories of Economics and the Power of the Storyteller', *History of Political Economy* 25, 1, pp. 147-65.

___ (1993b), 'Not a Free Market: The Rhetoric of Disciplinary Authority in Economics' in Ferber and Nelson, pp. 54-68.

Sunday Forum, prepared by The Family Centre and Business and Economic Research Limited (1991), *The National Government Budgets of the First Year in Office: A Social Assessment*, Wellington: New Zealand Educational Institute.

Sutch, W. B. (1974), *Women with a Cause*, Wellington: New Zealand University Press.

Sutton, F. (1985), 'Female-Male Pay Differentials in the Executive/Clerical Class of the Public Service', unpublished paper.

Symes, B. (1990), 'Pay Equity in Canada', paper delivered to Eighth Annual Labour Arbitration Conference, Calgary, Alberta.

Taylor, H. (1983), *The Enfranchisement of Women, 1851*, reprinted with a new introduction by Kate Soper, London: Virago.

Tennet, E. (1986), *Evidence in the case of New Zealand Federated Clerical, Administrative and Related Workers Industrial Association of Workers and Farmers Trading Company Limited and Others*, Wellington: NZFCARWIAW.
Thomson, D. (1991), *Selfish Generations? The Ageing of New Zealand's Welfare State*, Wellington: Bridget Williams Books.
Thurow, L. (1975), *Generating Inequality: Mechanisms of Distribution in the U.S. Economy*, New York: Basic Books.
Tickner, J. A. (1991), 'On the Fringes of the World Economy: A Feminist Perspective' in C. N. Murphy and R. Jooze (eds), *The New International Political Economy*, Boulder, Colorado: Lynne Rienner, pp. 191–206.
Treiman, D. and Hartmann, H. (eds) (1981), *Women, Work and Wages: Equal Pay for Jobs of Equal Value*, Washington D.C.: National Academy Press.

Urban Research Associates, Hyman, P. and Clark, A. (1987), *Equal Pay Study – Phase One Report*, Wellington: New Zealand Department of Labour.

Van Mourik, A., Poot, J. and Siegers, J. (1989), 'Trends in Occupational Segregation of Women and Men in New Zealand: Some New Evidence', *New Zealand Economic Papers* 23, pp. 29–50.
Vaughan, J. (1991), 'The Gift Economy', *Ms* I, 6, pp. 84–5.
Vogler, C. and Pahl, J. (1993), 'Social and Economic Change and the Organisation of Money within Marriage', *Work, Employment and Society* 7, 1, pp. 71–95.

Waller, W. and Jennings, A. (1990), 'On the Possibility of a Feminist Economics: The Convergence of Institutional and Feminist Methodology', *Journal of Economic Issues* XXIV, 2, pp. 613–21.
Ward, B. (1972), *What's Wrong with Economics?*, New York: Basic Books.
Ward, K. (1990), 'Introduction and Overview' in K. Ward (ed), *Women Workers and Global Restructuring*, Ithaca: Cornell University Press, pp. 1–22.
Waring, M. (1988a), 'Discussion Paper on the Role of the State' in *The Role of the State: Five Perspectives*, Wellington: Royal Commission on Social Policy.
___ (1988b), *Counting for Nothing: What Men Value and What Women Are Worth*, Wellington: Allen and Unwin/Port Nicholson Press.
Weitzman, L. (1985), *The Divorce Revolution*, New York: Free Press.
Wellington Women's Studies Association (1988), 'Submission to Royal Commission on Social Policy', *Women's Studies Association Newsletter* 9, 2, pp. 7–25.
Wheelwright, E. L. (1976), 'Thorstein Veblen and the American Institutionalists' in E. L. Wheelwright and F. Stilwell (eds), *Readings in Political Economy Vol I*, Sydney: A and NZ Book Company, pp. 177–80.
White, M. (1983), *Breaking the Circular Hold: Taking on the Patriarchal and Ideological*

Biases in Traditional Economic Theory, Toronto: Centre for Women's Studies in Education Occasional Paper 7.

Williams, R. M. (1993), 'Race, Deconstruction, and the Emergent Agenda of Feminist Economic Theory' in Ferber and Nelson, pp. 111–29.

Wilson, M. A. (1992), 'Employment Equity Act 1990: A Case Study in Women's Political Influence 1984–90' in J. Deeks and N. Perry (eds), *Controlling Interests – Business, the State and Society in New Zealand*, Auckland: Auckland University Press, pp. 113–31.

___ (1993), 'The Making and Repeal of the Employment Equity Act: What Next?', *Women's Studies Journal* 9, 2, pp. 68–86.

Wisconsin Task Force on Comparable Worth (1985), *Report*, Madison: University of Wisconsin.

Women's Legal Resources Group (1985), *She Works Hard for the Money . . . Equal Pay for Women*, Melbourne: Women's Legal Resources Group, Victoria.

Wood, S. (1985), 'Work Organisation' in R. Deem and G. Salaman (ed), *Work, Culture and Society*, Milton Keynes/Philadelphia: Open University Press, pp. 77–101.

Woodley, A. (1993), 'One Step Forward, Two Steps Back – The Pay Equity Campaign: A Study of Political Strategy', Master of Arts degree research essay, University of Auckland.

Woolley, F. (1988), *A Non-Cooperative Model of Family Decision Making*, London: London School of Economics TIDI/125.

___ (1993), 'Feminist Ideology and Welfare Economics', paper delivered to International Conference Out of the Margin: Feminist Perspectives on Economic Theory, Amsterdam.

Working Group on Equal Employment Opportunities and Equal Pay (1988), *Towards Employment Equity*, Wellington: Working Group.

Yates, G. G. (ed) (1985), *Harriet Martineau on Women*, New Brunswick, New Jersey: Rutgers.

Index

accident compensation 173–4, 188
advertising 33, 44
agency theory *see* principal agent
   problem
agendas for the future:
   liberal 223–4;
   radical 224–30
Air New Zealand air hostess case 140
Aitken job evaluation scheme 129
altruism 27–9, 57
Arbitration Commission 87, 121
Arbitration Court 81, 82, 83, 85, 221
Australia:
   government/trade union Accord 41, 113, 127;
   new-right strategies 41;
   and pay equity 99, 126–7, 132–3;
   social security system 164, 165, 168;
   supplementary Women's Budget 39

Batchelor, F. C. 222
benefits:
   accommodation benefit and supplement 208, 212, 213;
   child support and family benefit 161–2;
   domestic purposes benefit 168–9, 187–8;
   levels 70–6, 160, 166–70;
   seen as tax burden on business 75;
   targeted or universal 169–70, 184, 209, 223;
   units of assessment 163–4, 182–4;
   widows' benefit 168–9;
   see also income maintenance;
   labour force participation, women's
Birch, Bill 17

Bodichon, Barbara 82
Britain *see* Great Britain

Cammel Laird Shipbuilders Ltd 130
Campaign for Equal Value, Equal Pay 85–6, 150
Canada:
   and pay equity 127–9, 134;
   and superannuation 200
Canterbury Board of Education 80
Cartwright inquiry 172
Chicago school 20
childcare 65–70 *passim*, 162–3, 222, 223
choice and scarcity 15–18
Clark, Helen 6, 136
Clerical Workers Union 83, 85, 96, 120–1, 138, 142, 143
Combined Trades Unions (CTU) 113, 119;
   National Women's Committee 122, 136–7
comparable worth *see* earnings gap;
   job evaluation; pay equity
conflict:
   in families over consumer preferences 14, 25–6, 69;
   in industrial relations 113
'conjective economics' 58–9
consumer preferences:
   and conflict in families 14, 25–6, 69;
   in orthodox economics 32–4;
   see also utility functions
co-operative enterprise 57–8, 227–8
credit agencies 19, 224

Department of Labour *see* Labour, Dept. of

discrimination *see subject headings relating to economic theory and social and economic policies*
Distribution and General Workers Union 138
distributional change 30–2
division of labour *see* labour, division of

earnings gap:
  calculation of average earnings 90;
  decentralised industrial bargaining 132;
  direct and indirect discrimination 95;
  earnings function studies 97–8;
  historical trends in 219–20;
  impact of different hours of work 89–90;
  low pay in female-dominated occupations 89, 102, 133, 221;
  non-wage discrimination 95;
  role of occupational segregation 95–7, 133;
  wage-setting process 90–4;
  see also job evaluation; labour market; pay equity
Econometric Society 37–8
economic independence, women's:
  proposed right to share of husband's income 178–9, 181;
  of single women 180–1;
  see also benefits; income maintenance; labour force participation, women's; superannuation
economic modelling, oversimplicity of 20, 32
economic theory, feminist critiques of *see* orthodox economics, feminist critiques of
economics *see* 'conjective economics'; feminist theory; humanistic economics; institutional economics; new home economics; orthodox economics; political economy; socio-economics
economics textbooks and courses, feminist critiques of 52–3
economists: selfishness of 33–4; *see also* women economists
efficiency:
  and case for pay equity 98–9, 223;
  and costs of redistribution policies 31–2;
  in home production 70–6
Employment Contracts Act 1991 (ECA):
  and decentralised industrial bargaining 112, 118, 122;
  and disputes procedures 123;
  and EPA 136–53 *passim*;
  legislative changes arising from 139–40;
  more women than men opposed to 48;
  spurious symmetry of 17;
  and trade unions 84, 113, 120, 132, 138
Employment Equity Act 1990 6, 86–8, 100, 110, 121, 139, 148
Employment of Females Act 1873 220–1
Employment Tribunal 148
Engineers Union 116, 119
enterprise agreements 115–18
environment, activity detrimental to:
  and GDP 62;
  and Index of Sustainable Economic Welfare 64;
  and orthodox economics 14, 16
equal employment opportunities (EEO) 87, 95
Equal Employment Opportunities Trust 150

Equal Opportunities Tribunal
  (EOT) 140, 148
equal pay *see* pay equity
Equal Pay Act 1972 (EPA) 81, 84–5, 99,
  110;
  and ECA 136–53 *passim*
Equal Pay Amendment Act 1991 140
Equal Pay Study 86
European Economic Community 129,
  130, 135

families *see* new home economics
family wage 83, 180
female-dominated occupations:
  low pay in 89, 102, 133, 221;
  and shift away from occupational
    bargaining 120–3
feminist critiques *see* sub-headings under
    economics textbooks and courses;
    orthodox economics; social policy;
    science
feminist networks in economics 228
feminist theory:
  in economics 55–60;
  in theory of knowledge 35–7, 58
Fisher and Paykel 115
Fortex 115
free-rider behaviour 33–4, 59
Friedman, Milton 32

game theory 26
gender bias:
  in economics textbooks and
    courses 52–4;
  in macro-economic policy 39–44;
  in orthodox definitions of economic
    activity 14, 19, 24, 33, 38–9, 61;
  in 'Mitigating Misery' 68–9;
  in role of the state 43–4
gender differences:
  altruism and self-
    interestedness 27–8;

mathematical precision and language
  richness 55–6
gender roles *see* labour, division of
General Agreement on Tariffs and
  Trade (GATT) 42
Gibbs, Alan 159
Government Superannuation Fund
  198, 202
Great Britain:
  and pay equity 129–30, 133–4;
  and superannuation 200
Gresham, Peter (Minister of Social
  Welfare) 163, 184
Gross Domestic Product (GDP) 62–5

Hay job evaluation scheme 107–8
Hayward v. *Cammel Laird Ship-
  builders Ltd* 130
Henderson, Christina 80–1
Henderson, Stella 81
Hicks, Carol 137
Holidays Act 1981 146
home equity conversion schemes 203
home production, efficiency in 70–6
hours of work 89–90
Housing, Ministry of 213
Housing Corporation:
  home equity conversion schemes
    203;
  loans and rents 209, 210, 212, 216;
  Women's Unit 206
housing costs in minimum budgets 72
Housing New Zealand 213, 216
housing policy:
  Community Housing Improvement
    Plan (CHIP) 211;
  equity sharing 209–11, 212;
  fair market rents (FMR) 213;
  gender impacts of 213–16;
  and housing market 206–13;
  income maintenance, vouchers and
    direct provision 212–13;

housing policy *continued*:
  multiple ownership housing contracts 215;
  ownership v. rental 210–11;
  role of local government 211–12;
  second-chance loans 209;
  sweat equity schemes 209–10, 211
Human Rights Act 1993 139, 201, 202
Human Rights Commission 140
Human Rights Commission Act 1977 84, 139
humanistic economics 56–7

'incentives' as double-speak or euphemism 20–1, 70
income maintenance:
  categorical approach to entitlement 165–6;
  gender implications 165–70, 181–8;
  see also benefits; labour force participation, women's
Index of Sustainable Economic Welfare 64
'individuals in relation' 28, 161, 163
industrial bargaining:
  attitudes towards decentralisation 118–19;
  enterprise agreements 115–18;
  reforms of 1980s 112–15;
Industrial Relations Service 145
Infometrics 61, 224–5
Inland Revenue, Dept. of 193, 194
Inspector v. D. F. Jones 143, 144, 147
institutional economics 14, 22, 34–5
International Labour Organisation:
  ILO Convention 100 149
International Monetary Fund 19, 42, 224

job evaluation:
  credibility of schemes 111;
  inconsistencies and subjectivity in 85, 104;
  and job descriptions 103;
  off-the-shelf schemes 107–9, 129;
  policy capturing systems 104–6, 111;
  single or multiple schemes 109;
  and undervaluation of women's work and skills 102–4, 111–12, 134;
  and weighting of different factors 103;
  within-employer or cross-employer comparisons 109–10;
  and work of equal value 101–4;
  see also earnings gap; labour market; pay equity

Kerr, Roger 20

Labour, Dept. of 6, 89, 137, 140, 147
  inspectorate 146
labour, division of 24, 33, 46, 67–9, 186
labour force participation, women's:
  and effective marginal tax rates 182–4, 185;
  and gender roles 24, 33, 67–9, 186;
  historical trends in 80–3, 220–2;
  impact of ideology and policy on 181–8;
  and net value of second family income 65–70;
  by partnered women 182–4;
  related to decline in marriage rates 27;
  in Sweden 184, 185;
  by unpartnered women 184–8;
  see also benefits; economic independence, women's; income maintenance
labour market:
  dual 143;
  flexibility in 112, 138;
  orthodox explanation of wage

relationships 90–4, 102, 104;
power differences in 17–18, 93–4;
see also earnings gap; job evaluation;
  pay equity
Labour Relations Act 1987 112–15
Labour Relations Amendment Act
  1990 115, 121, 147, 148
lesbians:
  and economic independence of
    women 180–1;
  discriminated against in housing 215

Mackay, Jessie 81, 180
Manitoba 128
Maori Affairs, Dept. of 206
Maori
  cultural values of 228–9;
  and housing 208, 210, 212–13, 215;
  and Nissan enterprise
    agreement 115–17
markets:
  and economic power 34–5;
  public/private split 14, 27–8, 44–5;
  see also labour market
marriage, metaphors for, in neoclassical economics 23–4, 27, 30
Martineau, Harriet 82
Matrimonial Property Act 1976 214
Marx, Karl 22
methodology *see* orthodox economics,
  feminist critiques of
Mill, John Stuart 45–7, 81–2
minimum food budgets 72
minimum incomes 71
'Mitigating Misery':
  and net value of second family
    income 65–70;
  and efficiency in home
    production 70–6
Mitsubishi 115
Mondragon community 57–8
Moore, Mike 113

Morgan, Gareth 61

National Advisory Commission on the
  Employment of Women 5, 6
National and Local Government
  Officers Association (NALGO) 130
National Council of Women 80,
  178–9
National Housing Commission 5, 6,
  208, 214
National Women's Hospital 172
new home economics 22–30
New York State Pay Equity
  Study 105–6
New Zealand Association of
  Economists 47
New Zealand Business
  Roundtable 20, 118, 138
New Zealand Employers Federation:
  and EPA 85;
  and industrial bargaining 118
New Zealand Planning Council 112
New Zealand Steel 115
Nissan 115–17

occupational segregation 83, 95–7, 221
Ontario 128–9, 134, 150–1
Organisation for Economic
  Development and Co-operation
  (OECD) 224
Orr, Elizabeth 142–3
orthodox economics:
  concentration on efficiency
    costs 31–2;
  and consumer preferences 32–4;
  contrasted with political
    economy 14, 15–21, 34–5;
  and distributional change 30–2;
  double-speak 20–1;
  gender blind not gender neutral 13;
  imposed by international
    institutions 19–20, 41–3, 224;

orthodox economics *continued*:
  'no alternative' to 18;
  and understanding of power 34–5;
  and wage relationships 90–4, 102, 104;
  see also new home economics *and next entry*
orthodox economics, feminist critiques of:
  and analysis of policy outcomes 38–44;
  and assumptions of consumer theory 14, 22–30;
  neglect of 44–54;
  and 'positive' and 'value-free' methodology 18, 30–8;
  varieties of 14, 21–2
Otago University economy food plan 74, 167

Pacific Islanders:
  and housing 208, 210, 212–13;
  and Nissan enterprise agreement 115–17
participation *see* labour force participation, women's
pay equity:
  and decentralised industrial bargaining 132;
  and effectiveness of EPA 140–8;
  and efficiency 98–9, 223;
  equal pay for equal work 80–2;
  equal pay for work of equal value 79, 82, 84–5, 98–100;
  exclusion of women from workforce 82;
  future trends in 148–50;
  history of struggle for 80–8;
  international comparisons 124–35;
  key concepts 79–80, 124–6;
  and occupational segregation 79, 83, 95–7;

related issues 150–2;
  and trade unions 82;
  and undervaluation of women's work and skills 83, 92, 102–4, 111–12, 134;
  see also earnings gap; job evaluation; labour market
People's Select Committee 222
Picot report (1988) 161
political economy 14, 15–21, 34–5
Post Office 83
poverty lines 166–7
poverty trap 20–1, 183–4
power differences:
  in families and private households 25–6;
  in labour market 17–18
preferences *see* consumer preferences
Price Waterhouse job evaluation scheme 109–10
principal agent problem 20, 93, 212
public choice theory 20
Public Service Association (PSA) 82, 83, 122
public/private split (between markets and households) 14, 27–8, 44–5

Quarterly Employment Survey (QES) 136, 137
Quebec 128

rational maximisation *see* consumer preferences; orthodox economics; utility functions
redistribution:
  extent of 174–8;
  and orthodox economics 30–2
Residential Tenancies Act 1986 211
rest-home subsidies 203–5
Review Committee on Equal Pay (1979) 84, 85, 142, 143, 147
'Rosie the Riveter' phenomenon

Royal Commissions:
Social Security (1972) 72, 74;
Social Policy (1988) 8, 157–61, 164, 167, 168, 169, 177

scarcity and choice 15–18
science, feminist critiques of:
  feminist empiricism 36;
  feminist standpoint theory 36;
  post-modernism 37;
  strong objectivity 37;
  and types of reasoning 58;
  and value neutrality 35–7
second family income, assessing net value of 65–70
Service Workers Union 138, 139
Sheppard, Kate 80, 179
Shipley, Jenny 136, 151
Siedeberg, Dr Emily 222
Smith, Adam 57
Social Science Committee of Foundation for Research, Science and Technology 5
Social Science Research Fund Committee 5
social policy:
  basic concepts of fairness, equity and justice 157–61;
  gender impacts of 38–44, 165–78, 181–8;
  and role of the state 157–80 *passim*; *see also* accident compensation; benefits; housing policy; income maintenance; labour force participation, women's; redistribution; superannuation
Social Welfare, Dept. of 193, 194
Society for Research on Women 213–14
socio-economics 56–7
sole mothers 184–8, 215, 216

state, role of:
  Marilyn Waring's views 43, 59, 159;
  in social policy 158–80 *passim*
State Sector Act 1988 112
State Services Commission (SSC) 138
structural power:
  in capitalistic economy 26;
  in New Zealand 157;
  patriarchal 25–7
superannuation:
  Budget changes (1991) 191–5;
  and economic position of older women 190–1;
  occupational and other superannuation schemes 198–202;
  state pension 69–70, 192–8
sweated labour 80, 220
Sweden 184, 185

'tastes' *see* altruism; consumer preferences
taxation:
  flattening of income tax rates 170–2, 182;
  increase in indirect tax 171–2;
  seen as coercion 159
Taylor, Harriet 45–7, 81–2
Tenner, Elizabeth 146
Todd Task Force 197
Training Opportunities Scheme 186
transaction cost analysis 20, 26–7
Treasury:
  and calculation of minimum incomes 71–4;
  and earnings gap among its own employees 98;
  and housing policy 212;
  and redistribution policies 31, 167;
  and role of the state in social policy 159

INDEX 255

256 WOMEN AND ECONOMICS

union membership 138
unionism *see* industrial bargaining and
  names of individual organisations;
  see also Employment Contracts Act
  1991
United Nations System of National
  Accounts (UNSNA) 62–3
United States of America:
  and pay equity 131, 132–3;
  and superannuation 200
unpaid work:
  attempts to estimate value of 63–5;
  in 'Mitigating Misery' 65–76;
  omitted from orthodox analyses 14,
    22, 61–2;
  undervaluation of (19th cent.) 44–5
utility functions 25–6, 33, 182;
  see also consumer preferences
value and market price 16
value neutrality in economics 35–7

wage-setting process 90–4
Waring, Marilyn:
  and role of the state 43, 59, 159;
  and UNSNA 62–3
women economists:
  difficulties in getting published 50–1;
  and gender bias in textbooks and
    courses 52–4;
  and graduate training 51–2;
  number and position in
    profession 47–50;
  personal survival strategies 54
Women's Advisory Committee on
  Education 6
Women's Affairs, Ministry of 5, 6, 196,
  200, 205, 206
Working Group on Equal Employment
  Opportunities and Equal Pay 86, 99
Working Party on Equity in
  Employment 87
World Bank 19, 42